T5-ARX-008

The Economics of Agricultural Production

The Economics of Agricultural Production

Edward Witkowski
Webster College, Missouri

Arnold Wells
Mankato State College, Minnesota

Alfred Publishing Co., Inc.
Sherman Oaks, California 91403

Copyright © 1979 by Alfred Publishing Co., Inc.

All rights reserved.

No part of this book may be reproduced or transmitted in any
form or by any means, electronic or mechanical, including
photocopying, recording, or by any information storage and
retrieval system, without permission in writing from the
Publisher:

  Alfred Publishing Co., Inc.
  15335 Morrison Street
  Sherman Oaks, California 91403

Printed in the United States of America

Current printing last digit:
10 9 8 7 6 5 4 3 2 1

Library of Congress Cataloging in Publication Data
Witkowski, Edward.
    The economics of agricultural production.

    Includes index.
    1. Agriculture—Economic aspects. I. Wells, Arnold, joint
author. II. Title.
HD1411.W54   338.1   78-22717
ISBN O-88284-072-X

Contents

Preface

Since the purpose of a preface is to describe the nature of the work, the reasons for its existence, and the patterns of organization, is by its very nature introspective. As such it may be of some interest to a few and of absolutely no interest to others.

Our purpose in writing the book was threefold. First, most of the books extant in this area of the literature were somewhat dated. This, of course, suggested to us that it was time for a new text in the field. Additionally, many of the available texts concentrated heavily on institutional material which told the student a great deal about the nature of agricultural production but tended to obscure the theory which served as a base for decision making in the field. It has been our belief that the stuff of economics lies in the framework for decision making rather than in the collection of factual materials to be memorized by the hapless student. It is also our contention that economics is simple—that it is the collection of common sense into a pattern of analysis which is then dressed in a vernacular to amaze and amuse. Thus, if the student acquires the ability to think as an agricultural economist, he or she can do agricultural economics whether in a field or in a classroom. We have sought to emphasize method and process rather than facts and lists, in the hope that the student will leave with an appreciation of the thought processes of agricultural economics which can then be applied to the real world. Finally, we wanted to construct a textbook which was a teaching tool. Many books seem to be written to impress one's colleagues rather than to aid the student. In our own teaching we have found time and again that books tend not to speak to the student but to the professor. While the professor is of paramount importance in the acquisition of knowledge, the student is the person who must live with the book; who must be able to read and understand on those lonely nights before the exam when the professor is not there to help. We hope that this book will be understandable to students and have for this reason chosen to cover a limited number of concepts which we then reinforced thoroughly.

The organization whithin each chapter is designed to build important conclusions from simpler building blocks. In each chapter, the final conclusions evolve from the assumptions which underlie the model, from an explanation of any new concepts necessary, and from the use of these concepts in formulating rules of behavior. Within each chapter, three methods are used to convey each concept. Initially, concepts are presented in words. Thus, the determination of how much of a variable input, such as labor to hire, rests on a number of other variables such as the price of labor, its productivity, and the price of the product. The price of the product and the productivity of labor can be linked by the concept of marginal value product of labor. Following a description of the concept of marginal value product, a tabular example of the variation of marginal value product and labor utilization makes the relationship more explicit. The third exposure to the concept comes through a graphical depiction of the tabular values to reveal patterns or trends.

The purpose of going through these three steps in the development of each concept is that nearly every student will be able to understand the concept from one or more of the exposures. Some will obtain a thoroughgoing knowledge from understanding all three. In this methodology lies one of the keys to an understanding of the book. Rather than attempting an exhaustive coverage of agricultural economics, the book concentrates on a small number of important decisions that the producer must make. The rules evolve from the descriptive to the theoretical through numerical and graphical examples.

What should you, the student, be able to do when you complete the study of this book? You will not be a farmer, nor will you have any knowledge of animal husbandry. You will not know how to milk a cow or plow a field. What you will know are three simple things: how the producer decides how much and what kinds of inputs to use in the productive process; how the farmer decides how much and what kinds of products to produce to maximize profit; and finally, how to predict the optimum output, subject to constraints, that may be produced. These are not many things to master in one course, but, they will provide the basis for rational decision making should you enter the agricultural sector.

Clearly a book requires more than the diligence of its authors to come to fruition. Many have cooperated in this venture and we would like to thank them for their help. Dr. Barbara Barbato was most instructive in matters of style. Ms. Linda Michael, Lois Kodet and Barbara Lutz all took turns typing various otherwise indecipherable bits of manuscript. Finally, without the understanding and support of our wives the book would not exist. It would be nice to be able to blame others, but all errors are, of course, our own.

THE ECONOMICS OF AGRICULTURAL PRODUCTION

CHAPTER ONE

Introduction

The purpose of this introduction is to give the student and the instructor some insight into the nature of the subject matter and of the book. In this respect, it functions as a tour guide—a broad outline of what is to come. Toward this end, we shall examine the nature of the subject, then the organization of each chapter.

The topic, of course, is agricultural economics. But what does that mean? Why should students give over a whole block of their scarcest resource, time, to study it? For our purposes, the simplest definition will be the most useful. Agricultural economics is the application of the tools and logic of economics to the production of agricultural commodities. Each student of the discipline has learned the concepts or "tools" of the trade, such as supply-and-demand analysis, marginal analysis, and so on. These tools are but intellectual exercises, however, until they are applied and used to explain, predict, and ultimately to control some facet of the real world.

But why agriculture? Surely, the most salient feature of modern economies is the massive industrial sector. Most notably, the American economy is the economy of General Motors, DuPont, and U.S. Steel. If we have developed useful tools of analysis, should they not be applied here? The answer to that and the fulcrum of our interest is best explained by the simple classification of productive effort used in economics: Industrial production of the General Motors type is called *secondary production*. It takes refined products such as steel and shapes them into something useful, or at least something different. *Tertiary production* is the provision of services—that production sector that may have no physical product as its outcome. Examples of this are

1

obvious. The legal and medical professions, stockbrokers and business consultants, social workers, and even economists all provide a service that our society values but that yields no physical product in the way that steel production does.

Agricultural production is in the *primary* sector of production, and it is this important classification that commands our interest and concern. Since economists first began to explore why things worked as they did, the agricultural sector has been of uppermost importance. François Quesnay, in the development of his "Tableau Economique," stressed that all economic activity is ultimately dependent on agricultural production. It is easy to see how this view could develop. Modern economists and other scholars are interested in identifying human motivations. If we can discover "what makes Sammy run," we may alter his course somewhat and, perhaps, stop his flight altogether. Many theories have been advanced to explain human behavior. Humans are seeking love. Humans are seeking status. Humans are seeking riches or a familial dynasty. Each of these viewpoints are of some merit in explaining the rather complex phenomena known as man. Most theories, however, describe modern humans as having satisfied their most basic need—to survive. Whatever things may influence a human's path of activity, without survival, they are meaningless.

What constitutes the basis for survival? To exist physically from one day to the next, humans must satisfy certain physiological needs. They must have some type of protection from the elements. Their raiment need not be elaborate but they must clothe themselves or lose body heat and die of exposure. Even more basic is the fuel to produce that body heat. If humans lack sufficient caloric intake, they will die. They can live without the products of General Motors. They can do without the services of a barber and, certainly, a stockbroker. But they cannot "do" in the most basic sense without food.

This fundamental need is easily ignored in modern American society, which appears to have successfully provided more than enough food for survival. Yet, increasing signs point out the need to focus again on the primacy of agricultural production. One of these signs is the obvious discovery that in the present world there is not enough food to go around. In recent years, there have been many manifestations of this worldwide food scarcity. Newspapers tell of the needs of other industrialized nations for more food. One of the largest nations on earth, the Soviet Union, must import grain to feed its people. More disturbing is the actual starvation of many of the world's peoples. One does not have to view many pictures of children with swollen bellies and corpses of adults lying in the street to form a vision of a world food problem. This picture is buttressed by the neo-Malthusians who predict that the world will be so overpopulated that it will not be able to produce enough food to feed itself.

The question arises, why should Americans, who enjoy a relatively high standard of dietary living, be concerned? One reason is a sense of humanity. Another argument is that a healthy international community is the best safeguard for the continued growth of the present industrialized or "advanced" economies. It is reasonable to assume that, when the world food problem becomes the world food crisis, other people will not stand idly by and let the U.S. consume most of the scarce foodstuffs, but will provoke a conflict to redistribute these necessary resources. All these reasons why Americans should be concerned with agriculture in the international community.

But appeals to social conscience or international brotherhood seldom have much impact when in competition with self-interest. Are there food problems at home? At present, the answer would have to be a qualified "no." But this answer must be qualified by two facts. First, while most Americans enjoy a very rich diet, there are great numbers who do not. While starvation in India may affect Americans only marginally, malnutrition in American cities may be of greater import. In addition, the outward manifestation of a food shortage—an increase in the price of food—is a plague on American well-being.

What is the solution to this shortage of agricultural products? One might be tempted to throw up one's hands in despair or pray to "Science," that god that has thus far aided us in our struggles, to come up with the answer. Neither solution is very practical, and certainly not in the short run where most activity takes place. It is not sufficient to hope that scientists will come up with a way to make foodstuffs out of seaweed or develop new, more productive strains of food grains while people are starving to death each day and more are incapacitated in some way because of poor diets. The most important short-run solution is that of economizing on scarce agricultural resources to produce as much as possible, given the constraints that exist. In other words, if resources are too limited to turn out all the products that we want and need, it is important that none of these resources be wasted. Every acre of land must be used as efficiently as possible. Inefficiency cannot be tolerated in a world where people starve.

But how do we "economize"? What does this mean in the agricultural sector? It means rational decision making on the alternative uses of resources. There must be rules that will allow the agricultural producer to determine the best mix of products, resources, and techniques. Each producer must know what products are most needed. The delivery of these products must be accomplished in the most expeditious manner. The purpose of this book is the development of the rules or analysis that will enable the individual agricultural decision maker to make rational, economical decisions in a world not only of increasing scarcity, but also of increasing complexity.

The evolution of this set of rules will follow the basic nature of the economic process. It will begin by establishing the assumptions about behavior that reflect the world of the agricultural producer. Given these assumptions, several key concepts will be used throughout the book as points of departure. For example, what is production? How does the nature of the relationship between inputs and consequent outputs affect decision making? What decisions can be made given the technical circumstances of production? Once this essential base is established, it can be expanded to form a more comprehensive structure. Since the decisions made in the farm sector are made on the basis of dollar values rather than on a physical basis, the data from the chapter on production must be translated into dollars. This requires two steps: first, to translate the information of the production section concerning inputs in the production process into costs. Second, the outputs of the production process must be translated into revenues.

Once established, this basic information on production, costs, and revenues can be used to formulate some rules of behavior for the producer. An examination of questions that all agricultural producers face will generate a system of possible responses that will lead them to the correct, or most economical, conclusions. The first question that is encountered is really the most important one. How does the agricultural producer decide how much output to produce to maximize his profits? Within the scope of this text, the decision can be made, at least for a simple world with one input and one output. Chapter 6 follows as an elaboration of the basic factor-product decision concerning profit maximization by concentrating on the input side of the transaction to determine the profit-maximizing level of input utilization. This is analogous to the output decision above but is presented in terms of input use.

It goes without saying that the farmer in the real world does not operate under the economist's ideal circumstances—deciding how to use one input to produce only one product. Unfortunately, the real world is more complex than that. The next level of analysis is concerned with more closely approximating reality by considering decision making for profit maximization where there are multiple inputs and multiple outputs. Thus, Chapter 7 deals with the question of multiple inputs or factors of production and seeks to determine the rules or logic by which a producer can maximize profits by deciding how much of each input should be used in the production process. Chapter 8 completes the more sophisticated level of analysis by dealing with the concept of choice in the outputs produced, i.e., what products should be produced by the profit maximizing farmer when he has the option of producing one or several.

As a final note, it is all too easy for the study to view each chapter or each concept as totally unrelated to anything which has gone before or which will come later. Our system of educational testing seems, in many ways, to reinforce that rather unfortunate view of things. Nothing could be further from the truth. As was mentioned before, economics, to the extent that it is a scientific discipline, is so because it is a body of knowledge with the more complex parts built on simpler assumptions and hypotheses. To fully understand the process, the student must look at each chapter as part of a whole, drawing upon what has gone before and developing new tools for what will come later. This attitude will be reinforced whenever possible by making repeated references to the similarities in concepts developed previously and by the underlying theme that there is a producer who is endeavoring, like all of us, to make the best use of the things available to provide the best standard of living possible.

CHAPTER TWO

The Production Function

Up to this time, discussion has been expressed in such broad terms as "agricultural production" and the "agricultural industry." Such terms are so broad as to have no real meaning. Until it is known what the agricultural producer does, the term is useless. And since the agricultural industry is made up of agricultural producers, an adequate definition is doubly important.

The simplest description of what agricultural producers do is, of course, that "they produce." But what is meant by the term "produce"? Production can be defined as the combination of various inputs in such a way as to generate some output. But, again, this definition calls for more information. What are inputs or factors of production? What is output? These terms are best defined through the use of an example. Imagine a "free" field, one that has never been seen or touched by humans. In its natural state, this field will combine such things as seeds blown by the wind, rainfall, and sunlight to produce a variety of plants. There will be represented various types of weeds, flowers, bushes, trees, and, perhaps, some of the things commonly referred to as "crops." Each, however, grows randomly and no one plant is represented in any abundance. It is possible for humans to live or survive from this free field and, indeed, in early history they did survive this way merely by gathering the crops found in nature. However, a society whose means of support is gathering roots and berries from the free field has two built-in limitations. It cannot be very large because the crops produced by the free field will never grow in sufficient quantities to feed many people. It likewise cannot be very complex or specialized. Since the vast proportion of time is spent going from one free field to another to gather enough foodstuffs to survive another day, the inhabitants of such a society cannot allocate time to the production of other goods, pursuit of the arts, or other pastimes. Every man is a food gatherer; no man is anything else.

The free field does not produce desirable crops efficiently enough. To produce more corn, wheat, beans, or whatever foodstuffs are required, the free state must be altered. It is this alteration to produce a specified output that is defined here as production. Humans combine with the free field other types of products or resources in their efforts to generate a usable product.

To continue the example: in the alteration of this free field, the first undertaking would be to clear the field. To do this, the farmer would combine one factor of production—labor—with another—capital—to remove rocks, trees, and other obstacles from the field. This could be done by one person with a lever working several days or by a specialized crew with heavy construction equipment working for a much shorter period of time. The process is the same: a combination of inputs —labor and capital—with the free field to generate an output. Whatever technique is used, the process taking place is production, the combination of inputs to yield a product. The next step might be to loosen or till the ground so that a crop could systematically be planted. This could be done by using a number of different techniques, but again would require labor and capital goods to accomplish. Then, even before the field was seeded, the farmer might add other natural elements that the free field lacked, such as fertilizer. These natural products or resources used in the production process are called "land" by economists. (The free field itself is "land" in this example but will be ignored for purposes of explanation.) Following the tilling, the field is seeded, cultivated, and a crop ultimately harvested by using labor, capital, and such land resources as petroleum. In addition to these three factors of production, there is a fourth at work throughout the whole process commonly termed "entrepreneurial ability." Entrepreneurial ability in this example is the skill exhibited by the farmer in recognizing that, by combining various other factors of production with the free field, he or she could produce a product valued by society. It is also the willingness of that individual to take the risk involved in committing these resources in the hope that the value placed by society on the product will be sufficient to compensate for all his or her efforts.

Thus, production is the transformation of the free field into one that generates a final usable product through the application of four types of factors of production: land, labor, capital, and entrepreneurial ability. Put another way, it is the addition of value to the free field. As noted above, the free field will produce some amount of those crops valued by humans. When the entrepreneur combines the free field with other factors of production to produce systematically an output, he or she is adding value. This is accomplished in two ways. First, the amount of crops society desires will be greater from a cultivated field than from a free one. Whereas the free field may have randomly produced one bushel of corn on an acre, the cultivated field may produce one hundred bushels. One might view the difference as the value added by combining the free field with other factors of production. Second, the cultivated field has acquired value because of its enlarged capacity to produce—cleared land has a greater worth than uncleared land because it can be used for so many more things. Thus, an alternate definition of production might be the addition of value to some raw material, such as the free field, through a combination of the various factors of production.

It must be said, however, that the success of this process is dependent on elements other than these four factors. One of these influences is the state of nature. The success of the venture (i.e., the amount of crop produced) will depend on the amount of rainfall, the amount of sunlight, the presence or absence of insect pests, and a whole range of natural influences. The state of nature is, for the most part, beyond the farmer's control. Despite scattered attempts at cloud seeding and newly developed insecticides, humans have yet to exercise anything approaching complete control over these natural constraints. Any real-world farmer can provide many examples of how crops were washed away, burned out, or eaten by insects despite all his or her efforts.

The second state important to the production process is that of technology. It goes without saying that the amount of crop produced in a given field has changed over time. Much of the basis for this change has been a change in agricultural technology. New and more efficient machines have been developed to aid the farmer in cultivation, harvesting, and the many tasks involved in the agricultural production process. Hybrid seeds have produced new strains of crops that are more resistant to disease and have higher yields. New feed supplements and more scientific methods of feeding have made the production of livestock more efficient. Yet this is another area largely beyond the farmer's control and falls more rightly into the province of the inventor. Although farmers are interested in technology and readily seek its aid in his production, they are, by and large, not producers of technological advance. They may lack the scientific training required for experimentation with hybrid seeds or new types of animal-feed supplements. They may lack the mechnical training or aptitude necessary for the evolution of new or better machinery. They certainly lack the resources necessary to bring technology advances from the drawing board to the field.

In much of what follows, primary concern will be with how well the farmer can produce by varying the amounts of the four factors of production used. It will be assumed that, since the state of nature and of technology are beyond the farmer's purview, they do not change. Thus, the term *ceteris paribus* or "other things being equal," will be used to describe the situation where one input into the production process is allowed to vary but all other things, including the states of nature and technology, remain the same. One should always keep in mind, however, the magnitude of the world that lies beyond the producer's control.

DIMINISHING MARGINAL RETURNS

These very states nonetheless dictate the nature of the production relationship. This relationship can be described as the production function—the summarization of the technical relationships between inputs and outputs. The production function for corn, as an example, indicates how much corn might be produced using a given bundle of factors of production or how many units of the various factors of production must be used to produce an output of corn of a certain size. To refer again to the example of the free field, the farmer cannot produce enough foodstuffs on any free field to feed the world no matter how intensively he or she combines factors of production. Using any amount of land, labor, capital, and entrepreneurial ability in combination with the free field, the farmer will ultimately reach a production limit imposed by nature and technology, which dictates the technical relationships between bundles of inputs and outputs.

As the farmer adds more and more factors of production to the free field, he will find that, at some point, the extra output obtained from increased use of the factors of production begins to diminish. This constraint exists so widely that it has become a central concept in economics: the law of diminishing marginal returns, which states that successive applications of a variable factor of production (such as labor) to a fixed factor of production (such as the free field) will yield successively smaller increases in the total product. At some time, in fact, further increases in the use of factors of production may actually decrease the total product. The marginal returns, or extra physical product, associated with increased use of the factors of production decline in all facets of production. The law of diminishing marginal returns applies to industry, to agriculture, and to life itself. Each student has experienced decreasing marginal returns in his or her daily life. In preparing for an examination, the first hour of studying yields a much higher return in terms of comprehension than does the fourth hour. It is a fact of nature that the student's body and mind are subject to fatigue and, thus, cannot operate at the same level of efficiency throughout a long period of time.

Nature and technology also dictate that diminishing marginal returns will occur in the agricultural sector. Returning to the example, it is conceivable that the free field is lacking in some essential element such as potassium. Even with cultivation and systematic planting, the field may not yield any amount of corn without this essential nutrient. The farmer will seek to improve the fertility of the soil by having it tested and adding those minerals and nutrients that are lacking, thus increasing the yield. At first, the yield may even increase at an increasing rate. If an application of potassium to the free field takes ten units of potassium, the first ten units may produce an increase in yield of seven units of corn; the second ten units may produce an increase in yield of seventeen units. Note that the yield is increasing and also that the rate at which the yield increases is getting larger.

At some point, the yield will still increase with further applications of potassium but the *rate* of increase will be much slower. The fourth application of potassium may raise the yield of corn by nineteen units, while the fifth application increases yield by only eleven units. The yield is still increasing but at a decreasing rate. At this point, diminishing marginal returns have set in. Extra applications of potassium increase corn output by successively smaller amounts. Continued applications of potassium will, at some point, reduce the total product of the field and, at an extreme, enough potassium could be applied to the field so that nothing would grow. The law of diminishing marginal returns is illustrated by the application of potassium (the variable factor of production) to the free field (the fixed factor of production) with predictable results.

The production function linking the use of the various factors of production and the output of corn may be stated more explicitly. The production function described verbally thus far indicates that inputs (factors of production) and outputs are related. From the preceding discussion, it should be apparent that the output depends on the inputs used rather than the opposite. It is then possible to identify inputs into the production process as independent variables and outputs as dependent variables. The dependent variables change with, or depend upon, changes in those variables classified as independent.

This becomes much less cumbersome when the variables in question are represented symbolically and some mathematical notation is used. In traditional notation, if one variable is dependent on another, it can be said that it is a "function of" the second variable. If X is an independent variable and Y is a dependent variable, their relationship can be described by saying that "Y is a function of X." This is shown by the use of f( ) to represent "is a function of." Thus, the relation is shown as $Y = f(X)$, which is read "Y is a function of X." Suppose the following symbols are used to represent the variables already discussed:

Q   represents the quantity of corn produced
L   represents the land factor of production
K   represents the capital factor of production
M   represents the labor factor of production
E   represents the entrepreneurial ability
S_1 represents the state of nature
S_2 represents the state of technology

Then the production function between factors of production and the output of corn becomes:

$$Q = f(L, K, M, E, S_1, S_2)$$

or, "the quantity of corn produced is a function of the factors of production used and the states of nature and technology."

As indicated above, the states of nature and technology are usually assumed to be constant or unchanging. This is the *ceteris paribus* assumption. It can be shown in the new notation by using a vertical bar to separate those independent variables which change from those which, by assumption, do not change. Holding the nature and technology constant, the production function for corn becomes:

$$Q = f(L, K, M, E \mid S_1, S_2)$$

or "the quantity of corn produced is a function of the four factors of production *given* the states of nature and technology (holding the states of nature and technology constant)." As already mentioned, Y is usually used as the symbol for dependent variables and X is used as the symbol for independent variables. To state the production function in more general terms, the dependent variable (Y) is a function of any number of independent variables (Xs). Thus, a general statement of the production function between inputs and outputs would take the form:

$$Y = f(X_1, X_2, X_3 \ldots X_n)$$

It is possible to discuss any production function using this notation by designating what the independent and dependent variables represent in the individual situation. As an example, in describing the relationship between potassium and the output of corn, we showed the effect of the application of increasing amounts of a variable factor (potassium) to a group of fixed factors (all other factors of production including the free field). In this instance, the independent variable in the production function is potassium and the dependent variable is the output of corn. Using X_1 to represent potassium, Y to represent the output of corn, and the other Xs to represent the remaining factors of production and the "states," the relationship becomes:

$$Y = f(X_1 \mid X_2, X_3 \ldots X_n)$$

read "the output of corn is a function of potassium used when all other independent variables are held constant." Note that the dependent variable is represented by Y and the independent variables by Xs. Thus, it is possible to fit any production function into this general format.

This is, however, a very general statement of the production function between potassium and the output of corn produced. From the producer's perspective, it is important to know precisely the relationship which exists. To return to our example, assume that, without potassium, the free field produced no corn. The first application of potassium increases the total product of corn to seven units. The second application increases the output to twenty-four units. Thus, the extra, or marginal, output associated with the first application of potassium is seven units; the extra output from the second application is seventeen units. The third unit of potassium used may increase output still further, say to forty-five units and, thus, have a marginal contribution of twenty-one units. The relationship between input of potassium and output of corn can be summarized as in Table 2–1 for several levels of input use.

When information used in this example is presented in tabular rather than narrative form, the phenomenon described as diminishing marginal returns becomes more apparent. The gain in yields (the extra output associated with another application of potassium) rises initially from seven units at the first application to twenty-one units at the third. When the fourth unit of potassium is applied, however, the extra output from additional potassium begins to decline. In this example, the extra output from the fourth application of potassium is nineteen units of corn as opposed to twenty-one units for the third application. This decline in the contribution of potassium to the total product continues until further applications of potassium actually decrease output. This happens at application six, where using more potassium decreases the total output from seventy-five units to seventy-two units. Thus, the extra output associated with the sixth application of potassium is negative. Further negative returns continue until the total output is reduced to zero with the eighth application of potassium. The applica-

TABLE 2-1: Production function for corn with potassium as a variable input

Applications of Potassium Units	*Output of Corn Units*	*Extra Output from an Extra Application of Potassium Units*
0	0	
1	7	7
2	24	17
3	45	21
4	64	19
5	75	11
6	72	− 3
7	49	−23
8	0	−49

tion of potassium (a variable factor of production) to fixed factors of production (the free field and all other factors of production which were held constant by assumption) causes the extra output attributable to an extra unit of input to decline at some point.

Decreasing marginal returns are illustrated even more clearly when the information from the above example is plotted graphically as in Figure 2-1. In this depiction of the data from the production function for corn, using potassium as a variable factor, the effect of additional units of potassium on the total output of corn is clearly seen. More importantly, it is possible to note the decline in the extra output associated with the increased use of the variable factor.

STAGES OF PRODUCTION

Figure 2-2 repeats the information on total production found in Figure 2-1. The total product curve can be divided into three stages of production. In the first stage, two different relationships exist between inputs of potassium and the output of corn. Initially, increases in input utilization increase the output of corn at an increasing rate. Thus, while the first application of potassium increases yield by seven units, the second application increases yield by seventeen units—an even greater amount. During Stage I, however, this changes at the point of inflection.[1] Applications of potassium in Stage I, past the point of inflection, still increase output but at a decreasing rate.

---

1. Mathematically, that point at which the total product curve changes from being convex to the origin to being concave to the origin. This is identified by the point P_1 in Figure 2-2.

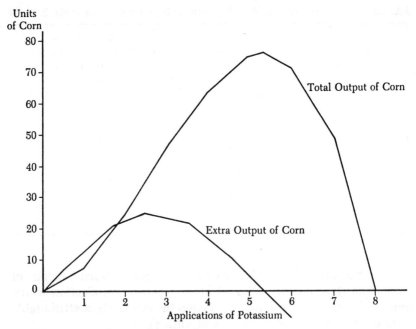

FIGURE 2-1: Production function for corn
(variable input: potassium)

In Stage II, output of corn is still increasing at a decreasing rate. Increases in input utilization produce less than proportionate increases in output. So, in Stage II, a ten percent increase in the amount of potassium used will generate a less than ten percent increase in the amount of corn produced. The point of separation between Stage I and Stage II comes at that level of input use at which a ray from the origin is tangent to the total product curve. This is designated as P_2 in Figure 2-2.

The shift from Stage II to Stage III comes at point P_3. At this point, the slope of the total output curve is zero.[1] As production enters Stage III, increased use of the variable input actually produces declines in the output of corn. So, if the amount of potassium used increases from six applications to seven, the output of corn declines from seventy-two units to forty-nine units. Put a different way, the extra output associated with extra inputs is positive in Stages I and II and negative in Stage III.

1. Slope is defined as the change in the vertical distance moved, divided by the change in the horizontal distance moved between two points. In this example, it is the change in the amount of corn produced divided by the change in the applications of potassium.

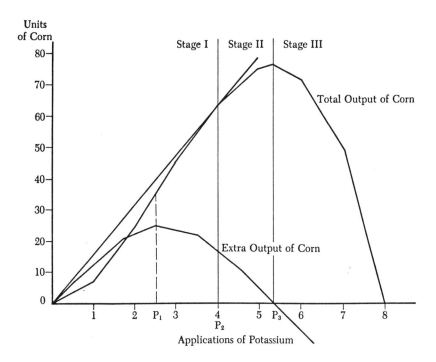

FIGURE 2-2: Production function for corn
(variable input: potassium)

To summarize the stages of production:

Stage I: Extra applications of the variable factor increase production, initially at an increasing rate but later at a decreasing rate.

Stage II: Extra applications of the variable factor increase production but at a decreasing rate throughout the stage.

Stage III: Extra applications of the variable factor decrease the amount of total output produced, eventually reducing production to zero.

Economically, the first two stages of production are the most important; Stage III will not be reached very often. The producer may, in error, slip over the line between Stage II and Stage III from time to time, but not for long. The rational producer will not add costly resources to the production process in order to diminish the total amount of output. Thus, the producer will be making decisions about the application of potassium or any other variable input primarily in Stages I and II.

Given the empirical relationship described above through the tabulation of data and its graphical representation, it is possible to make a much more specific statement of the relationship between the number of applications of potassium and the output of corn. The general relationship was expressed as:

$$Y = f(X_1 \mid X_2, X_3 \ldots X_n)$$

From this data, it is possible to derive the specific equations that describe the functional relationship between inputs and outputs.[1]

While the equation used in the above example is a "made up" or hypothetical one, econometricians have endeavored to discover the precise relationships which exist between production variables in agriculture.[2] With this equation, it is possible to predict what output will be at any level of input use or, conversely, to predict what amount of input will be required to produce a specific output.

A second example will again illustrate the concept of decreasing marginal returns and the stages of production. Part of the process described above as production (i.e., the application of factors of production to the free field) involved the use of labor. Concentrating for the moment on the labor input, it is possible to describe the relationship between the amount of labor used and the amount of corn produced, once again beginning with the general functional relationship:

$$Y = f(X_1 \mid X_2, X_3 \ldots X_n)$$

where Y represents the dependent variable, the amount of corn produced, and X_1 represents the independent variable, in this case, the amount of labor used. All other factors of production and the two external variables (nature and technology) are, of course, held constant. The relationship under scrutiny is thus the production function for corn with labor as a variable factor.

The production function can also be described in narrative form. The free field may, in fact, produce no corn without the input of some labor resources. Surely, without the labor involved in harvesting, any corn that might volunteer in the free field will not be "produced." For purposes of this example, it may be assumed that if one unit of the

1. While the derivation of equations from empirical data can be found in most general mathematical texts and particularly in such texts as R. G. D. Allen, *Mathematical Analysis for Economists*, the most concise text concerning the mathematics germane to this type of theory can be found in Clark Lee Allen, *Elementary Mathematics of Price Theory*.
2. The equation for the production function for corn with potassium as a variable input is:

$$Y = 8X_1{}^2 - X_1{}^3$$

TABLE 2-2. Production function for corn with labor as a variable input

Units of Labor	Output of Corn Units	Extra Output from an Extra Unit of Labor
0	0	
1	9	9
2	16	7
3	21	5
4	24	3
5	25	1
6	24	-1
7	21	-3
8	16	-5

labor factor of production is used, nine units of corn can be garnered from the free field. Further application of labor in conjunction with the free field will yield more corn. A second unit of labor used to remove rocks or weeds from the free field will increase the amount of corn produced to sixteen units. A third unit of labor used to till the soil or seed corn more systematically will increase the output of the field to twenty-one units. Table 2-2 indicates the possible outputs of corn for various inputs of the labor resource.

It is important to note that when a variable factor of production is applied to a bundle of fixed factors of production, the extra contribution to total product associated with another unit of the variable factor begins to decline at some point due to the law of diminishing marginal returns. The first unit of labor used produces nine extra units of corn. With the second unit, diminishing marginal returns begin to set in. The second unit of labor contributes only seven units of corn to the total output. Diminishing marginal returns continue until, with the sixth unit of labor, the extra product produced is negative and the total product diminishes also.

When this data is plotted in Figure 2-3, the concept of diminishing marginal returns is reillustrated in more graphic form. After the first unit of labor, it is easy to see that the extra product from each additional unit of labor used becomes smaller. Repeating this production function, or total product curve, in Figure 2-4 allows separation of the production function into the various stages of production. As in the previous example, Stage I, where output first increases at an increasing rate and then increases at a decreasing rate, terminates at the point where a ray from the origin is tangent to the total product curve. In Figure 2-4, this occurs when one unit of the labor resource is

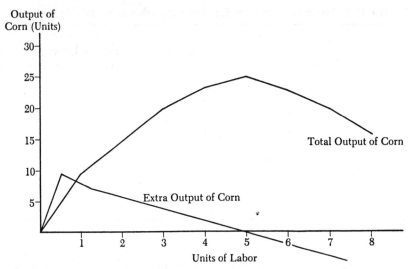

FIGURE 2-3: Production function for corn
(variable input: labor)

used. Stage II, where total output still increases but at a decreasing rate throughout, ends at the point at which the slope of the total output curve is zero; when total product is at a maximum. This occurs at five units of labor used. Any further use of the labor resource beyond five units takes the producer into Stage III, that stage where the additional product associated with more units of labor is negative. Again, the producer is concerned about where to produce in Stages I and II, though he or she may occasionally, through error, slip into Stage III.

ALTERNATE PRODUCTION FUNCTIONS

Up to now, attention has centered on one type of production function —that which illustrates diminishing marginal returns.[1] There are two other types of production relationships which may exist at least conceptually. Varying one factor of production with all other factors of production and the external variables held constant may produce either constant or increasing changes in the extra product produced. As indicated above, either of these relationships certainly is possible in

---

1. This is true in general, although each of the production functions examined exhibits increasing marginal returns over a limited range of production.

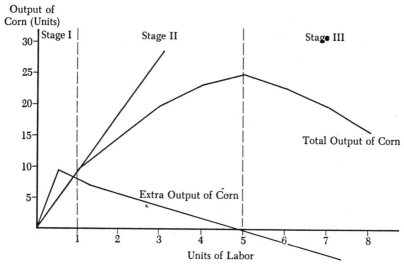

FIGURE 2-4: Production function for corn
(variable input: labor)

concept and may exist in the real world for some production relationships or for many over short periods of production.

Constant marginal returns to the variable factor exist when each
additional unit of that factor used adds exactly the same amount to
total production. If the first unit of the variable factor used adds ten
units to total production so will the fifth unit, the tenth unit, and so on
to n units. An example of constant returns can be found, to a certain
degree, in egg production. The production function for eggs, using
feed, can be expressed in the familiar form of the production function
$Y = f(X_1 \mid X_2, X_3 \ldots X_n)$, where Y represents the number of eggs
produced and X_1 represents the variable input feed. The other factors
of production and the external variables are, of course, held constant so
that the relationship between feed and egg production can be
examined more specifically. Since egg production involves the use of a
living organism as the "machine," the relationship is somewhat different than for industrial production. The first portion of feed, ten units
in this example, goes to maintain the producing organism—the hen. In
other words, the first ten units of feed constitute a maintenance ration
required for the survival of the hen and generate no eggs. Over and
above this maintenance ration, however, every extra unit of feed
produces the same increase in egg production. If the second ten units of
feed produce ten eggs, so will the third ten units of feed, the fourth ten
units of feed, and so on. The production function for eggs, with feed as

TABLE 2-3. Production function for eggs with feed as the variable input

Units of Feed	Output of Eggs (Units)	Extra Output from an Extra Unit of Feed
0	0	
		0
10	0	
		1
20	10	
		1
30	20	
		1
40	30	
		1
50	40	

a variable factor, exhibits constant marginal returns inasmuch as each increment in input generates the same increase in output. This relationship is described in Table 2-3.

When this data is plotted in Figure 2-5, it can be determined that the slope of the total output curve (the change in egg production divided by the change in feed used) is constant and that the contribution of each additional unit of input to total output is also constant.

The third possible type of production function shows increasing marginal returns to the variable factor of production, which occur when each additional unit of the variable factor used adds an increasing amount of extra output to the total. Referring again to the production function for corn, using potassium as a variable factor, the student will recall that, in the initial stages of production (the first three applications), total output increased at an increasing rate. Each additional application of potassium generated larger increases in extra output than the one before.

While examples of increasing marginal returns are uncommon in agriculture and generally exist only over a limited range of output, as in the potassium example, it is possible to illustrate the phenomenon using the production function for corn with micronutrients as the variable factor of production. Micronutrients are those elements such as iron, manganese, and other minerals important to the growth of this crop but not necessary in large quantities. Using the familiar notation of Y representing the output of corn and X_1 representing the amount of micronutrients used, the production function again takes the form, *ceteris paribus*, of:

$$Y = f(X_1 \mid X_2, X_3 \ldots X_n)$$

Since increasing marginal returns to the variable input implies increasing amounts of extra output generated by additional units of the

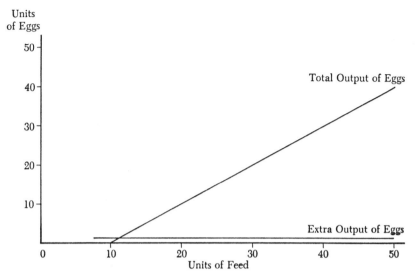

FIGURE 2-5: Production function for eggs
(variable input: feed)

variable factor, the second application of micronutrients will yield a greater increase in corn output than did the first. The third application will produce a greater increase in the output of corn than did the second, and so on. The relationship takes the form described in Table 2–4.

While the first unit of micronutrients applied generates three extra units of corn, by the time the producer has applied the last unit of micronutrients the rate of increase in production has increased to twenty-seven units. Graphically, the total output curve in this situation has an increasing slope as depicted in Figure 2–6.

The concept of increasing marginal returns to the variable factor of production provides insight into economic reasoning. While increasing marginal returns certainly exist conceptually, and may exist in isolated instances in the real world, widespread occurrence of such a phenomenon has little relationship to economic reality. If the above example held true, output could be increased without bounds on a given piece of land merely by using increasing amounts of micronutrients. The world could then be fed by intensive working of one field of corn, one of wheat, and so on. Any acquaintance with reality demonstrates that this does not happen. While many phenomena are conceptually or theoretically possible, it is important that theory be tested by reference to the real world to determine its validity.

So far, in this chapter, the production process has been described in

TABLE 2–4. Production function for corn with micronutrients as a variable factor

Micronutrient Units	Output of Corn Units	Extra Output from an Extra Unit of Micronutrients
0	0	
1	3	3
2	12	9
3	27	15
4	48	21
5	75	27

vague terms, using very general terminology. The purpose here was to acquaint the student with some of the concepts of agricultural production before the analysis was complicated by introducing new terminology. The basic problem with the use of common words to describe the rather complex phenomena discussed is that it increases the chances for confusion. Two simple examples will illustrate what is meant.

Part of the prevailing stereotype of farmers is that they go to bed early. *Early*, however, is one of those vague, general words that is subject to interpretation by both the speaker and the listener. If a college student says that he went to bed early, is this the same *early* the farmer would use? Probably not. As long as the farmer and the student talk with each other using such imprecise terms, however, they will go on thinking each understands what the other meant and never really communicate any accurate information or understanding.

A second example of the problems brought about by the use of vague or inaccurate language is provided by the military establishment. At some time, almost everyone has encountered the military system of referring to time of day on the basis of a twenty-four-hour clock. Using this system, 4:00 P.M. becomes 1600 hours. The purpose of the system is clearly to designate whether the time is morning or past morning. Since military activity, presumably, may take place at any time of the night or day, one can imagine the perils encountered by ordering an attack at six o'clock and having it happen at the wrong six o'clock. Precision in the description of time eliminates this worry.

While the discipline of economics can hardly be likened to warfare, it is, nonetheless, important that students of the subject learn to communicate in the same language and that their use of it be as precise as possible. Without a vernacular, economists are like the student and the farmer—mouthing words at each other but never really communicating. For this reason, the casual, descriptive phrases that have been used

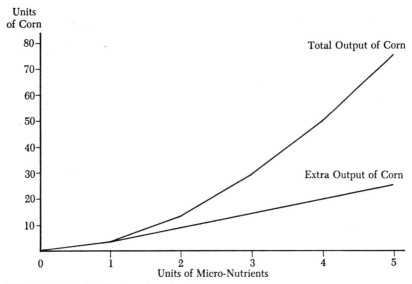

FIGURE 2-6: Production function for corn
(variable input: micronutrients)

up to this point must be abandoned. A new language must be developed. Once this is done, discussion can be carried further and be more accurate than before.

TOTAL, AVERAGE, AND MARGINAL PHYSICAL PRODUCT

Since this chapter examines the production function in some detail, it is sensible that the first three terms to be fitted into the new vernacular deal with production. Since the subject area is the agricultural sector, the terms will focus on physical production or output. The terms relevant to the previous discussion are: *total physical product*, *average physical product*, and *marginal physical product*.[1] These terms will allow discussion of the production relationship in several different ways, as each is very important in a different set of decisions.

---

1. In many industries in a developed economy, the products produced are not physical, concrete items. It is quite inaccurate to talk about the physical product that a lawyer or stockbroker produces. Yet, in the agricultural sector, emphasis is placed on the production of physical things and the terms are appropriate.

Total Physical Product

> *Total Physical Product* (TPP) is the amount of output associated with any level of input use.

All that is required to assimilate this new term is to use it in place of output or product in our discussion. Thus, in the first example used in the chapter (the production function for corn with potassium as a variable factor), the intent is to determine how the total physical product of corn varies with the amount of potassium used. The production function, hence, can be expressed in different terms as:

$$TPP_{corn} = f(X_1 \mid X_2, X_3 \ldots X_n)$$

Table 2–1 is thus modified in such a way that the column for "output of corn" is, in actuality, the total physical product of corn, and it can be determined that, with three applications of potassium, the total physical product of corn is 45 units; with six applications of potassium, the total physical product of corn is 72 units, and so on. Figure 2–1 and all graphic displays dealing with the total output of corn, eggs, or other products can be presented in terms of total physical product.

Average Physical Product

> *Average Physical Product* (APP) is the amount of output produced per unit of variable input. APP = TPP divided by the number of units of the variable input used.

Table 2–1 can be modified to show the calculation of average physical product as illustrated in Table 2–5 by dividing the total physical product of corn by the number of units of potassium used.

For this production relationship, average physical product increases through the fourth application of potassium. This corresponds to the first stage of production indicated in Figure 2–2, at the beginning of which total physical product increases at an increasing rate, resulting in an increase in APP. Even when total physical product begins to increase at a decreasing rate, the rate will be greater than the average and will increase the average. Another way to determine the point separating Stage I from Stage II is to determine that point at which average physical product stops increasing.[1] If APP has stopped increas-

1. APP can be measured geometrically as the slope of a ray to the total physical product curve. The point at which this slope and APP are at a maximum is the point of tangency between the ray and the TPP curve. This is the dividing point between Stages I and II.

TABLE 2-5. Production function for corn with potassium as a variable input

Applications of Potassium	TPP of Corn Units	Calculation of Average Physical Product, APP	APP (Units) of Corn Per Unit of Potassium
0	0	0/0	—
1	7	7/1	7
2	24	24/2	12
3	45	45/3	15
4	64	64/4	16
5	75	75/5	15
6	72	72/6	12
7	49	49/7	7
8	0	0/8	—

ing and has not quite begun to decrease, it must be at its maximum value. More directly stated, the breakpoint between Stage I and Stage II comes at that point when APP is at a maximum. Following this point, more inputs into the production process generate increases in total physical product at a decreasing rate and average physical product declines. Average physical product will continue to decline throughout Stages II and III, but will remain positive as long as total physical product is positive. Plotting average physical product on the same set of axes as total physical product produces Figure 2-7, which demonstrates more visually the discussion above.

Marginal Physical Product

The third term to be introduced, and the concept most important to the agricultural decision maker, is *marginal physical product.* Many of the decisions a farmer makes are made at the edge, or margin, of production. He or she must decide whether to produce one more or one less field of corn, to use one more or one less application of fertilizer, and so on. The farmer's interest, therefore, lies in the effect of an additional, or marginal, application of a variable input on production. The measure of this effect is marginal physical product.

> *Marginal Physical Product* (MPP) is the amount of additional output produced by one additional unit of the variable input. It is the change in total physical product divided by the change in the variable input used.[1]

1. Mathematically, the marginal physical product is the first derivative of the total physical product function. It can be estimated by finding the slope of a line tangent to the total physical product curve.

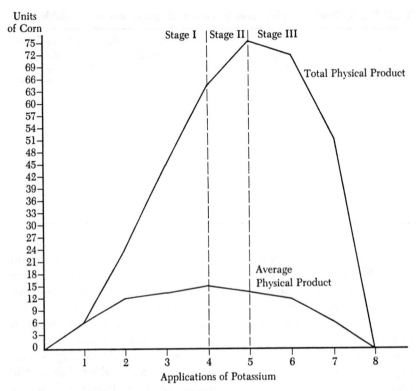

FIGURE 2-7: Production function for corn
(variable input: potassium)

In earlier examples, mention was made of the extra output that resulted from an extra application of potassium, an extra unit of labor, or of any variable input. This is the marginal physical product. Referring again to Table 2-1, as the first application of potassium is used, total physical product changes from zero to seven units. The change in TPP of seven units divided by the change in input use of one unit produces a marginal physical product of seven. When the second unit of potassium is applied, the total product of corn increases to twenty-four units. The change in TPP is twenty-four minus seven, or seventeen units. The change in the variable factor is, again, one unit. Dividing the change in TPP (17) by the change in input use (1), the marginal physical product of the second application of potassium is seventeen units.

One problem encountered in the calculation of MPP is that the value determined represents an average rate of change between two points. Thus, the values of the MPP should be placed midway between the

TABLE 2-6. Production function for corn with potassium as the variable input

Applications of Potassium	TPP of Corn Units	Calculation of Marginal Physical Product (MPP) [ΔTPP/ΔINPUT]	MPP of Corn Units
0	0		
		7/1	7
1	7		
		17/1	17
2	24		
		21/1	21
3	45		
		19/1	19
4	64		
		11/1	11
5	75		
		– 3/1	– 3
6	72		
		–23/1	–23
7	49		

inputs for which the change in production is calculated. In all of the previous discussions of the extra output associated with an additional unit of input, the figures have been so placed as to indicate that they represent an average rate of change. Using Δ to represent "change in" in the formula for the calculation of MPP, it is possible to revise Table 2–1 to show the calculation of MPP. This is done in Table 2–6.

Marginal physical product is also a measure of the rate of growth in total physical product. When MPP is increasing, this means that the rate at which TPP is growing is also increasing. When MPP is declining, the rate at which TPP is growing is also declining. When TPP stops growing and begins to decline, MPP, as a measure of the rate of growth, is negative. The calculations in Table 2–6 indicate that TPP is growing at an increasing rate through the first three applications of potassium. Thus, MPP is increasing. TPP continues to grow, though at a decreasing rate, through applications four and five. In this case, MPP is declining but still positive. Earlier, the point of inflection was defined as that point at which TPP continued to increase but at a decreasing rate. At this point, MPP is at a maximum. Plotting the total physical product and marginal physical product data from Table 2–6 in Figure 2–8 demonstrates this relationship between TPP and MPP.

The notion of total physical product, average physical product, and marginal physical product can be strengthened by reviewing these calculations for the second example cited previously—the production function for corn, with labor as a variable factor. Table 2–7 shows this production relationship as well as the mechanics of calculating APP and MPP. From this table, it is apparent that diminishing returns to the variable input set in almost immediately. MPP declines steadily from nine, when the first unit of labor is used; it becomes negative

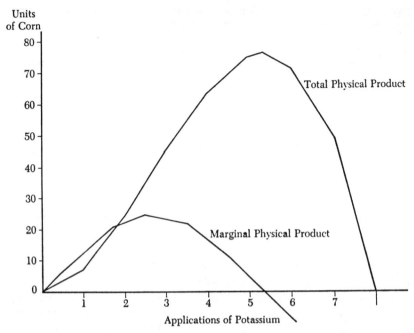

FIGURE 2-8: Production function for corn (variable input: potassium)

when the sixth unit of labor is used. thus, the marginal contribution of each unit of labor declines as more and more labor is applied to the fixed set of factors of production, illustrating the law of diminishing marginal returns.

Since the MPP of each additional unit of labor is declining, so is the APP. From Table 2-7, it can be readily observed that APP follows MPP in its decline. When the information from Table 2-7 is plotted, as in Figure 2-9, the relationships observed in the previous examples again hold true.

RELATIONSHIPS BETWEEN TOTAL, AVERAGE, AND MARGINAL PHYSICAL PRODUCT

All that has been done thus far is to express the kind of information available in Table 2-1 in somewhat more precise language. There remains one additional task necessary for a complete discussion of the production function: an examination of the relationships between the various measures of output that have been developed. To illllustrate, the various measures of production for the corn production function are put together in Figure 2-10.

TABLE 2-7. Production function for corn with labor as the variable input

Units of Labor	TPP of Corn Units	APP_{labor} (TPP/Q_{labor})	MPP_{labor} $(\Delta TPP/\Delta Q_{labor})$
0	0	0/0 = —	
1	9	9/1 = 9	9–0/1–0 = 9
2	16	16/2 = 8	16–9/2–1 = 7
3	21	21/3 = 7	21–16/3–2 = 5
4	24	24/4 = 6	24–21/4–3 = 3
5	25	25/5 = 5	25–24/5–4 = 1
6	24	24/6 = 4	24–25/6–5 = –1
7	21	21/7 = 3	21–24/7–6 = –3
8	16	16/8 = 2	16–21/8–7 = –5

Total Physical Product and Marginal Physical Product

The first relationship of consequence is that which exists between total physical product and marginal physical product. MPP has been defined as the change in TPP with respect to the change in the variable input. The formula for the calculation of MPP is $\Delta TPP/\Delta X_1$, where X_1 represents the variable input—in this case, potassium. This formula is also a measure of the slope of the TPP curve. Thus, in Figure 2-10, when the amount of potassium used increases from one to two units (from P_0 to P_1), the quantity of corn produced increases from seven units to twenty-four units (Q_0 to Q_1). The slope of the curve is $(Q_1-Q_0)/(P_1-P_0)$, or $(24-7)/(2-1)$, which is exactly equal to the value of MPP at the midpoint between P_0 and P_1; thus, MPP is the slope of the TPP curve.

Reasoning from the other perspective, total physical product is the summation of the marginal physical products at each stage of input use. When the MPP of the first unit of potassium used is seven and the MPP of the second unit is seventeen; the total physical product produced using two units of potassium is the sum of these two marginal physical products (7 + 17). As indicated by Figure 2-10, the total physical product of two units of potassium is twenty-four.

Finally, if marginal physical product is the measure of the rate of change in total physical product, it should signal when that rate of growth changes. That it does is apparent by the reference to two points. In Stage I, total physical product first increases at an increasing rate, then reaches the point of inflection and begins to increase at a decreasing rate. This is reflected in the behavior of MPP. When TPP is increasing at an increasing rate, MPP is rising; at the point of inflection (when the rate of growth continues increasing but at a decreasing rate)

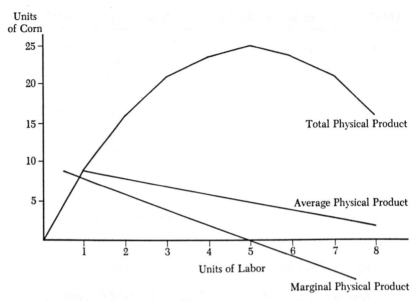

FIGURE 2–9: Production function for corn (variable factor: labor)

MPP is at a maximum. Finally, through the rest of Stage I, while TPP is still increasing but at a decreasing rate, MPP is still positive but declining. At the juncture between Stages II and III, total physical product changes from growth at a decreasing rate to a decline. Also, at this point, MPP changes from being positive though declining to being negative. Thus, as the rate of growth changes from positive to negative, so does the marginal physical product.

Total Physical Product and Average Physical Product

The relationship between the total physical product and the average physical product is a simple one. At any level of input use, the APP can be determined by dividing the TPP by the number of inputs used. Thus, in Figure 2–10, at P_1 number of applications of potassium, the APP is the output OQ_1 divided by the number of applications of potassium (OP_1). Since OP_1 represents two applications of potassium and OQ_1 represents twenty-four units of corn, the APP is equal to 24/2, or twelve. Reading APP from the lower graph, it is observed that the APP for two units of potassium is twelve.

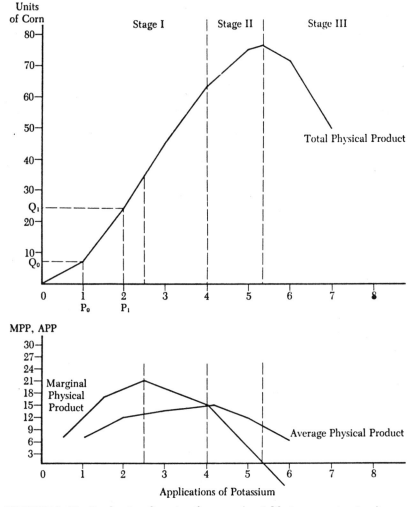

FIGURE 2-10: Production function for corn (variable input: potassium)

Average Physical Product and Marginal Physical Product

The last relationship of significance is that which exists between average physical product and marginal physical product. In simplest terms, it can be said that the average follows the marginal. Two examples will illustrate how this is true.

One descriptive measure of any class of students is height. It might be of some interest to an educational researcher to determine the average height of students in an agricultural economics class. This number is easily obtained. One would simply add the heights in inches of all class members and divide that total by the number of students in the class. In a class of ten students whose heights are (in inches): 72, 60, 63, 70, 65, 73, 61, 66, 68 and 71, the average height could be found by dividing the sum of the heights (669 inches) by the number of students (10) to determine the average height of students in this class (66.9 inches). What happens to this average if an extra, or marginal, student enters the class? Above, it was noted that the average follows the marginal. Thus, if the extra student is taller than the average, the average should rise. If he is shorter than the average, the average should fall.

The class total was 669 inches, yielding an average height of 66.9 inches. If the marginal student is 74 inches tall, the new average is calculated as:

$$\frac{669 \text{ inches} + 74 \text{ inches}}{10 \text{ students} + 1 \text{ student}} = \frac{743 \text{ inches}}{11 \text{ students}}$$

for a new class average of 67.54 inches. Since the marginal contribution to class height was greater than the average height, the average does, indeed, increase.

If the average follows the marginal, the class average should fall if the extra student is shorter than the class average. Were the student 60 inches tall, the new class average would be calculated as:

$$\frac{669 \text{ inches} + 60 \text{ inches}}{10 \text{ students} + 1 \text{ student}} = \frac{729 \text{ inches}}{11 \text{ students}}$$

for a new class average of 66.27 inches. Since the marginal contribution to class height was less than the average height, the class average fell. The average again followed the marginal.

A second example may be drawn from baseball. If a batter enters a game with a batting average of .250, this indicates that, in his previous games, he has had one hit for every four official times at bat. If, in this game, the batter gets no hits in four official times at bat (i.e., bats .000 on the day), what happens to his batting average? The answer is, of course, that it declines. Because the marginal contribution to his batting average is less than the average itself, his batting average declines. Should he get four hits in four times at bat, however, his average would increase in that the marginal contribution would be greater than his average. Again, the average follows the marginal.

With these examples in mind, examine the average and marginal physical product curves in Figure 2-10. When marginal physical product is greater than average physical product, as it is up to four units of input, the average is being pulled up by the marginal. To this point, then, average physical product is increasing. At any point beyond four units of input, the marginal physical product is less than the average physical product. Since the marginal is less than the average, it pulls the average down. Consequently, at any level of input use greater than four units, the average physical product is decreasing. Given that when MPP is greater than APP, APP is rising, and, when MPP is less than AP, APP is falling, when are they equal? It can be determined from the data presented and through the use of logic that they are equal at that point at which APP is neither increasing nor decreasing (i.e., when APP is at a maximum), four units of input use in Figure 2-10. To summarize briefly the relationship between APP and MPP:

If MPP > APP, APP is increasing
If MPP < APP, APP is decreasing
If MPP = APP, APP is at its maximum

As a final note, these relationships are useful in analyzing the three stages of production in economic rather than in strictly mathematical terms. In Stage III, total, average, and marginal physical products are all decreasing. This indicates that not only is the average rate of return from the variable factor declining, but also, and more importantly, that the absolute amount of product produced declines as more and more units of potassium are used. Thus, the producer would not be rational, given the production relationship in Figure 2-10, in using more than five applications of potassium. He or she would find that profits were doubly diminished by using more than five units. First, revenues would decline in that there would be less product to offer on the market than had five or fewer applications of potassium been used. Second, costs would increase as additional units of this variable input were used, which again would diminish profits. Even if potassium were a free good and there were no costs involved in its application, the producer's return would be cut by the diminished amount of product produced. In short, it is irrational for the producer to operate in Stage III of the production function.

In Stage I, average physical product is always increasing. The producer is obtaining an increased average return from the variable factor each time he or she increases its use. As long as this holds true, it will be rational for the producer to increase the use of the variable factor. This will be true at least until the average physical product reaches a maximum and begins to decline. Since average physical product increases throughout Stage I, it would be advantageous for the producer to continue production until Stage II is reached. Again, to refer to the profit the producer makes, if the variable input provides an increasing average return while its costs remain the same, a positive change in profits will result. Since the assumption upon which models of behavior are based is that the producer desires to maximize profits, he or she would continue production into Stage II.

It has been shown that the producer will generally not operate in Stages I and III of the production function. The question then becomes to determine where in Stage II he or she should produce. The answer to this question cannot be obtained from the physical production information alone; it is also necessary for the producer to know the prices of inputs and the prices at which the output can be sold. Once this information is ascertained, he or she can decide how much output to produce (i.e., where in Stage II to produce). To determine this, the farmer will compare the extra costs incurred by adding more inputs to the extra revenue the product generated by these extra inputs will yield. If using additional inputs adds more to revenue than to costs, the rational producer will do so and the result will be an increase in profits. The discussion of the profit-maximizing output will be undertaken once the concepts of costs and revenues have been fully developed.

SUMMARY

This chapter represents the first exposure to the technical data of production and the models and concepts that have been formulated to explain it. This production information is the foundation upon which all of the following descriptive and decision-making models rest. Coupled with information about the prices of output, it becomes the basis for a study of revenues. Linked with data about input prices, it becomes the basis for the determination of costs. Finally, through these costs and revenues, it is the foundation upon which profit maximization decisions are made.

Discussed in this chapter were the concepts of total, average, and marginal physical product. Conceptually, each will find an analog in the chapters on the costs and revenues of production and in the various decision-making moels. These linkages are of importance in that they illustrate the completeness of the subject under study. Without a constant reminder that costs and revenues are not isolated but are closely tied to the constraints of production, effective decision making is impossible.

QUESTIONS

1. Assume a farm firm has the following production function:

FEED	BEEF	APP	MPP
0	0		
10	100	_____	_____
20	180	_____	_____
30	240	_____	_____
40	290	_____	_____
50	330	_____	_____

A. Calculate the average physical product associated with each level of feed used.

B. Calculate the marginal physical product associated with varying levels of feed used.

C. How much feed is used when the law of diminishing returns begins?

D. Plot total physical product, average physical product, and marginal physical product on graph paper. Study these graphs and note relationships and stages of production.

2. Assume a farm producer finds the following relationship of corn yield to fertilizer:

FERTILIZER	CORN	APP	MPP
0	90	_____	
100	110	_____	_____
200	125	_____	_____
300	135	_____	_____
400	140	_____	_____
500	138	_____	_____

A. Calculate the average physical product associated with each level of fertilizer used.

B. Calculate the marginal physical product associated with varying levels of fertilizer used.

C. Determine the level of fertilizer where diminishing returns begins.

D. Plot the total physical product, average physical product, and marginal physical product on graph paper. Study these graphs and note relationships and stages of production.

3. Explain why a rational firm would not produce in Stage III of production. Give numerical support for your answer.

CHAPTER THREE

Costs of Production

The last chapter centered on the development of the technical aspects of production. It established the kinds of natural constraints the producer faces in the transformation of the "free" field into a useful and valuable crop. The most important constraint is clearly diminishing marginal returns to the variable factor, which force the producer to make decisions. Without this, producers could happily labor in their fields with the knowledge that each additional input of variable factors would increase yield either at a constant or increasing rate. Since this situation does not exist, producers are forced to answer a number of questions about their endeavors. They must decide on the best combination of inputs or factors of production to use. They must determine how much of a crop to produce. They will select the course of action that maximizes profits. This choice will depend upon knowledge of the elements in the profit equation. Profit, to the farmer, is what remains after the costs associated with production are subtracted from the revenues associated with production. These profits (π) are dependent on revenues and costs in the following way:

$$\pi = \text{Revenues} - \text{Costs}$$

In this chapter, the production function serves as the basis for understanding the cost component of the profit equation. The discussion on costs is divided into three parts: First comes a general discussion of

36

different ways in which the costs of production can be classified. Second comes a discussion on how various measures of costs of production are developed. It should be noted that these measures are analogous to those developed for the production function in the previous chapter. As such, they constitute new applications rather than new concepts. Third, measures of cost developed are examined for interrelationships. Explanations are then presented for these relationships.

EXPLICIT AND IMPLICIT COSTS

One way to look at the costs associated with production is to differentiate between those costs, or payments, that are made between the farm-firm unit and an outside agency, and those costs that are made to resource suppliers within the firm. The former are called *explicit costs* of production. They are paid directly to an agency or supplier outside the farm-firm unit for resources and are reported by the farm accountant as cash expenses for supplies. The costs that result from resources supplied from within the firm are *implicit costs*. They are viewed as noncash expenses. The nature of explicit costs can be shown by the following examples.

One of the inputs into the production process for corn is seed. In an effort to diminish the susceptibility of corn to blight, insects, and other natural predators and to increase yield, most farmers use some type of hybrid seed in their planting. Some farmers may attempt to save seed from the hardiest plants in the harvest to use as seed for the following crop. However, most lack the skills and equipment necessary to produce seed with high yield qualities. This function has been taken over by the major agribusiness firms, which supply everything from seed to equipment. Thus, it is very likely that the farmer will not have seed on hand to plant a corn crop and will have to purchase it from the local seed dealer. If the farmer plans to plant 200 acres of corn and uses one-fourth bushel of seed per acre, the seed requirement is fifty bushels of hybrid seed. At a price of $50 per bushel, a cash outlay to the seed dealer of $2,500 is required. Money changes hands and the farmer records the transaction as an expense. This expense results in an explicit cost of production. It is explicit in that it involved the payment of money to an outside agency in return for some good or service involved in the production process.

Another resource which the farmer may have to purchase from an outside agency is labor. Many farmers hire local teenagers to "walk the fields" to pull out weeds that the herbicide and cultivator have missed. If a farmer hires five teenagers who walk the fields for ten hours each and are paid at a rate of $2.00 per hour, the $100 spent on labor is again an explicit cost of production. Again, a payment was made by the farm-firm unit to an agency outside that unit.

While the farmer purchases many of the production inputs from outside agencies, many of the required inputs are provided from within the farm-firm unit. Most agricultural producers are not brokers who bring together a set of purchased inputs to produce a crop. Rather, they are intimately involved in the production process. They provide many of the inputs themselves. The most common resource supplied from within the farm-firm unit is labor. In the traditional family farm, most of the labor used in production is supplied by the family itself. While this practice is becoming increasingly less prevalent, most farmers will still provide a large proportion of the labor input into the production process. What is the value of that labor to the production unit? Before discussing the determination of that value, it is helpful to examine what happens if no value is assigned to the farmer's labor. First, if no value or cost is assigned to internally held resources, they may be used in an uneconomical fashion. The farmer who attributes no cost to internally held land may be careless in laying out fields and in attempting to maximize the product derived from the fields. A second consequence of not charging a price for internally held resources is that it overstates the return on the farmer's labor. For example, when a farmer is asked how he did on his farm, he may say that he did very well. He paid out $30,000 and took in $35,000 for his crops. Thus, he made a profit of $5,000. However, if the same farmer is asked what he could have received by selling his labor resource in town, he may say $10,000. If the farmer has not included his labor as an implicit cost of production, he has actually lost $5,000 by employing his resources in the farm-firm unit. He may go on assuming that he is doing well while, in reality, he is doing poorly. This misconception is of great importance in that it frustrates the movement of resources to where they are most valued by society. In the above situation, society values the farmer's labor more in town than it does on the farm. When the farmer remains where he is, he provides more farm goods and less town goods than society wants. In short, if both explicit and implicit costs are not charged against the production of the farm-firm unit, uneconomical use of society's resources will result. Society will produce less output than desired or produce the wrong mix of output.

The determination of the value of internally held resources is shown by the following examples. Assume that a farmer supplies all of the labor necessary in the production process. Although he does not hire labor from an outside agency, there is still a labor cost, which must be charged against the revenues generated. If this is not done, profits or losses will not be determined accurately. The determination of this labor cost comes through an assessment of what the farmer could receive for his labor resource if it were not employed in the farm-firm unit. What could he earn if he sold his labor, skills, and experience to someone else? There might be a number of alternate buyers for this resource. It might be sold to a factory in town for $8,000 per year. It might be sold to the local municipality for use in garbage collection for $9,000 per year. It might be sold to the corporate farm in the next county, which needs agricultural experience and expertise, for $15,000 per year. The measure of the cost of the farmer's labor is the sacrifice he must make to use it in his own production process. In this example, the best alternative use of his labor would be to sell it to the corporate farm for $15,000 per year. If the farmer chooses to retain his labor resource in his own business, he must realize this amount through farming. If he does not, it would be rational for him to give up farming and transfer his labor resources to the corporate farm. The salary that the corporate farm would pay the farmer for his labor is equal to the *opportunity cost* of his using his own labor on the farm, that is, the amount of money that he sacrifices by contributing his resources to his own business rather than selling them to the corporate farm. Opportunity cost does not take the same form as the explicit costs previously discussed. However, as a measure of implicit costs, it must be assessed against total revenues associated with the production of the farm-firm unit. If this is not done, the true costs of production are not accurately stated.

Another example resulting in implicit costs is where the farmer furnishes all or part of the capital required in the production process. Some farmers rent their capital from others through such services as custom combining, resulting in explicit costs of production. However, most farmers have a sizable investment in machinery such as tractors, combines, and so on. An estimation of the cost of capital provided from within the farm-firm unit is analogous to that previously used to determine the cost of labor. It is necessary to find the opportunity cost of capital used in that way. The opportunity cost of capital will be equal to the amount that it could earn at its best alternative use. If a farmer uses $100,000 of capital in the production process, the best alternative use for that capital might be to invest it in a certificate of deposit paying seven percent interest. The opportunity cost of using capital within the farm-firm unit would then be $7,000 per year—the interest on $100,000 at seven percent. This $7,000 is the implicit cost of capital in this example. It must be assessed against revenues if the farmer is to determine profits accurately. Again, if the revenues from production do not cover both explicit costs and implicit costs, the farmer would be better off financially to employ his resources in their best alternative uses.

Thus, one perspective on the costs of production comes through the summation of all explicit costs and implicit costs of production. Only by considering both types of costs can the farmer estimate accurately the value of the factors of production required to produce his product. If the return, or revenue, received from the production of this crop does not cover both types of costs, it will be economically advantageous for the farmer to employ his resources and talents in some alternative type of endeavor. Many times, this means producing a different crop or leaving agricultural production altogether.

FIXED AND VARIABLE COSTS

Another way to view costs involved in the production of a product is to separate them into two parts: *fixed costs* and *variable costs*. This division will help the farmer determine how much output, if any, to produce. This decision will be aided by the knowledge of which costs are dependent upon the amount of output produced and which are not.

Fixed Costs

Fixed costs are those costs that do not vary with the amount of output produced. They are the same whether the amount of product produced is one unit or one hundred units. They are incurred and must be paid whether the farmer has a bounteous harvest or none at all. There are many examples of fixed costs. The main ones can best be remembered as the DIRTI five: depreciation, interest, rent, taxes, and insurance.

Depreciation may take two forms: (1) that resulting from wear and tear and (2) that resulting from obsolescence. To demonstrate both types, assume that each of two farmers purchased a new front-mounted corn cultivator. Farmer A stores his cultivator in a machine shed for five years without using it. Farmer B uses her cultivator to cultivate 400 acres of corn per year for the same five years. At the end of the five-year time period, both pieces of machinery are worth less. They have both depreciated. Farmer A's cultivator depreciated through obsolescence. It may have become obsolete because rear-mounted, more efficient cultivators were developed during that five-year period or the development of new chemicals for controlling weeds may have eliminated the need for cultivation. Whatever the reason, depreciation through obsolescence has taken place. It is a fixed cost, which must be borne by the farmer.

Farmer B used her cultivator and caused it to decline in value or depreciate because of wear and tear. This depreciation was a function of the output produced. It is more properly termed a variable cost since it could have been avoided by not producing any crop. However, Farmer B must still assign a portion of the depreciation incurred to obsolescence and view it as a fixed cost.

Interest charges are a second broad type of fixed cost. They vary with the size of the obligation incurred rather than with the size of the output produced. If a farmer purchases an 80-acre farm and finances it through the owner on a contract for deed, he or she agrees to repay the principal amount in a certain number of years. In addition to the repayment of the principal, the borrower will also pay an interest charge each year to the person who does the financing. Assuming the borrower finances $80,000 at seven percent interest, the yearly interest payment will be $5,600 the first year. Each following year it will be less, depending on how much the principal is reduced. This cost goes on irrespective of the size of the harvest produced on the land. Whether the farmer raises 800 or 8,000 bushels of corn on those acres, the interest charge will not change—it is a fixed cost of production and as such is not dependent on output produced.

Some types of taxes are also a fixed cost to the farm operator. For example, real estate taxes depend on the size of the farm and not on the amount of crops produced thereon. One year a wheat farmer may raise 40,000 bushels of wheat on his 1,000-acre wheat farm. That year he receives a $5,000 real estate tax bill from the county. The next year conditions are less conducive to wheat production and the 1,000 acres produces only 15,000 bushels. Again, the farmer receives a notice that his real estate taxes are $5,000. The tax bill remains the same even though the output produced has changed dramatically. This tax typifies fixed costs.

Rent is a fourth general type of fixed cost. One way in which the farmer may acquire or enlarge the amount of land that he or she uses is to rent it. This rent may take the form of a cash payment. A given amount for each acre of land rented may be payable at two periods during the year—March 1 and October 1. Thus, a farmer might rent 80 acres of land for $100 per acre. The yearly rent would be $4,000 per payment date. The amount paid on each date has no bearing or relationship to the amount of the product generated by the rented fields during the production period. If production is only fifty percent of that in a normal period, the $8,000 payment stays the same and therefore is a fixed cost.

In some cases, however, the rent payment takes the form of a portion of the crop. The landlord may receive two-fifths of the crop produced and the renter three-fifths. Assume a farmer raises forty bushels of soybeans per acre: the landlord would receive sixteen of these bushels. If the landlord receives $5.00 per bushel for his soybeans, the rent is $80 per acre. In a less successful year, the farmer might produce only twenty-five bushels of soybeans per acre. The landlord's rent would then decline to $50 per acre. In this instance, rent payments would be a variable cost. They would change with the amount of crop raised during the production period.

The last of the fixed costs is insurance. Many farmers insure their buildings and equipment against fire or wind. Payment for this insurance is dependent on the value of the property and equipment insured and on the probabilities of damage to them from fire or wind. Basically, the insurance premium is independent of the amount of crops or livestock produced by those buildings or equipment. For example, a farmer with a swine-finishing operation might have $100,000 worth of buildings and equipment, which when fully utilized can process 900 pigs each year. The insurance premium covers the $100,000 value of buildings and equipment. It remains the same whether the buildings are used to capacity to finish 900 pigs per year or only produce 300 pigs per year. Thus, yearly insurance premium represents a fixed obligation independent of pork produced.

Variable Costs

What types of costs constitute variable costs? The simplest answer would be to say that variable costs are all those costs of production other than the DIRTI five. More generally, they are those costs that are dependent on the output of crops or livestock produced. They increase as output increases and decrease as output decreases.

As has been continually noted, the production of any commodity requires a great number of inputs, which are reflected in the production function:

$$Y = f(X_1, X_2, X_3 \ldots X_n)$$

Examples of inputs into the production process are obvious. Potassium, labor, feed, herbicide, and many other items have been mentioned as inputs into the production process for various commodities. The thread of commonality that links these inputs is that they are variable inputs. The total amount used increases as the output increases and decreases as output decreases.

To illustrate more directly the difference between fixed and variable costs, consider a production function for corn with two fixed inputs:

TABLE 3-1: Production function for corn

Fixed Inputs		Variable Input	TPP
Units of Land	Units of Capital	Units of Labor	Units of Corn
1	1	0	0
1	1	1	3
1	1	2	7
1	1	3	12
1	1	4	15
1	1	5	17
1	1	6	18

land (X_2) and capital (X_3), and one variable input: labor (X_1). The production function is as follows:

$$Y = f(X_1 \mid X_2, X_3)$$

An example of the relationship that might exist between labor and the output of corn produced with two fixed inputs is shown in Table 3-1.

To translate this information into cost data, it is necessary to know the prices paid for the inputs used. Assume that the price of capital is $5 per unit, the price of land is $15 per unit, and the price of labor is $5 per unit. Now it becomes possible to calculate fixed and variable cost for each level of output in Table 3-1 by multiplying the number of inputs used at each output by their price. These calculations have been done in Table 3-2. In column 5, total fixed cost was calculated by multiplying the amounts of land and capital used from columns 1 and 2 by their prices. Since one unit of land was used at a price of $15 per unit and one unit of capital was used at a price of $5 per unit, the total fixed cost for each level of output was $15 + $5 = $20. In column 6, total variable cost was found by multiplying the number of units of labor used from column 3 by the price of labor. In column 7, total cost was found by adding the total fixed costs and total variable costs found in columns 5 and 6.

Several insights into the production and cost relationship may be gained when the information on total cost, total variable cost, and total fixed cost is plotted. This has been done in Figure 3-1. First, total fixed costs stay the same at every output of corn. The total fixed cost is $20 even when no corn is produced. This fact is of importance to the decision maker in deciding whether it is more advantageous to produce or to shut down production. Variable costs begin at zero and then increase as output increases. They assume the traditional S shape of

TABLE 3–2: Total costs of production for corn

Fixed Inputs		Variable Input				
(1)	(2)	(3)	(4)	(5)	(6)	(7)
Units of Land	Units of Capital	Units of Labor	Output Units of Corn	Total Fixed Cost (1) × $15 + (2) × $5	Total Variable Cost (3) × $5	Total Cost (5) + (6)
1	1	0	0	15 + 5 = 20	0 × 5 = 0	20
1	1	1	3	15 + 5 = 20	1 × 5 = 5	25
1	1	2	7	15 + 5 = 20	2 × 5 = 10	30
1	1	3	12	15 + 5 = 20	3 × 5 = 15	35
1	1	4	15	15 + 5 = 20	4 × 5 = 20	40
1	1	5	17	15 + 5 = 20	5 × 5 = 25	45
1	1	6	18	15 + 5 = 20	6 × 5 = 30	50

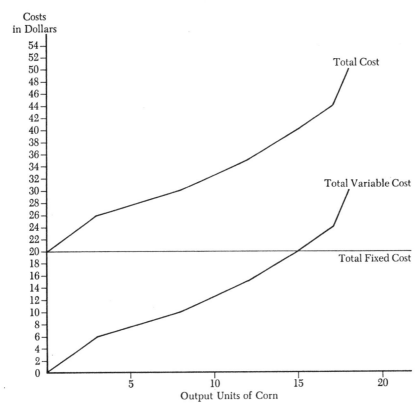

FIGURE 3-1: Costs of production for corn

total cost functions. The S shape is determined by the nature of the production function, which exhibits first increasing and then decreasing
returns. When total product is increasing at an increasing rate, total
variable cost is increasing at a decreasing rate. When total product is
increasing at a decreasing rate, total variable cost is increasing at an
increasing rate. This accounts for the S shape of the total variable cost
and total cost curves. The difference between total cost and total
variable cost is constant at every level of output. This difference is fixed
cost. Thus, total costs take the S configuration from the total variable
cost curve.

AVERAGE AND MARGINAL COSTS

Once total costs of production are established, it is possible to develop
several other measures of cost that are helpful to the decision maker,

TABLE 3-3: Average fixed cost for corn production

TPP Units of Corn	Total Fixed Cost	Calculation (TFC / TPP)	Average Fixed Cost
0	$20	$20 / 0	—
3	20	20 / 3	$6.67
7	20	20 / 7	2.86
12	20	20 / 12	1.67
15	20	20 / 15	1.33
17	20	20 / 17	1.18
18	20	20 / 18	1.11

with the focus on average and marginal measurements. The measures relevant to the costs of production are: average fixed cost, average variable cost, average total cost, and marginal cost. It should be noted that these measures are analogous to those developed in the last chapter to describe various aspects of production.

Average Fixed Cost

Average fixed cost is a measure of the proportion of overhead or fixed cost assigned to each unit produced. In contrast to total fixed cost, it decreases as output increases. Average fixed cost can be determined by dividing total fixed cost by output or total physical product. The formula for the determination of average fixed cost is:

$$AFC = TFC/TPP$$

Using the information from Table 3-2, Table 3-3 is constructed to show average fixed cost at different levels of corn output. Graphically, average fixed cost for this example is shown in Figure 3-2. AFC graphs as a rectangular hyperbola. Both end points are asymptotic to the axis. As production increases, AFC declines, tending toward, but never reaching, a limit of zero. At the opposite extreme, as output gets smaller and smaller, AFC tends toward infinity. Thus, for any output chosen, there will always be the same area under the AFC curve, in this case, equaling $20. For example: at three units of output, the average fixed cost is $6.67. The area under the curve at this point is shown by the hatched rectangle. It equals 3 × $6.67 or $20. At twelve units of output, the AFC is $1.67. Again, the area represented equals $20. It is shown by the heavy-lined rectangle. Any rectangle chosen will have the same area. Again, this fact shows that total fixed cost is the same

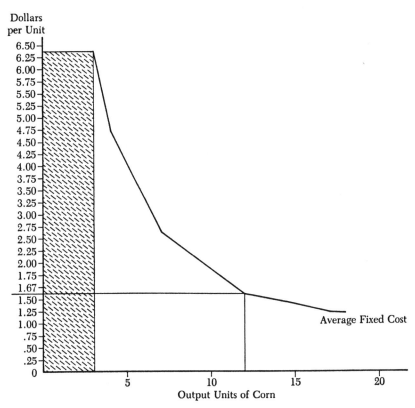

FIGURE 3-2: Average fixed cost for corn production

irrespective of output. However, as output increases, AFC will always decrease.

Average Variable Cost

The second measure of cost is average variable cost, which tells the decision maker how many dollars' worth of the variable input are associated with each unit of output. Average variable cost is important to the producer in deciding whether it is more advantageous to continue production or to shut down. The calculation of average variable cost or per unit variable cost is a simple process: dividing total variable cost by total physical product. The formula is:

$$AVC = TVC/TPP$$

TABLE 3–4: Average variable cost for corn production

(1) Variable Input Units of Labor	(2) TPP Units of Corn	(3) Total Variable Cost (1) × $5	(4) TVC / TPP (3) ÷ (2)	=	(5) Average Variable Cost	(6) Average Physical Product
0	0	0	—		—	—
1	3	$ 5	$ 5 / 3		$1.67	3
2	7	10	10 / 7		1.43	3.5
3	12	15	15 / 12		1.25	4
4	15	20	20 / 15		1.33	3.75
5	17	25	25 / 17		1.46	3.40
6	18	30	30 / 18		1.67	3

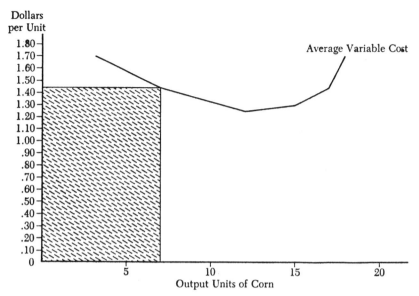

FIGURE 3-3: **Average variable cost for corn production**

Column 4 in Table 3-4 shows the calculation of average variable cost. Note that average physical product, which underlies average variable cost, is also shown. When the average physical product is increasing, the variable cost per unit of output is decreasing. When the average physical product is decreasing, average variable cost is increasing. Up to the third unit of the variable input used, average physical product is increasing from three to four, while average variable cost is declining from $1.67 to $1.25. At three units of input, average physical product is at its maximum and average variable cost is at its minimum. Beyond three units of variable input, average physical product decreases while average variable cost increases. These facts indicate the close relationship between production and cost data. When average variable cost is plotted graphically in Figure 3-3, it takes the normal U shape, which results from the nature of the production function. When APP is increasing, AVC is decreasing and conversely. When APP is at a maximum, AVC is at its minimum.

Since AVC equals total variable cost divided by total physical product, it is possible to calculate total variable cost for any output by reversing the process:

$$\text{Since AVC} = \text{TVC/TPP,}$$

multiplying both sides of the equation by TPP gives:

$$\text{TPP} \times \text{AVC} = \frac{\text{TVC}}{\text{TPP}} \times \text{TPP}$$

which reduces to:

$$\text{TPP} \times \text{AVC} = \text{TVC}$$

Thus, for any output, TVC can be calculated by multiplying the total physical product by its corresponding average variable cost. In Figure 3–3, the average variable cost for seven units of output is $1.43. Total variable cost for seven units of output will be represented by the rectangle, whose measurements are seven units of output by $1.43. This is the crosshatched rectangle and has a value of $10, which equals the total variable cost.

Average Total Cost

Average total cost is cost per unit of output of all inputs used in the production of that output. It is possible to calculate average total cost in two ways. The first way is to add AFC and AVC for each output:

$$\text{ATC} = \text{AFC} + \text{AVC}$$

Alternatively, average total cost can be calculated by dividing total cost by the output produced:

$$\text{ATC} = \text{TC/TPP}$$

Table 3–5 shows average total cost calculated by both methods. Columns 5, 6, and 7 show the calculation by the first method discussed. Column 3 shows the calculation of ATC by the division of TC by TPP. When average total cost is plotted, as in Figure 3–4, it assumes the U configuration.

It should be noted that, in the initial stages of production, ATC declines. This happens because both AFC and AVC are declining. Average total cost will decline even when AVC is increasing, as long as AFC decreases at a faster rate than the rate of increase in AVC. When the rate of increase in AVC is faster than the rate of decline in AFC, ATC begins to increase. This happens when TPP reaches eighteen units. Because ATC is influenced by the declining AFC, the minimum

TABLE 3-5: Average total cost for corn production

(1) TPP Units of Corn	(2) Total Cost	(3) TC / TPP (2) ÷ (1)	(4) ATC	(5) AFC	(6) + AVC	(7) = ATC
0	$20	$20 / 0	—	—	—	—
3	25	25 / 3	$8.33	$6.67	$1.67	$8.34
7	30	30 / 7	4.29	2.86	1.43	4.29
12	35	35 / 12	2.92	1.67	1.25	2.92
15	40	40 / 15	2.66	1.33	1.33	2.66
17	45	45 / 17	2.64	1.18	1.46	2.64
18	50	50 / 18	2.78	1.11	1.67	2.78

point of the ATC curve comes at a greater output than that of the AVC curve.

Marginal Cost

The third cost measurement to be examined is marginal cost. The term *marginal* is applied to an extra or additional unit, in this instance, the extra cost associated with an additional unit of output. There are two ways to calculate marginal cost. One is to divide the change in total cost by the change in output:

$$MC = \Delta TC/\Delta TPP$$

Since total cost changes only because of the change in total variable cost, the change in total cost equals that in total variable cost. Thus, marginal cost can also be calculated by dividing the change in total variable cost by the change in output:

$$MC = \Delta TVC/\Delta TPP$$

In Table 3-6, the calculation of marginal cost by both methods is shown. In column 4, marginal cost is calculated by dividing changes in total variable cost by changes in output. In column 7, marginal cost is

1. In this case, marginal cost is the first derivative of total cost with respect to output: dTC/dTPP.
2. MC = dTVC/dTPP.

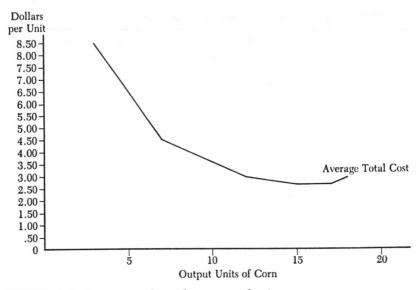

FIGURE 3–4: Average total cost for corn production

calculated by dividing changes in total cost by changes in output. As would be expected, both methods produce the same result. The marginal cost calculated in columns 4 and 7 is an average of the rates of change in cost with respect to output. Thus, it is placed between the changes in output in the table.

It should also be noted that marginal cost is based on the physical production measure of marginal physical product. When marginal physical product is increasing, marginal cost is declining. This takes place through the first three units of input. When marginal physical product is at its maximum, at three units of input, marginal cost is at its minimum. Finally, beyond three units of input, when marginal physical product decreases, marginal cost increases.

In Table 3–6, as corn production increases from zero to three units, the total variable costs increase from zero to $5. For this change in output, the marginal cost is $5 divided by three units, or $1.67 for each extra unit produced. When the change in total cost is used to calculate marginal cost, the answer is the same. If zero output is produced, total costs are $20, which also represents the fixed costs of production. When output is increased to three units, total costs increase to $25. The increase of $5, divided by three units of output, produces a marginal cost of $1.67. Figure 3–5 shows graphically how marginal cost changes as output is increased.

TABLE 3-6: Marginal cost for corn production

(1) Variable Input Units of Labor	(2) TPP Units of Corn	(3) Total Variable Cost	(4) ΔTVC / ΔTPP	(5) MC	(6) TC	(7) ΔTC / ΔTPP	(8) MC	(9) MPP
0	0	0			$20			
1	3	$ 5	$5 / 3	$1.67	25	$5 / 3	$1.67	3
2	7	10	5 / 4	1.25	30	5 / 4	1.25	4
3	12	15	5 / 5	1.00	35	5 / 5	1.00	5
4	15	20	5 / 3	1.67	40	5 / 3	1.67	3
5	17	25	5 / 2	2.50	45	5 / 2	2.50	2
6	18	30	5 / 1	5.00	50	5 / 1	5.00	1

53

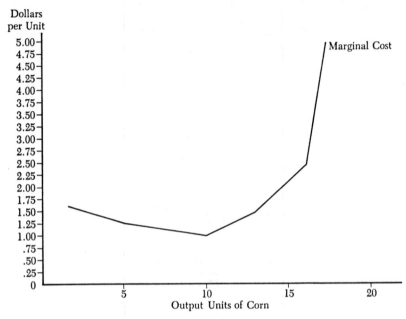

FIGURE 3-5: Marginal cost for corn production

RELATIONSHIPS BETWEEN AVERAGE TOTAL, AVERAGE VARIABLE, AND MARGINAL COST

To this point, each cost concept has been examined individually. Discussion has focused on the calculation of average fixed cost, average variable cost, average total cost, and marginal cost. In Figure 3-6, these various cost measures are put together to show their relationship. Average fixed cost, as such, has been omitted from the graph—it can always be calculated by determining the difference between average variable and average total cost. Its omission from this and future graphs also minimizes the number of curves appearing in one figure.

The relationships between average total cost, average variable cost, and marginal cost are analogous to those that were developed between average physical product and marginal physical product in the last chapter. Average cost follows marginal cost: Anytime the firm's marginal cost of production is below its average variable cost, average variable cost is declining. Anytime marginal cost is above average variable cost, average variable cost is increasing. The point at which they are equal is the minimum point of the average variable cost curve.

The same holds true for the relationship between marginal cost and average total cost. When marginal cost is less than average total cost,

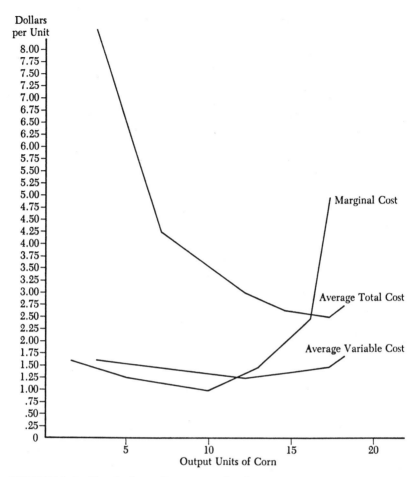

FIGURE 3-6: Marginal cost for corn production

average total cost is declining. When marginal cost is greater than average total cost, average total cost is increasing. The point at which these two cost measures are equal is the minimum point of the average total cost curve. Figure 3–6 shows the relationships just discussed. It should be noted that the minimum point of the average total cost curve comes at a greater output than does the minimum point of the average variable cost curve. This is because average total cost is affected by a continuously declining average fixed cost, which, for a time, counterbalances the rising average variable cost component of average total cost.

The use of examples will make these relationships clearer. If a farmer is initially producing 20,000 bushels of corn at an average total cost of $2 per bushel and decides to expand output, what happens? How will average total cost be affected if the farmer rents an additional farm and produces another 10,000 bushels of corn at an additional cost of $15,000? Total output has increased by 10,000 bushels. Total cost has increased by $15,000. The marginal cost of production is $1.50 per bushel ($15,000/10,000 bushels). Marginal cost of production on the rented land is fifty cents per bushel ($2.00–1.50)—less than the average total cost of production on the initial farm. The new average cost can be found by adding the cost of production of both farms—$40,000 for the first farm plus $15,000 for the second. This total is then divided by the number of bushels of corn produced on both farms (20,000 + 10,000 = 30,000) to derive an average cost of production of $1.83 per bushel. Thus, when the marginal cost of $1.50 was less than the average total cost of $2, the new average total cost declined to $1.83.

To demonstrate that the opposite holds true, a variation of this example is in order. Again, the farmer is initially producing 20,000 bushels of corn at an average cost of $2 per bushel. This time the additional rented land is less suitable for corn production and produces an additional 10,000 bushels of corn at a cost of $30,000. The marginal cost of production is $3 per bushel ($30,000/10,000 bushels). The average cost of production for the two farms can be calculated by adding together total costs from the two farms ($40,000 + $30,000 = $70,000). This figure is divided by the number of bushels of corn produced on both farms (20,000 + 10,000 = 30,000 bushels). Average total cost is then $70,000/30,000 bushels, or $2.33 per bushel. Since the marginal cost of $3 per bushel was greater than the average cost of $2 per bushel on the initial farm, the average cost increased to $2.33 per bushel.

The following summarizes the relationships that exist between average total cost, average variable cost, and marginal cost:

If MC < ATC, ATC is falling
If MC > ATC, ATC is rising
If MC = ATC, ATC is at its minimum

and

If MC < AVC, AVC is falling
If MC > AVC, AVC is rising
If MC = AVC, AVC is at its minimum

SUMMARY

This chapter has examined one component of the profit equation—cost. It developed certain concepts and measures of cost that can be used by agricultural decision makers. It expressed the notion that cost is intimately connected to the production function. The close tie of financial aspects of agriculture to the production function will be further established in the chapter which follows on the revenues of production. Presenting information concerning the production function and its financial manifestations—costs and revenues—will make it possible to discuss the actual decisions that the agricultural producer must make.

APPENDIX

The cost relationships that have been determined in this chapter can be briefly summarized through the use of equations. Total cost was first divided into two parts—fixed and variable cost. The relationship is described by equation 1.

$$(1)\ TFC + TVC = TC$$

To determine how much of each type of cost was borne by each unit of output, the concept of an average cost was developed. This concept can be applied to each type of cost in equation 2.

$$(2)\ \frac{TFC}{TPP} + \frac{TVC}{TPP} = \frac{TC}{TPP}$$

Equation 2 results in the averages in equation 3.

$$(3)\ AFC + AVC = ATC$$

Once an average cost of each unit of output was established, the focus changed to the calculation of extra or marginal cost. This was accomplished by dividing equation 1 by the change in output. The result is equation 4, which shows how costs change as output increases.

$$(4)\ \frac{\Delta TFC}{\Delta TPP} + \frac{\Delta TVC}{\Delta TPP} = \frac{\Delta TC}{\Delta TPP} = MC$$

By definition, the change in total fixed cost as output changes is zero. Thus, the change in total cost with respect to changes in output is marginal cost. The change in total variable cost with respect to changes in output is also marginal cost.

AVERAGE PHYSICAL PRODUCT AND AVERAGE VARIABLE COST

From equations 2 and 3, it has been determined that average variable cost may be calculated according to the equation:

$$(5) \quad AVC = TVC/TPP$$

Total variable cost can also be determined in another way: by multiplying the number of units of the variable input used by the price of the input. This is shown in equation 6:

$$(6) \quad TVC = Quantity_{Input} \times Price_{Input}$$

Average variable cost can be found from equation 6 by dividing TVC by output. Average variable cost then takes the form of equation 7:

$$(7) \quad AVC = \frac{Q_{Input} \times P_{Input}}{Total\ Physical\ Product}$$

Multiplying both sides of equation 7 by total physical product produces equation 8:

$$(8) \quad TPP \times AVC = P_{Input} \times Q_{Input}$$

When dividing both sides of equation 8, the quantity of input used produces equation 9:

$$(9) \quad \frac{TPP}{Q_{Input}} \times AVC = P_{Input}$$

Output, or TPP, produced divided by the quantity of input used is average physical product. Equation 9 can, thus, be restated:

$$(10) \quad APP \times AVC = P_{Input}$$

Dividing both sides of equation 10 by average physical product produces equation 11, which clearly shows the relationship between AVC and APP:

$$(11) \quad AVC = P_{Input}/APP$$

This confirms earlier statements concerning the relationship between average physical product and average variable cost. When APP increases, AVC must decrease to preserve the equality. When APP decreases, AVC must increase. Thus, average variable cost is inversely related to average physical product.

Marginal Product and Marginal Cost

The same types of manipulations can be performed to show the relationship between marginal physical product and marginal cost. One way to calculate marginal cost is to look at changes in the total variable cost with respect to changes in output. This is shown in equation 12:

$$(12) \quad MC = \frac{\Delta TVC}{\Delta TPP}$$

The change in total variable cost can be found by taking the change in the amount of variable inputs used and multiplying by the price of the input. When this substitution is made, equation 12 becomes equation 13:

$$(13) \quad MC = \frac{\Delta Q_{Input} \times P_{Input}}{\Delta TPP}$$

Multiplying both sides of equation 13 by the change in output produces equation 14:

$$(14) \quad \Delta TPP \times MC = \Delta Q_{Input} \times P_{Input}$$

Dividing both sides of equation 14 by the change in input produces equation 15:

$$(15) \quad \frac{\Delta TPP}{\Delta Q_{Input}} \times MC = P_{Input}$$

The change in TPP divided by the change in inputs used is marginal physical product. Thus, equation 15 becomes equation 16:

$$(16) \quad MPP \times MC = P_{Input}$$

Dividing both sides of this equation by MPP produces equation 17, which clearly shows the relationship between MC and MPP:

$$(17) \quad MC = P_{Input}/MPP$$

When marginal physical product increases, marginal cost decreases. When marginal physical product decreases, marginal cost increases.

QUESTIONS

1. A firm has the following production function. It must pay labor $20 per unit and rents its fixed inputs for $25 per unit.

Units of Fixed Inputs	Labor	Output
3	0	0
3	1	4
3	2	9
3	3	16
3	4	20
3	5	23
3	6	24

 A. Determine total fixed cost, total variable cost, and total cost for all levels of output.

 B. Determine average fixed cost, average variable cost, average total cost, and marginal cost for each level of output.

2. Explain the importance of the Law of Diminishing Marginal Returns on the shape of the marginal cost and average variable cost curves.

3. Explain carefully the difference between a fixed cost and a variable cost of production. How would the following costs be classified in the short run?

 A. fire insurance premiums

B. shipping charges

C. sales tax

D. raw materials

E. rent on grain storage facilities

F. interest on money borrowed to buy raw materials

CHAPTER FOUR

Revenues from Production

The last chapter developed concepts relevant to one part of the profit equation: the costs of production. In this chapter, the focus is on the revenue component of the equation. To adequately discuss the revenues that are generated by production, it is first necessary to establish the nature of the farm market and the individual farmer's position in that market. The nature of the agricultural market dictates how the price of agricultural commodities will be determined. It has an important influence on the revenues of the farm firm. These revenues can themselves be examined from different perspectives in order to aid the decision maker. Not only are farmers concerned with such measures of revenue as marginal revenue and average revenue, but they are also concerned with the variation in revenue with respect to both inputs and output. Once the revenue associated with production is explained, it is possible to discuss the production and profit-maximization decisions that the farmer makes on the basis of this data.

THE AGRICULTURAL MARKET

Many of the problems that the farmer encounters in the sale of farm products have to do with the rather unique nature of the market for such products. The market mentioned here is not a specific gathering of farmers and their customers. It is, rather, a generic description of that mass of buying and selling transactions by which agricultural goods move from field to their ultimate consumption. While the U.S.

economy is generally described as a "competitive" one, the market for agricultural commodities is perhaps the only market in which reality approximates the economist's definition of "competitive." A number of conditions produce this competitiveness. The three most important are: (1) the number of firms in the industry, (2) the way in which they make their decisions, and (3) the type of product produced.

First, the number of farms in the U.S. has steadily declined over time. However, the agricultural industry is still made up of a very large number of small producers, a condition that affects the market in three ways: First, the large number of producers in the industry increases the number of options available to the consumer. Second, when consumers are dissatisfied with one producer, they do not have to go far to find another producer. Third, the existence of a large number of options prevents producers from arbitrarily setting conditions on the sale of their crop.

Since there are a number of producers in the market, each individual producer supplies a very small amount of the total commodity produced. If Farmer Brown is dissatisfied with the price he is offered for his wheat and decides to withhold it from the market, the effect will be unnoticed. His wheat crop is so small relative to the total amount produced that it will have no effect at all on the price or availability of wheat. In contradistinction, consider the effect on the automobile market if the Ford Motor Company were to withhold its product.

Finally, the existence of a large number of firms in the industry is almost a guarantee against collusive agreements. American economic history contains many examples of producers attempting to combine to fix prices, market shares, and other aspects of economic life—all to the betterment of company profits and to the detriment of the consumer. Such behavior is illegal under present antitrust statutes, yet instances of collusion are reported almost daily in the press. Collusion is easiest when the number who are party to the agreement is very small. As the number increases, the probability of one of the colluders reporting the agreement increases. More practically, as the number of firms increases, the probability of their agreeing to something declines. As the National Farmers Organization has discovered, to its dismay, it is difficult to persuade enough farmers to agree to withhold their production to have any effect on the market.

The absence of collusion results in the second condition influential on the market—independence in decision making. Producers make their own decisions on what crops to plant, how to raise them, and how and where to market them. Each producer is an independent decision maker who makes an individual estimation of the future. The result is a set of decisions that determines the shape of the market. There is no cohesion or coercion in the decision of what to plant or in the decision of what to sell. In short, the market that emerges is the result of the decisions of a great number of independent, atomistic decision makers.

The final factor that influences the competitiveness of the market relates to the type of product produced. In economic terms, the product produced by the agricultural industry is homogeneous; every unit produced is a perfect substitute for every other unit. For each commodity, there is no difference in the product of any of the producing units. Corn from the fields of northern Illinois is exactly the same as that produced in southern Minnesota. Corn produced by Farmer Brown is a perfect substitute for corn produced by Farmer Jones. This increases the number of options for consumers of agricultural output in that where they purchase their product is totally irrelevant. At the same time, it reduces the ability of the producer to influence the market. Should the farmer advertise his corn for sale at a price higher than that existing in the marketplace, he would be greeted with derision. Should he attempt to set an arbitrary price on his output, he would be rejected and buyers would go elsewhere for their corn.

All of this dictates the position of the individual farmer relative to that exogenous influence termed *the market*. Farmers accept as given the information the market provides. Rather than setting their own product prices, they are "price takers." They determine how much they will plant and what techniques will be used in producing their products, but they are helpless in determining one of the most important aspects of their venture—the price of their products. This point cannot be stressed too strongly in that it affects all of the farmers' decisions. The market determines the prices of the products they produce. This is the stimulus to which they react, the basis for their decisions.

Since the market plays an overwhelming role in the determination of product price, the process by which this is accomplished is of major importance. Price determination in a competitive market is explained best by the simple supply-and-demand model.

SUPPLY

For purposes of this model, the most useful definition of supply is as follows:

> Supply is a schedule that links together various product prices and the quantities of a product that producers are willing and able to supply at those prices over a given period of time.

From a different perspective, it might be said that supply is a schedule of intentions. If producers were asked: "How much corn do you intend

TABLE 4-1: Supply of corn—one firm

Price Per Unit of Corn	Quantity of Corn Supplied Per Year (Units)
$5	20,000
4	15,000
3	10,000
2	5,000
1	0

to bring to the market if the price of corn is $3 per unit?" and "How much corn do you intend to bring to the market if the price of corn is $4 per unit?" and the question were repeated for a number of other prices, the result would be a schedule of intentions called *supply*. The price of the output is the stimulus to which the producer responds. In this part of the model, price is the independent variable; the quantity of corn supplied is the dependent variable. Obviously, the manner in which the producer responds to these questions will depend on a number of factors such as input costs, technology, and so on, all of which are assumed to have been considered before a response is given.

Economists have examined over time the types of responses that producers make to the price stimulus and have discerned enough commonality of behavior to generalize about this response. This generalization has taken the form of a "law" of economics—the *law of supply*. Simply stated, the law of supply says that the quantity of output producers are willing and able to bring to the market is directly related to the price of that output, and that larger quantities of the product will be supplied at higher prices than will be supplied at lower prices. Table 4–1 illustrates both the nature of supply as a schedule of intentions and the law of supply.

This table shows that supply is indeed a schedule from which the firm's intentions can be determined. For any price chosen, there is a corresponding quantity supplied. Thus, supply is a schedule linking together product price and quantity supplied. A second fact drawn from Table 4–1 is that supply is expressed in terms of a specific time period. It is not particularly enlightening that a firm is willing and able to supply 10,000 units of corn for $3 per unit unless the period of time in question is known. Ten thousand units per day is very different from 10,000 units per decade. Thus, this example shows the importance of designating the time period.

Finally, the table illustrates the law of supply. It shows that quantity supplied is directly related to price. As the price of corn increased from

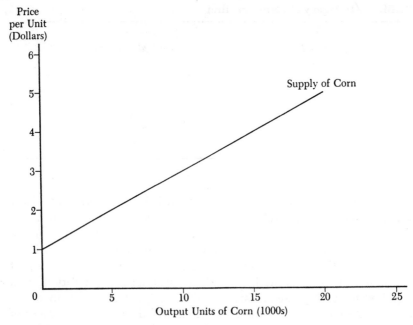

FIGURE 4-1: Supply of corn, individual firm

$2 per unit to $5 per unit, the quantity supplied increased from 5,000 to 20,000 units per year. Also, as the price of corn decreased from $4 a unit to $3 a unit, the quantity supplied decreased from 15,000 to 10,000 units per year. There are two basic reasons found for this direct relationship. First, higher product price provides an incentive to producers to offer more on the market to increase profits. If unit costs can be held constant, higher product prices will mean higher profits for the producer. Second, higher product prices allow the producer to expand output by adding more expensive inputs. As an example, a farmer may have a field that is unsuitable for the production of soybeans without the installation of drain tile. At low soybean prices, this field may stand idle or be used to produce other crops. However, as the price of soybeans increases, the farmer will, at some point, be able to convert the field to soybean production through the installation of drainage tile. In doing so, a profit will be added to the farm firm. Thus, the quantity of soybeans supplied increased in response to higher prices. The firm's supply schedule is plotted in Figure 4-1 and takes the form of a curve sloping upward to the right, again indicating the direct relationship between price and quantity.

An alternate way in which to view supply is through the more generalized form of an equation. For the example just cited, the relationship between price and quantity supplied is a linear one. Supply is a straight line. The equation for a straight line takes the general form:

$$Y = mX + b$$

where X is the independent variable, Y is the dependent variable, m is the slope of the line, and b is the Y intercept—the value of Y when X is equal to zero. In the previous example, the amount of corn supplied (Y) when price equals zero is a negative 5,000 units.[1] The slope of the supply line is found by dividing the change in the dependent variable by the change in the independent variable (5,000 units ÷ $1 per unit = 5,000). The equation descriptive of the firm's supply of corn is then:

$$Qs_{corn} = -5,000 + 5,000\ P$$

The slope has a positive sign since the relationship between price and quantity of corn supplied is direct; when price increases, quantity of corn supplied also increases.

Given this equation, it is possible to: (1) determine the quantity of corn that will be supplied at any price and (2) determine what price will be necessary to call forth a specific amount of corn. As an example, if the price of corn is $6 per unit, the units supplied are 25,000. The $6-per-unit price is substituted into the equation and the units supplied is found in the following manner:

$$Qs_{corn} = -5,000 + 5,000\ P$$
$$Qs_{corn} = -5,000 + 5,000\ (\$6)$$
$$Qs_{corn} = -5,000 + 30,000$$
$$Qs_{corn} = 25,000 \text{ units}$$

If it is important to know what the price of corn would have to be for the firm to supply 50,000 units, this equation again provides the answer through appropriate substitution. In this case, the price of corn needs to be $11 per unit:

1. The use of mathematical models to describe behavior often leads to conclusions that do violence to reality. In the real world, it is extremely unlikely that a price of zero will exist. Also, a supply of negative 5,000 units has no meaning. This again points out the importance of measuring the results of a model against the real world.

TABLE 4–2: Supply of corn, industry

Price Per Unit of Corn	Quantity of Corn Supplied Per Year (Billions of Units)
$5	10
4	7.5
3	5
2	2.5
1	0

$$Qs_{corn} = -5{,}000 + 5{,}000\ P$$
$$50{,}000\ units = -5{,}000 + 5{,}000\ P$$
$$55{,}000 = 5{,}000\ P$$
$$\frac{55{,}000}{5{,}000} = P$$
$$P = \$11$$

Thus far, it is clear that the quantity of product supplied by the individual firm is a function of the price of the product. To a large extent, the supply of product available for the industry as a whole is also dependent on price. There are, however, other factors that influence the industry supply curve, such as the number of firms in the industry, the state of technology, the prices of related goods, the prices of inputs, and future price expectations. Before discussing these factors, however, it would be helpful to know how the industry supply of a product is determined. The process is simple. Assume there are 500,000 corn producers in the industry and each has the same schedule of intentions as the firm in Table 4–1. The industry supply schedule can be found by multiplying the amount offered at each price by the number of firms. One firm would offer 10,000 units of corn to the market at a price of $3 per unit, while the industry as a whole would offer five billion bushels (10,000 × 500,000). The industry supply schedule is represented in Table 4–2. Since the relationship between price and quantity supplied remains direct, the graphical expression of the industry supply schedule also slopes upward and to the right, as shown in Figure 4–2.

When all firms in the industry do not have identical supply schedules, the construction of an industry supply curve is still relatively easy. Rather than multiply the supply schedule of the representative firm by the number of firms in the industry, it is necessary to determine how much product would be offered by each firm in the industry at various prices and add the responses. For example: If three firms were in the industry and Firm A would offer 10,000 units of corn at a price

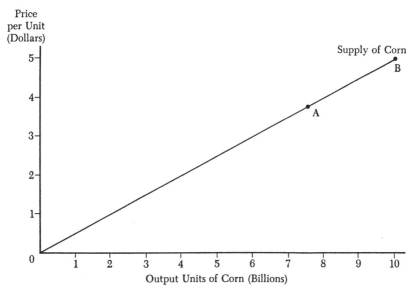

FIGURE 4-2: Supply of corn, industry

of $3, Firm B 6,000 units, and Firm C 16,000 units, one point on the industry supply schedule would be at $3 and 32,000 units (10,000 + 6,000 + 16,000 = 32,000). The entire industry supply schedule could be obtained by applying the same method to other prices.

In discussing factors that influence the firm or industry supply curve, it is essential to draw a distinction between a change in quantity supplied and a change in supply. From Tables 4-1 and 4-2, it may be determined that the quantity of corn supplied changed in response to a change in price. As price increased from $4 to $5 per unit, the quantity of corn supplied by the industry increased from 7.5 billion units to 10 billion units. The schedule of intentions remained the same. Price changes only caused a change from one position on the schedule to another. Thus, a change in quantity supplied is a movement along the same supply schedule or curve. In Figure 4-2, a change in quantity supplied is illustrated by a move from point A to point B on the supply curve.

Factors That Affect Supply

If price is the factor that causes a change in quantity supplied, what factors cause supply to change? That is, what causes supply to shift to a

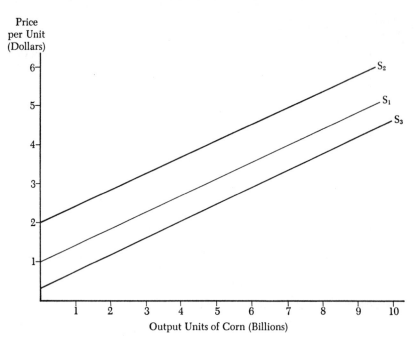

FIGURE 4-3: Supply of corn, industry

new position? In general, the supply of corn (as opposed to the quantity of corn supplied) will be influenced by the number of firms in the industry, the state of nature and technology, the prices of related products, the prices of inputs, and future price expectations. Changes in these factors will produce changes in the supply schedule, and different quantities will be offered at each price.

Assuming the size of the firms stays the same, a change in the number of firms in the industry will cause a change in the supply schedule. If firms leave the industry, reducing the number of producers, *ceteris paribus*, less corn will be offered at each and every price. This is shown in Figure 4-3 by a leftward move of the supply curve from S_1 to S_1. An increase in the number of firms in the industry would increase the quantity of corn supplied at each and every price and cause the supply curve to shift to the right. This is shown as a shift from S_1 to S_3 in Figure 4-3.

External factors are also important to the position of the supply schedule. Excellent weather conditions or a technological advance increasing the yield of corn will shift the supply curve to the right (S_1 to S_3). Producers are now willing to offer more corn at each price. A drought will have the opposite effect on industry supply—the supply curve will shift to the left (S₁ to S₂) and producers will now offer less corn at each price.

The prices of related products will also have an effect on the supply of corn. For example, when the price of soybeans increases relative to the price of corn, farmers will revise their planting intentions. They will plant more soybeans and less corn, causing the supply curve of corn to shift to the left. The opposite also holds true: If the price of soybeans drops relative to that of corn, the supply of corn at a given price will increase.

Prices of the inputs used by the farmer in the production processes will also help determine the position of the supply curve. If the price of feed supplement increases, the farmer who feeds out cattle will experience higher costs, which will make him less willing to produce cattle. As a result, the supply curve for cattle will decrease or shift to the left. A decrease in input prices will have the opposite effect: more output will be offered at given prices.

Another factor that affects supply is the farmer's future price expectations for the product he or she has produced. For example: If a farmer expects the price of corn to be higher six months in the future, he will withhold his corn from the current market. This will cause a decrease in the present supply of corn. The opposite will be true for lower future price expectations: An expected increase in price will bring forth a smaller supply on the current market.

The supply of the commodity represents only one portion of the market—production. But consumers play an equally important part. They represent the demand side of the market. It is the forces of supply and demand together that determine market prices. Thus, a discussion of demand is necessary.

DEMAND

The discussion of demand closely follows that of supply. First, by way of definition:

> Demand is a schedule that links together various product prices and the quantities of product that consumers are willing and able to purchase over a given period of time.

Like supply, demand is a schedule of intentions. It expresses the desires of consumers and their intentions toward consumption of a product at varying prices. It should be noted, however, that it is not sufficient for a consumer just to "want" or "desire" a product. For that desire to be recorded by the market, it must be backed by purchasing power. When this happens, demand will be effective and recorded in the market.

TABLE 4-3: Market demand for corn

Price Per Unit of Corn	Quantity of Corn Demanded Per Year (Billions of Units)
$5	0
4	2.5
3	5.0
2	7.5
1	10.0

The responses that consumers make to the stimulus of price have been studied by economists and found to be generally predictable. From this study has emerged the *law of demand*, which describes the relationship between price and the quantity of product demanded: As the price of a product increases, the quantity demanded decreases; as the price decreases, the quantity demanded increases. This is the law of demand and shows that price and quantity demanded are inversely related. An example of the functional relationship between the independent variable price and the dependent variable quantity demanded is shown in Table 4-3. To simplify the analysis, the market demand for corn will be considered.

The law of demand is explicitly confirmed through Table 4-3. As the price of the product increases from $4 per unit to $5 per unit, the quantity demanded decreases from 2.5 billion units to zero.[1] Conversely, when price decreases from $3 to $2 per unit, the quantity demanded increases from 5 to 7.5 billion units. Since price and quantity demanded move in opposite directions, the relationship is termed inverse.

The information on market demand for corn is plotted in Figure 4-4. The curve assumes the shape characteristic of an inverse relationship— it slopes downward.

Expressing the market demand for corn in equation form involves the same process as previously used to express supply. The general form for the demand function is:

$$Qd = A - mP$$

1. In reality, it is extremely unlikely that the quantity demanded of a product would ever decline to zero. For purposes of this explanation, however, the hypothetical data aid in understanding without doing violence to the applicability of the model to the real world in any way.

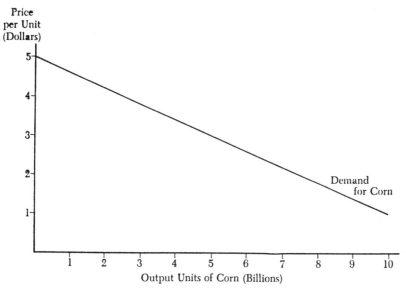

FIGURE 4–4: Market demand for corn

where Qd represents the quantity demanded, m the slope of the curve, P the price of the product, and A the quantity demanded when price equals zero. In this instance, the slope is negative because price and quantity demanded move in opposite directions. In the example used in Table 4–3, A equals 12.5 billion units. The slope equals the change in the dependent variable divided by the change in the independent variable, or 2.5 billion ÷ $1 per unit = 2.5. Thus, the equation describing this relationship is:

$$Qd = 12.5 \text{ Billion} - [2.5 \text{ Billion}] P$$

Again, using the equation it is possible to predict how much would be demanded at any price or what price would be necessary for market demand to equal a certain amount. For example: if the price of corn is $1.50 per unit, the units demanded equal 8.75 billion. This answer is found by substituting the price into the demand equation:

$$Qd = 12.5 \text{ Billion} - 2.5 \text{ Billion } P$$
$$Qd = 12.5 \text{ Billion} - 2.5 \text{ Billion } (1.50)$$
$$Qd = 12.5 \text{ Billion} - 3.75 \text{ Billion}$$
$$Qd = 8.75 \text{ Billion Units}$$

Likewise, it is possible to determine the price at which 6.25 billion units of corn would be demanded, again by substituting the appropriate numbers in the demand equation. The answer is $2.50 per unit.

$$Qd = 12.5 \text{ Billion} - 2.5 \text{ Billion P}$$
$$6.25 \text{ Billion} = 12.5 \text{ Billion} - 2.5 \text{ Billion P}$$
$$2.5 \text{ Billion P} = 6.25 \text{ Billion}$$
$$P = 6.25 \text{ Billion}/2.5 \text{ Billion}$$
$$P = \$2.50$$

Factors That Affect Demand

As it was important to distinguish between supply and quantity supplied, it is also important to distinguish between demand and quantity demanded. As previously noted, quantity demanded comes in response to a change in the price of the product. This is shown graphically by a movement along a given demand curve. A change in demand means that the whole schedule of intentions has been altered. While a change in product price is the only thing that will bring about a change in quantity demanded, several factors will produce a change in demand: the number of consumers in the market, the tastes or preferences of consumers, consumers' income, the prices of related goods, and expectations about future prices.

The number of consumers in the market influences the position of the demand curve in a very predictable way. As the number of consumers increases, more quantity will be demanded at each and every price. This is shown in Figure 4–5 by a shift of the demand curve for corn to the right from D_1 to D_2. This shift could be caused by more foreign consumers such as the Soviet Union entering the market for American farm commodities, thus increasing the demand. Should the number of consumers decrease, market demand will decrease. This is shown in Figure 4–5 by a shift of the demand curve to the left from D_1 to D_3.

The income of consumers is a factor influencing the demand for goods and services. As the per capita income of the U.S. and other countries such as Japan has increased over time, so has their demand for agricultural products. This increase in demand can be shown as a shift in the demand curve from D_1 to D_2 in Figure 4–5. A reduction in income would shift the demand curve in the opposite direction from D_1 to D_3, indicating that consumers would purchase less at every price.

In many cases, a change in income will precede a change in tastes or preference. As the per capita income in Japan has increased, food preferences have changed to include more beef in the diet of the Japanese.

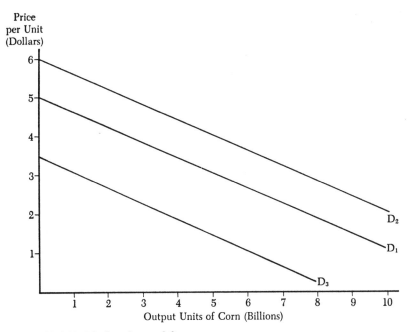

Price
per Unit
(Dollars)

FIGURE 4–5: Market demand for corn

This change in tastes has had a direct impact on the U.S. soybean market. Because soybeans are important as a feed supplement in cattle production, a preference for more beef means an increase in demand for soybeans. Likewise, a change in tastes adverse to a particular commodity will cause demand to decline. Recent concern over cholesterol intake has produced a change in consumer preference for eggs. The decrease in demand for eggs would take the form of a leftward shift in the demand curve.

The demand for specific agricultural products is also influenced by the prices of related goods. Products can be related in one of two ways: (1) they can be substitutes for one another or (2) they can be complements to one another. When the price of one good rises relative to its substitute, the demand for the substitute will increase as more and more consumers use it instead of the first good. If the price of the second good increases relative to the price of the first, demand for the first good will increase. Thus, to the extent that corn and wheat are substitutes, the price of one will affect the demand for the other.

The second type of relationship is that of complementarity. This relationship exists when goods are used together. Some examples of complementary goods are gasoline and rubber tires, bacon and eggs, and stereo and records. When complementarity exists, the price of one good will affect the demand for the other just as in the case of substitutes, but in the opposite direction. Given that product A and product B are complements, when the price of A increases, less A will be demanded. Since less A is purchased, demand for good B will decrease. If the price of A had declined, more A would have been purchased. This would require that more B be used and, consequently, increase the demand for B.

The following briefly summarizes the relationship that exists between two goods, A and B:

If A and B are substitutes:
An increase in the price of A increases the demand for B.
A decrease in the price of A decreases the demand for B.
If A and B are complements:
An increase in the price of A results in a decrease in the demand for B.
A decrease in the price of A results in an increase in the demand for B.

The final factor affecting product demand is future expectations about product prices. Should consumers expect price increases to be forthcoming in the future, they may elect to purchase more of a commodity now to avoid expected price increases. This increase in purchases will shift the demand curve outward to the right. On the other hand, if the price is expected to decline in the future, demand in the current period may decline, the reason being that consumers may postpone present purchases to take advantage of expected lower prices in the future.

MARKET EQUILIBRIUM AND PRICE DETERMINATION

With this background about supply and demand, it is now possible to discuss the method by which the price of agricultural products is determined. Essential to an understanding of this process is the concept of *equilibrium*. Equilibrium is defined as a state or position from which there is no tendency to move. It can be illustrated by a concept borrowed from the biological sciences: the concept of homeostasis. Homeostasis is the tendency of an organism to maintain a stable relationship between its components and can be illustrated through the example of blood temperature. The human organism functions normally when his or her blood temperature is 98.6° Fahrenheit.

TABLE 4-4: Market supply and demand for corn

Price Per Unit of Corn	Quantity of Corn Supplied Per Year (Billions of Units)	Quantity of Corn Demanded Per Year (Billions of Units)	Surplus (+) or Shortage (-) of Corn Per Year (Billions of Units)
$5	10	0	+ 10
4	7.5	2.5	+ 5
3	5	5	0
2	2.5	7.5	− 5
1	0	10	−10

When some outside stimulus raises or lowers the temperature of the blood, reactions are set off to regain the normal blood temperature. An external force, such as a chill wind, lowers blood temperature below the normal point, and the organism responds. Goose pimples appear as the capillaries on the surface of the skin contract to expose less blood to the chilling stimulus. Shivering begins, which burns energy to increase the blood temperature. In short, automatic forces are set into motion to raise the temperature of the blood and restore it to its normal level.

If the outside stimulus raises the blood temperature above the normal level, the organism again responds. Sweating begins and wets the surface of the skin, which cools the organism when it evaporates. This lowers the blood temperature toward the normal 98.6°. The normal blood temperature of 98.6° may be thought of as an equilibrium blood temperature. When an external force serves to raise the blood temperature above or below this norm, forces are automatically set into motion to restore it to its equilibrium level. What happens when the blood temperature is at 98.6°? The answer is nothing. The equilibrium state of 98.6° is one from which there is no tendency to change. Any other blood temperature is a disequilibrium, a condition which cannot endure. The body always seeks a state of equilibrium.

The notion of equilibrium can also be applied to prices determined in a competitive market. An equilibrium price is one from which there is no tendency to change. In distinction, a disequilibrium price is one that tends to change and is unstable. When price is out of equilibrium, forces will be set into motion to restore equilibrium. An examination of market supply and demand for corn will demonstrate more clearly the meaning of equilibrium. Table 4-4 shows both market supply and demand for corn.

At a price of $1 per unit, consumers are willing and able to purchase 10 billion units of corn per year. On the other hand, producers are not willing to produce any corn at a price of $1. The net result at this price is that consumers are frustrated. While they want to purchase 10 billion units of corn, they find none available. Given the intentions of producers and consumers, there is a shortage of 10 billion units. When this occurs, consumers will bid up the price of corn. Two things happen as the price increases. One, the law of demand indicates that consumers will be willing and able to purchase less of the product. As the price rises from $1 to $2 per unit, the quantity demanded declines from 10 billion units to 7.5 billion units. Two, the law of supply indicates that producers are willing and able to offer more of the product. As the price increases from $1 to $2 per unit, the quantity supplied increases from 0 to 2.5 billion units. At the new price of $2 per unit, the shortage has declined from 10 billion units to 5 billion units. However, a shortage still exists and will produce another round of bidding up of prices by consumers.

If the other extreme in price is chosen, there will again be frustrated intentions. At a price of $5 per unit, producers are willing and able to offer 10 billion units of corn per year. However, consumers are not willing to purchase any corn at that price. There is a surplus of 10 billion units of corn. What can be done? Grain dealers, finding themselves with large amounts of unsold corn, will reduce the price of corn in an effort to get consumers to purchase it. As the price falls, consumers, acting in accord with the predictions of the law of demand, will buy more. Producers, as predicted by the law of supply, will offer less corn on the market. As the price falls from $5 to $4 a unit, the quantity demanded increases from 0 to 2.5 billion units. At the same time, quantity supplied declines from 10 billion to 7.5 billion units. The surplus has now shrunk from 10 billion units to 5 billion units. With a surplus still in existence, prices will decline still further. When the price of corn falls to $3 per unit, the intentions of both producers and consumers are satisfied. At this price, consumers want to purchase 5 billion units of corn, and producers want to sell 5 billion units. The intentions of consumers are fulfilled in that there is exactly as much corn available as they desire at that price. Producers find that they may sell all the corn they were willing and able to produce at that price. There are neither surpluses to drive down the price nor shortages to drive it up. There is no tendency for this $3 per unit price to change once it is reached. In short, it is an equilibrium price.

The definition of the equilibrium price is that it is a price that "clears" the market, leaving neither surpluses nor shortages. It is the price at which quantity supplied equals quantity demanded. The market supply-and-demand curves for corn are plotted as in Figure

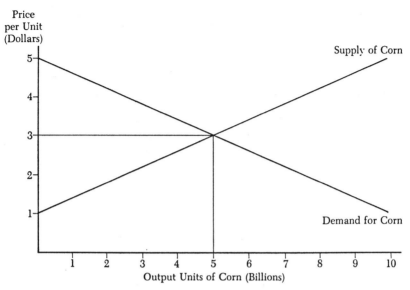

FIGURE 4-6: Market supply and demand for corn

4-6. It is apparent that the equilibrium price is the one accompanying the intersection of the two curves. At this price, and only at this price, does the quantity supplied equal the quantity demanded. At this price, and only at this price, will there be stability. In short, it is the market's equilibrium price.

The equilibrium price can also be determined if the equations describing supply and demand are known. For this example, the equation describing the market supply of corn is:

$$Qs_{corn} = -2.5 \text{ Billion} + [2.5 \text{ Billion}] P$$

The market demand equation is:

$$Qd_{corn} = 12.5 \text{ Billion} - [2.5 \text{ Billion}] P$$

It is known that the equilibrium price is one which will clear the market; i.e., the one at which quantity supplied equals quantity demanded. The equilibrium condition is thus:

$$Qs_{corn} = Qd_{corn}$$

Substituting the appropriate numbers into this equation results in:

$$-2.5 \text{ Billion} + [2.5 \text{ Billion}] P = 12.5 \text{ Billion} + 2.5 \text{ Billion}$$
$$[5 \text{ Billion}] P = 12 \text{ Billion}$$
$$P = \$3$$

Once the equilibrium price is shown, the equilibrium quantity supplied and quantity demanded can be found by substituting this price into the appropriate equation.

$$Qs = -2.5 \text{ Billion} + [2.5 \text{ Billion}] P$$
$$Qs = -2.5 \text{ Billion} + 2.5 \text{ Billion} (3)$$
$$Qs = -2.5 \text{ Billion} + 7.5 \text{ Billion}$$
$$Qs = 5 \text{ Billion Units}$$

Likewise:

$$Qd = 12.5 \text{ Billion} - [2.5 \text{ Billion}] P$$
$$Qd = 12.5 \text{ Billion} - 2.5 \text{ Billion} (3)$$
$$Qd = 12.5 \text{ Billion} - 7.5 \text{ Billion}$$
$$Qd = 5 \text{ Billion}$$

Of course, it is already known in equilibrium that Qs = Qd, so determining one determines the other.

TOTAL REVENUE FOR THE FIRM

As previously mentioned, once the market determines the price of the product, each individual producer accepts this information and responds to it. Of greatest interest to the producer is the total revenue brought in from the firm's production. It is total revenue, coupled with information about the total costs, which allows the producer to assess the profitability of the firm's operation. Total revenue to the firm is simply calculated by multiplying the number of units of product sold by the market-determined price.

Total Revenue (TR) = Total Physical Product (TPP) × Price

If the price of a product is $3 per unit and the producer sells fifteen units, total revenue is 15 × $3 = $45. The relationship between output and total revenue for the firm given a market price of $3 per unit of corn is shown in Table 4–5.

Since the price of corn is determined by the market for corn, and since each individual producer supplies such a small proportion of the total production, the price remains the same no matter how much any

TABLE 4–5: Total revenue and output

Output Units of Corn	Price Per Unit of Corn	Total Revenue
0	$3.00	0
3	3.00	$ 9.00
7	3.00	21.00
12	3.00	36.00
15	3.00	45.00
17	3.00	51.00
18	3.00	54.00

one producer supplies. Thus, the price of $3 per unit remains constant. Total revenue is plotted graphically in Figure 4–7. The total revenue curve has a constant slope. This fact again shows that one producer cannot change market price no matter how much or how little output he or she brings to the market.

AVERAGE REVENUE

There are other methods of viewing revenue than from the total aspect. One such measure is *average revenue*, which measures the amount of total revenue attributable to each unit produced. It is calculated by dividing total revenue by the output produced.

$$\text{Average Revenue (AR)} = \text{TR/TPP}$$

From the previous discussion, it is clear that the amount of revenue brought in by each unit of product is exactly the same. It does not change no matter what output the individual producer chooses to offer on the market. Thus, average revenue is the same as the market-determined price. This can be demonstrated by a manipulation of the equations below:

$$\text{TR} = \text{TPP} \times \text{P}$$

This equation measures the total revenue of the firm. If both sides of the equation are divided by output, the equation takes a different form:

$$\text{TR/TPP} = \text{P}$$

and

$$\text{TR/TPP} = \text{AR}$$

FIGURE 4–7: **Total revenue corn production**
(price of corn $3 per unit)

Therefore:

$$AR = P$$

in a competitive market such as the one for agricultural products. Calculating average revenue from the data in Table 4–5 shows the equality of average revenue and price. These calculations are shown in Table 4–6. The information from Table 4–6 is shown graphically in Figure 4–8. Now it can readily be seen that average revenue and price are the same.

MARGINAL REVENUE

A third measure of revenue is *marginal revenue*. Marginal revenue is the additional or extra revenue associated with an additional or extra

TABLE 4-6: Average revenue

Output Units of Corn	Price Per Unit of Corn	Total Revenue	AR = TR/TPP	Average Revenue
0	$3.00	0	0/0 = 0	0
3	3.00	$ 9.00	9/3 = 3	$3.00
7	3.00	21.00	21/7 = 3	3.00
12	3.00	36.00	36/12 = 3	3.00
15	3.00	45.00	45/15 = 3	3.00
17	3.00	51.00	51/17 = 3	3.00
18	3.00	54.00	54/18 = 3	3.00

unit of output. It can be calculated by dividing the change in total revenue by the change in total output produced.[1]

$$\text{Marginal Revenue (MR)} = \Delta TR/\Delta TPP$$

Table 4-7 shows the calculation of marginal revenue. Marginal revenue is placed between the levels of output for which it is calculated because it represents an average rate of change. Each extra unit of output brings in the same amount of extra revenue. This means marginal revenue will be constant at all levels of output. Thus, price and marginal revenue will also be equal at all levels of output. This is

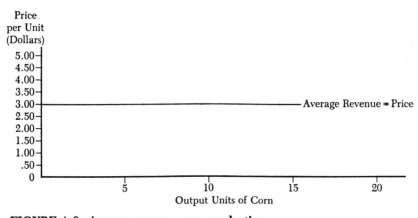

FIGURE 4-8: Average revenue, corn production

1. Expressed in terms of calculus, it is the first derivative of the total revenue function with respect to output: dTR/dTPP.

TABLE 4-7: Marginal revenue, corn production

Output Units of Corn	Total Revenue	MR = $\Delta TR / \Delta TPP$	Marginal Revenue
0	$ 0		
3	9	9-0/3-0 = 9/3	$3.00
7	21	21-9/7-3 = 12/4	3.00
12	36	36-21/12-7 = 15/5	3.00
15	45	45-36/15-12 = 9/3	3.00
17	51	51-45/17-15 = 6/2	3.00
18	54	54-51/18-17 = 3/1	3.00

shown in Table 4-7, where marginal revenue is equal to the market-determined price of $3. Figure 4-9 shows graphically this same relationship.

DEMAND FOR THE FIRM'S PRODUCTS

It has been noted that the competitive market environment in which the farmer operates is created by the very special characteristics of farm production. The product produced is homogenous. The number of producers is great. Decisions are made independently. Each producer supplies to the market a negligible share of the total output produced. While these characteristics form the basis of the competitive market, they also impose special operating constraints on the individual producer. The market determines the price. The farmer reacts to it. Thus, for the individual firm, the market price is the demand curve for the firm's products.

Figure 4-10 shows a recapitulation of the analysis of the relationship of firm demand to the market. Market supply and demand combine to produce an equilibrium price of $3 per unit. This price is viewed as given by the individual firm and is, in fact, the demand curve for the products of the individual firm. At the market price, each firm can sell all of the product that it desires. Should the firm seek to raise the price of its product above that market-determined price, there will be no demand for its product—consumers, confronted with a very large number of alternate sources, will go elsewhere. The firm may charge less than the market price. However, at any price less than the market-determined price, it will sell exactly the same output that it could have at the market-determined price. The difference is that it will derive less revenue by doing so. The only way in which it would be rational for

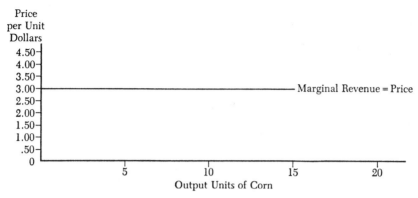

FIGURE 4-9: Marginal revenue, corn production

the firm to sell at less than the market price would be if the firm were ignorant of the market price. This situation may occur for individual producers from time to time. However, it is generally assumed, and accurately so, that producers in the agricultural market will be very well informed about the market price of their products.

Given the above, it will be irrational for the firm to offer its product to the market at a price below the market-determined price. It will also be impossible for the firm to sell any of its product at a price higher than the market-determined price. This means the individual producer is faced with what economists call a perfectly elastic demand curve at the market-determined price of $3 per unit. This demand price for the individual firm is also equal to the firm's average and marginal revenue. This is shown graphically in Figure 4-10.

REVENUE AND INPUT USE

Thus far, all of the measures of revenue have been associated with the output produced. Measures of total, average, and marginal revenue are all dependent on the amount of output produced. It is useful many times for the individual producer to be able to calculate the amount of revenue generated by the inputs used. Before the firm expands its labor force or purchases new equipment, it must have some idea of how much revenue it can expect to receive from that additional labor or equipment. Two alternate ways of measuring this revenue are through the calculation of *total value product* and *marginal value product*.

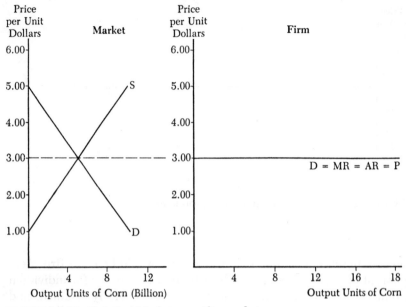

FIGURE 4–10: Relationship between the market
and the firm's demand

Total Value Product

Total value product is the total value of the products produced by any
level of input utilization. It can be calculated by multiplying the total
physical product of the inputs used by the price of the product
produced. Table 4–8 shows how total value product is related to
various levels of labor input. Three units of labor used produce 12 units
of corn. The total value product of this labor is the TPP of 12 units
multiplied by the $3 price of the product produced, or $36.

Total value product is plotted in Figure 4–11. The difference between this measure of revenue and total revenue is clear. Since total
value product is related to input use rather than to output produced,
the TVP curve assumes the shape of the production function. It does
not have the linear form of the total revenue curve.

Marginal Value Product

In its decision-making process, the firm will be more concerned with
the value added to its revenue by adding another unit of input than

TABLE 4–8: Total value product use

Units of Labor	Output Units of Corn	×	Price Per Unit of Corn	=	Total Value Product of Labor
0	0		$3.00		$ 0
1	3		3.00		9
2	7		3.00		21
3	12		3.00		36
4	15		3.00		45
5	17		3.00		51
6	18		3.00		54

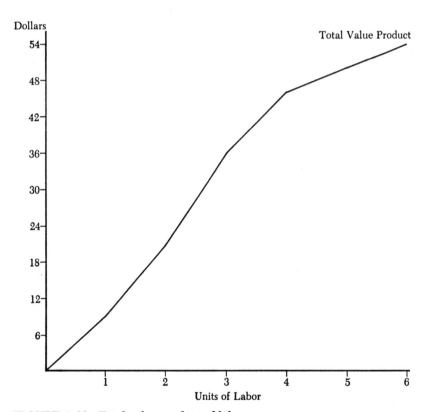

FIGURE 4–11: Total value product of labor

TABLE 4–9: Marginal value product

Units of Labor	Total Value Product of Labor	$MVP = \Delta TR/\Delta Q_{input}$	Marginal Value Product
0	$ 0	9–0/1–0 = 9/1	$ 9
1	9	21–9/2–1 = 12/1	12
2	21	36–21/3–2 = 15/1	15
3	36	45–36/4–3 = 9/1	9
4	45	51–45/5–4 = 6/1	6
5	51	54–51/6–5 = 3/1	3
6	54		

with the total revenue generated by a set of inputs, the reason being most decisions made in agricultural production are made on an incremental basis. Should the firm hire another hired man? Should it use another unit of capital to dry the corn? These are questions that can only be answered if the farmer has some idea of how the extra unit of input affects revenues and costs. The extra revenue generated by the use of an extra unit of input is called the *marginal value product*. It measures the change in total revenue associated with a change in input use. It can be calculated by dividing the change in total revenue by the change in input use.[1]

$$\text{Marginal Value Product (MVP)} = \Delta TR/\Delta Q_{input}$$

Table 4–9 shows the calculation of marginal value product. As the producer increases level of input use from four units to five, total revenue increases from $45 to $51. Marginal value product is then ($51–$45)/ (5–4), or $6.

A second way in which marginal value product can be calculated is to multiply the marginal physical product of the variable input by the price of the output. This results in the following equation:

$$MVP = MPP_{input} \times Price_{output}$$

Table 4–10 shows the calculation of the marginal value product by the second method.

The data on marginal value product is plotted graphically in Figure 4–12. It can be seen that the curve takes on the same shape as the mar-

---

1. The marginal value product is the first derivative of total value product with respect to input use: $dTVP/dQ_{input}$.

TABLE 4–10: Marginal value product

Units of Labor	Output Units of Corn	MPP	× Price of Corn	= MVP
0	0			
1	3	3	$3.00	$ 9
2	7	4	3.00	12
3	12	5	3.00	15
4	15	3	3.00	9
5	17	2	3.00	6
6	18	1	3.00	3

ginal physical product curve. This shows the close relationship between the physical details of production and the value from this production.

SUMMARY

This chapter completes the discussion of the rudiments of production in the agricultural industry. At this point, the technical details of production are well established. The relationship to costs and revenues has been examined. The producer is now in a position to make decisions about input use, output produced, whether to continue production or

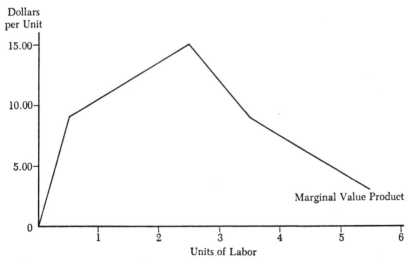

FIGURE 4–12: Marginal value product

shut down, types of products to produce, and a myriad of other things. In all of these decisions, the producer will refer to the basic information that has been developed in the last three chapters. Given the goal of profit maximization or loss minimization, this information will allow the producer to control rationally his or her future.

QUESTIONS

1. Explain the effects of the following on a firm's total revenue schedule for wheat.

   A. an increase in demand for barley
   B. an increase in consumer income
   C. an increase in livestock on farms

2. For the production function below, develop a total revenue schedule for output. Also, show this schedule graphically. Assume output sells for $5 per unit.

Units of Land	Units of Labor	Units of Output
10	0	0
10	5	5
10	10	12
10	15	16
10	20	19
10	25	20

3. Using the information found in question 2, determine the marginal value product and total value product for labor. Explain how total value product differs from total revenue.

CHAPTER FIVE

Decision-Making: The Profit-Maximization Decision

With the information on the production function and its attendant costs and revenues, the farm firm can make analytical decisions concerning its operation. The most fundamental decision it must make is the amount of output to produce in order to maximize profits. This seemingly simple decision is the focus of this chapter. To obtain some insight into the decision-making process, the model developed here will be a very crude approximation of the real world. The assumptions upon which it is built are very restrictive. It is assumed that the farmer is producing only one product and using only one variable to produce it. All other inputs are held constant. Thus, the model deals with the familiar production function:

$$Y = f(X_1 \mid X_2, X_3 \ldots X_n)$$

By dealing initially with this simplified model, the logic of the decision-making process is more clearly revealed. This logic is of the greatest importance. It is impossible for the economist or the agricultural producer to foresee all possible contingencies that may be encountered. Thus, it is more important to develop a framework of analysis suitable to a great number of different circumstances than to attempt to generate answers that apply only to specific circumstances. Once the logic of this model is established, it will be possible to bring decision-making models closer to reality. This is accomplished by relaxing the constraining *ceteris paribus* assumption. However, this task is left for later chapters.

The model dealt with now shows how the farmer decides the amount of output to produce to maximize profits or minimize losses. Two approaches can be used to determine this output. Both yield the same results but rely on different sets of information. The choice of which one to use depends more on the availability of data than on any innate superiority of one over the other. The two approaches are: (1) the total-cost, total-revenue approach, and (2) the marginal-cost, marginal-revenue approach.

Before dealing with these two approaches to determining output, it is necessary to establish the time frame within which the decision occurs. Time acts as a constraint on the firm, circumscribing its range of decision making. It may react very rapidly to some stimuli, while the reaction to other stimuli may require considerably more time. For example: decisions concerning the size of plant to construct take much longer to make than decisions concerning the amount of fertilizer to apply. Since the actual amount of time involved varies so widely, economists have separated time into two periods: the long run and the short run. As the model is developed, the importance of these two time periods in the decision-making process will be shown.

THE LONG RUN AND SHORT RUN

The distinction between the long run and the short run lies in the kinds of decisions that may be made within each time period. The long run is defined as a period of time long enough to change all of the inputs in the production process. There are no fixed inputs in the long run; all inputs are variable. Thus, the long run is, in reality, a planning period for the firm. The short run is a period of time when certain inputs in the production process can be varied and others cannot. This distinction determines which of the costs of production vary in the short run and which remain fixed. In general, the costs associated with the variable inputs will be variable costs, while the costs associated with the fixed inputs will be fixed costs. Thus, in the long run, all costs will be variable costs because all inputs are considered to be variable. An example will more adequately illustrate the distinction between these two time periods. It will also show how the time period within which the decision takes place is a constraint on the range of the producer's decisions.

Assume, for the moment, that a farmer calculates revenues and costs of production at year's end and finds that he has incurred a rather sizable loss on his operation. Since his goal in producing is to make a profit, he has failed. What is his reaction? How does he make decisions regarding future operations? If he expects the same result in future years, will he rationally choose to leave farming for some other line of endeavor? This decision, since it involves the liquidation of fixed inputs, is not one which may be carried out in a short period of time. It not only requires time to dispose of fixed inputs, such as his plant and land, but it also takes time before contractual obligations, such as insurance or any other types of long-term commitments, can be ended. During the period he is attempting to dispose of his fixed inputs, he also faces a number of short-run decisions. What crop should be planted to minimize the loss? How much fertilizer should be used? How much labor should be hired? Does it make sense to produce a crop at all? Is it more economical to let the land lie fallow? The answers to these questions depend, partially, on which costs are subject to change for the farmer and which are not. When this information is put together with revenues, it becomes possible for the farmer to decide how much output to produce in both the short run and the long run.

THE TOTAL-COST, TOTAL-REVENUE APPROACH

The profit equation:

$$\pi = TR - TC$$

is the difference between total revenue and total cost. Clearly the most obvious way for the farmer to determine profit-maximizing or loss-minimizing output is to compare total revenue and total cost for each level of output. This comparison yields the level of profit for each output. It allows the farmer to determine which level of output provides the greatest profit or smallest loss. To illustrate this procedure, Table 5–1 combines the cost-and-revenue data from the preceding two chapters. A calculation of the profit has been made for each level of production. From this calculation, the output that produces the greatest profit can be determined.

A comparison of total revenue (column 3) with total cost (column 6) shows that the most profitable level of output for the farmer to produce is seventeen units. At this output, total revenue is $51 and total cost is $45. This results in a $6 profit to the farmer. Other levels of output, such as fifteen and eighteen units, will also produce a profit, but less than the $6 which occurs at seventeen units of output. The producer seeking to maximize profits will therefore choose to produce an output of seventeen units.

It should also be noted that maximum revenue does not necessarily coincide with maximum profits. The total revenue generated by eighteen units of production ($54) is greater than that associated with

TABLE 5-1: Total revenues, total costs, and profits

(1) Output Units of Corn	(2) Price of Corn	(3) TR	(4) TFC	(5) TVC	(6) TC	(3) – (6) Profit + Loss –
0	$3	$ 0	$20	$ 0	$20	–$20
3	3	9	20	5	25	– 16
7	3	21	20	10	30	– 9
12	3	36	20	15	35	+ 1
15	3	45	20	20	40	+ 5
17	3	51	20	25	45	+ 6
18	3	54	20	30	50	+ 4

seventeen units of production ($51). While it is tempting to look for the output that generates the most revenue as the optimal one, this output will not always yield the optimal result. While revenues increase as output increases from seventeen to eighteen units, costs also increase, at a faster rate than the increase in revenues. Consequently, profit is reduced by an increase in output from seventeen to eighteen units. This again demonstrates that the profit-making calculation requires information on both revenues and costs. A simple examination of revenues alone will not suffice to determine the producer's best output.

Using the information developed in Table 5-1, it is possible to derive a graphical solution to the output question using the total-revenue, total-cost approach. In Figure 5-1, the total profit at each level of output is represented by the vertical distance between total revenue and total cost. This distance will be the greatest at that point at which the slope of the total revenue curve is equal to the slope of the total cost curve. The slope of the total revenue curve is equal to the price of the product. The slope of the total cost curve is the slope of a line segment tangent to the curve at that point. Thus, the slopes of the two curves are equal at seventeen units of output, indicating it as the profit-maximizing level of production.

Thus far, the total-revenue, total-cost approach has been used to determine the profit-maximizing output for a firm making a profit in the short run. This explains only one of the possible outcomes of production. There will be occasions when short-run production yields a loss rather than a profit. Under these circumstances, the total-revenue, total-cost model can be used to determine the output that minimizes losses rather than maximizes profits. The firm incurring losses in the short run is faced with two alternatives: (1) continue production in the short run and leave the industry in the long run, or (2) shut down the operation in the short run and leave the industry in the long run. The

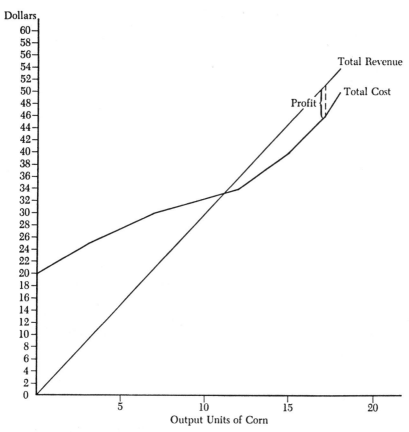

FIGURE 5-1: Total revenue, total cost, and profits

total-revenue, total-cost approach can provide solutions to both alternatives.

The event most likely to change the firm's operating situation is a change in the price of the product it sells. Events totally beyond its control may lower the price of the product to the point where it incurs a loss no matter what output is produced. Should the price per unit of output decline to $2, the profitability of the operation will change. Table 5-2 is a modification of Table 5-1 and shows the effects of a lower price on profit and output produced. Given a price of $2 per unit, any output the firm chooses to produce generates a loss. Since it is irrational to devote resources to an activity producing a loss, the firm will leave the industry. However, leaving the industry is a long-run decision. Until enough time passes for that decision to become operational, the firm is faced with short-run decisions. While there are no

TABLE 5-2: Total revenues, total costs, and profits

(1) Output Units of Corn	(2) Price of Corn	(3) TR	(4) TFC	(5) TVC	(6) TC	(7) Profit + Loss −
0	$2	$ 0	$20	$ 0	$20	−$20
3	2	6	20	5	25	− 19
7	2	14	20	10	30	− 16
12	2	24	20	15	35	− 11
15	2	30	20	20	40	− 10
17	2	34	20	25	45	− 11
18	2	36	20	30	50	− 14

profits to be maximized in the short run, it is possible to minimize losses. Determination of the loss-minimizing output can again be accomplished by using the total-revenue, total-cost approach.

A comparison of total revenue with total cost for each level of output indicates that losses will be minimized when fifteen units of output are produced. Production of fifteen units generates a loss of $10. This is a smaller loss than that associated with any other level of output. If no output was produced, the producer would lose $20 or an amount equal to total fixed cost. Thus, in the short run, it pays to continue production to minimize the firm's losses. When the information of Table 5-2 is plotted graphically in Figure 5-2, the farmer's circumstances are illustrated even more clearly. Total revenue is less than total cost at every output level. The vertical distance between the two curves measures the magnitude of the loss incurred. The producer's task in the short run is to find that output at which the vertical distance is least. This, of course, is the output of fifteen units. This output occurs where the slopes of the two curves are equal.

The firm may also be faced with circumstances where reducing output to zero is rational in the short run. To determine when this will be true, the farmer must examine those costs that continues even though no production takes place; i.e., fixed costs. In the example discussed in Table 5-2, the farmer's fixed costs of production are $20. Again, this would be the loss if no production took place. Producing an output of fifteen units reduces the loss to $10. This amount is $10 less than would be lost by reducing output to zero; i.e., discontinuing production. In short, the production of fifteen units generates a total revenue that covers all of the variable costs of producing that output and contributes something toward fixed costs. In this situation, it is to the farmer's advantage to produce in the short run. However, if total revenue had fallen short of covering total variable cost, the farmer

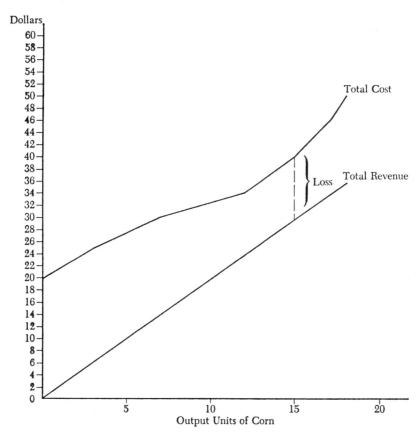

FIGURE 5–2: Total revenue, total cost, and losses

would have incurred **a** smaller loss by shutting down than by operating. Table 5–3 shows total-revenue and total-cost data with the price of corn at $1 per unit.

This table shows the farmer is again making a loss at each and every level of output. Additionally, if a comparison is made between total revenue and total variable cost for each output, it is clear that no level of output exists where total revenue exceeds total variable cost. Thus, the farmer is in the peculiar situation of having to add to the production process dollars over and above fixed costs.[1] When the farmer

1. Lest this be dismissed as a theoretical, unrealistic situation, during one of President Nixon's price freezes, the cost of feed required to raise baby chicks to market weight was greater than the price at which they could be sold. As a consequence, producers found it economically advantageous to drown the chicks rather than feed them. Thus, output was reduced to zero in the short run.

TABLE 5-3: Total revenues, total costs, and profits

(1) Output Units of Corn	(2) Price of Corn	(3) TR	(4) TFC	(5) TVC	(6) TC	(7) Profit + Loss −
0	$1	$ 0	$20	$ 0	$20	−$20
3	1	3	20	5	25	− 22
7	1	7	20	10	30	− 23
12	1	12	20	15	35	− 23
15	1	15	20	20	40	− 25
17	1	17	20	25	45	− 28
18	1	18	20	30	50	− 32

compares the costs of producing to the costs of shutting down, it emerges that: (1) by producing no output at all, losses are $20 or an amount equal to fixed costs, and (2) since total revenue does not cover variable costs, every level of output produced generates a loss greater than $20. Thus, it is to the farmer's advantage to produce no output in the short run and to leave the industry in the long run.

From this discussion, it is possible to develop a set of generalizations regarding rational behavior for the producer. When the producer is making a profit in the short run, this profit will be maximized by choosing that output at which the difference between total revenue and total cost is the greatest. In this situation, the producer will have no incentive to leave the industry in the short or long run. However, when conditions result in a loss, the producer may find the situation entirely different. In the short run, production should be continued if, and only if, the losses from doing so are less than fixed costs. This means total revenue must exceed total variable cost to continue production. If the losses incurred while producing an output are greater than fixed costs, it will be advantageous to halt production in the short run.

THE MARGINAL-COST, MARGINAL-REVENUE APPROACH

While the total-revenue, total-cost approach is the most obvious way to determine the profit-maximizing or loss-minimizing output, it does have its disadvantages. First, it requires the farmer to think in terms of totals rather than the more familiar terms of increments in output or

TABLE 5–4: Marginal revenues, marginal costs, and profits

(1) Output Units of Corn	(2) AFC	(3) AVC	(4) ATC	(5) MC	(6) MR = P	(7) Profit + Loss –
0	—	0			—	–$20
3	$6.67	$1.67	$8.34	$1.67	$3.00	– 16
7	2.86	1.43	4.29	1.25	3.00	– 9
12	1.67	1.25	2.98	1.00	3.00	+ 1
15	1.33	1.33	2.66	1.67	3.00	+ 5
17	1.19	1.46	2.64	2.50	3.00	+ 6
18	1.11	1.67	2.78	5.00	3.00	+ 4

inputs. Most farmers do not rise with the sun to make a decision as to whether they should farm that day or shut down altogether. Normally, their decisions concern the effect that adding another unit of output has on revenues and cost—the marginal revenue and the marginal cost of adding another unit of output. The second disadvantage of the total approach is that it requires data that may not be available during the production process. Information concerning the marginal cost and projected marginal revenue associated with an extra unit of production may be more easily obtained. The third disadvantage is that the total approach requires a large number of calculations. For each possible level of output, the farmer must ascertain total revenue, total cost, and the consequent profit or loss. Far fewer calculations are required by using the marginal approach. For these reasons, the marginal approach is simpler and more often used.

The most basic explanation of the marginal approach is that the farmer examines the effect of each incremental unit of production on profit. If the effect is positive, the farmer will produce that unit. If the effect is negative, he or she will not produce it. The effect on profit is a function of costs and revenues. Thus, the farmer must examine the marginal cost and marginal revenue of each increment in output. Table 5–4 illustrates the marginal approach. It repeats the cost-and-revenue data for the now familiar production function for corn, with special emphasis on marginal cost and marginal revenue.

As production expands from zero to three units in Table 5–4, MC = $1.67 per unit and MR = $3 per unit. Since MC is the change in total cost as output increases, such an action would add $1.67 per unit to total cost. Since marginal revenue is the change in total revenue as output increases, such an action would add $3 per unit to total revenue. The difference between the increase in total revenue and the increase in total cost is the net effect on, or change in, profits. In this instance, the increase in production from zero to three units increases profits (decreases loss) by $1.33 per unit ($3.00 – $1.67). Since three more units are produced, profit is increased (loss is decreased) by $4. The amount of loss declines from $20 when no output is produced to $16 when three units are produced. Thus, the farmer finds it profitable to expand output from zero to three units.

Once this decision to expand production is made, the farmer must examine the effect of the next increment of production on profits. Should production be increased from three to seven units? Table 5–4 shows the marginal cost associated with this increase is $1.25 per unit. The marginal revenue, of course, remains constant at $3 per unit. The net return for each unit is $1.75 ($3.00 – $1.25). The production of each unit of corn from four to seven will add $1.75 to per-unit profits or diminish losses by the same amount. Increasing production by four units diminishes losses by $7 (4 units × $1.75). The loss incurred declines from $16 to $9. The decision to expand production again takes place. In both cases, it was clearly in the interest of the producer to produce those units of output where marginal revenue was greater than marginal cost. By doing so, more was added to total revenue than to total cost. Consequently, the amount of profit earned increased or the size of the loss incurred decreased.

Another reference to Table 5–4 illustrates what the producer should do when marginal cost is greater than marginal revenue. Is it in the producer's interest to increase output from seventeen to eighteen units of corn? The marginal cost associated with the eighteenth unit of output is $5. The marginal revenue of that same unit is $3. Production of the eighteenth unit of corn adds $2 more to total cost than it does to total revenue ($3.00 – $5.00). The net effect of this change is to decrease profits by $2. Total profits decline from $6 to $4. Since it is assumed that the farmer is a profit maximizer, such a move would be irrational. The profit-maximizing farmer will not produce the eighteenth unit of corn. Hence, when marginal cost of an extra unit of production is greater than the marginal revenue of that unit, it is not economically rational to produce it.

The three examples discussed so far represent situations where the farmer decides to increase production (the first two cases) and not to increase production (the third case). The farmer need not make calculations and comparisons of marginal cost and revenue for each and every possible level of output. If the assumption is made that output is infinitely divisible, the solution to the determination of the profit-maximizing or loss-minimizing output is an easy one. As indicated above, any unit or fraction of a unit of output for which marginal revenue is greater than marginal cost should be produced. Likewise, any unit or fraction of a unit of output for which marginal cost is greater than marginal revenue should not be produced. There is only one output at which marginal revenue is neither greater than nor less than marginal cost. At this output, the farmer has no incentive to increase or to decrease production. It is the output where profits are at a maximum or losses are at a minimum. Thus, the farmer can simply look for that output where marginal cost and marginal revenue are equal rather than to make these calculations for each and every level of output.[1]

To briefly summarize, the decision maker will react to marginal-revenue and marginal-cost signals in the following manner:

1. When marginal revenue is greater than marginal cost, he or she will increase output and increase profits or decrease losses.
2. When marginal revenue is less than marginal cost, he or she will decrease output and increase profits or decrease losses.
3. When marginal revenue and marginal cost are equal, profit is at a maximum or loss is at a minimum. Increasing or decreasing output from this point will only decrease profits or increase losses.

The information from Table 5–4 is plotted graphically in Figure 5–3. This graph further clarifies the relationship between marginal revenue and marginal cost and profit. For the first 16.2 units of production, marginal revenue exceeds marginal cost. As each of these units is produced, it adds more to total revenue than it does to total cost and, therefore, increases profit. It is obviously to the farmer's advantage to produce each of these units. For any output larger than 16.2 units of production, marginal cost exceeds marginal revenue. Each of these units produced adds more to total cost than it does to total revenue. Consequently, profits decrease. It would be foolish for the farmer to produce any of these units of output. Thus, the profit-maximizing output is where marginal revenue equals marginal cost; in this case, 16.2 units. The farmer can only reduce profits by producing a larger or smaller output than this.

Once the profit-maximizing output is determined, the total amount of profit earned can be shown graphically as in Figure 5–4. The profit-maximizing output is again determined at that point where marginal

1. In reality, since inputs and outputs are not infinitely divisible, the producer will choose the output where marginal revenue is greater than or equal to marginal cost.

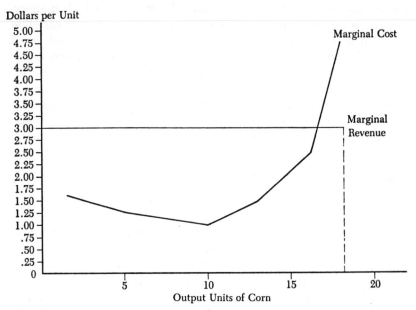

FIGURE 5-3: Marginal cost, marginal revenue

cost is equal to marginal revenue. This output is measured by line segment OE. Total revenue is calculated by multiplying each unit of output by marginal revenue or price. Marginal revenue or price is measured by the line segment OC or BE. Therefore, total revenue is graphically the rectangle OEBC. Total cost for this output is calculated by multiplying output (OE) by average total cost (OD or AE). This multiplication yields rectangle OEAD as the graphic measure of total cost. The different between total revenue and total cost is total profit. Thus, total profit, in this instance, is the shaded rectangle DABC. An alternate method of showing profit is to calculate the profit per unit and multiply it by the number of units produced. Profit per unit can be found by subtracting the average total cost (EA) from the price received per unit (EB). Thus, profit per unit is AB. Total profit is then AB multiplied by the output OE, or rectangle DABC.

This method of calculating profit or loss is especially helpful when examining the production decision under loss conditions. The determining factor in whether or not to produce under loss conditions is whether the price received per unit will cover the average variable costs. Figure 5-5 reproduces the cost data of Figure 5-4, but assumes that the price of corn has fallen to $2 per unit. The initial decision the producer must make is that of the best output to produce—the one that maximizes profits or minimizes losses. Marginal analysis indicates this output is at OA, where marginal costs equal marginal revenue. It can

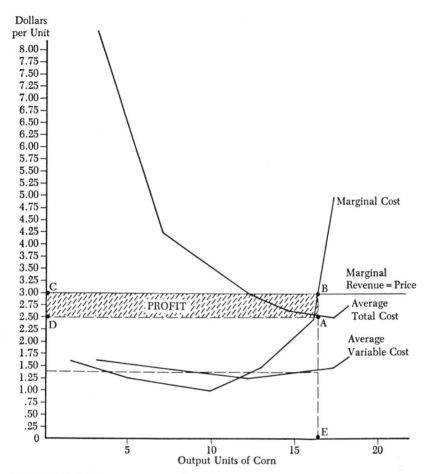

FIGURE 5–4: Revenue, cost, and profits

be seen that this output results in a loss. The decision facing the producer now is whether to continue production or to shut down operations. To make this decision rationally, the producer must compare the losses incurred by producing output (OA) with the losses incurred by producing no output.

The amount the producer would lose by producing no output is, of course, an amount equal to total fixed costs. In Figure 5–5, the difference between average variable cost and average total cost is average fixed cost. Thus, for an output of OA, the average fixed cost is BD. Total fixed cost is output (OA) multiplied by average fixed cost (BD). Total fixed cost is shown graphically by rectangle GBED. By producing output OA, the producer would lose on a per-unit basis the difference between average total cost and price. In Figure 5–5, average total

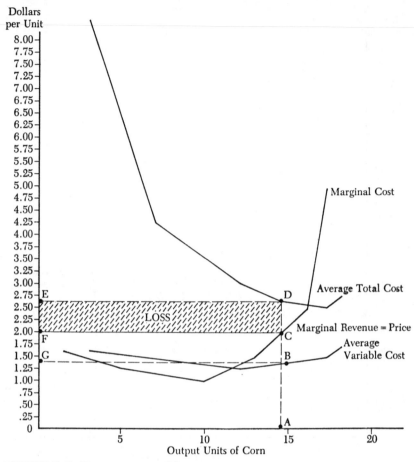

FIGURE 5–5: Revenue cost and losses

cost is AD while price is AC. The loss per unit is then CD. When this loss per unit is multiplied by output produced, the total loss incurred is rectangle FCDE. Rectangle FCDE is obviously smaller than the fixed-cost rectangle GBED. Thus, the producer would lose a smaller amount by producing in the short run than would be lost by shutting down. Put another way, revenues not only cover the average variable costs of producing, but also make a contribution to the average fixed costs of production. This contribution, measured on a per-unit basis, is equal to BC.

The case where it is more rational for the firm to shut down than to continue production in the short run can also be easily demonstrated. Figure 5–6 shows the case where the price of corn has fallen to $1 per unit. In this situation, marginal cost is equal to marginal revenue at an output of OA or ten units of corn. Once the farmer has determined this

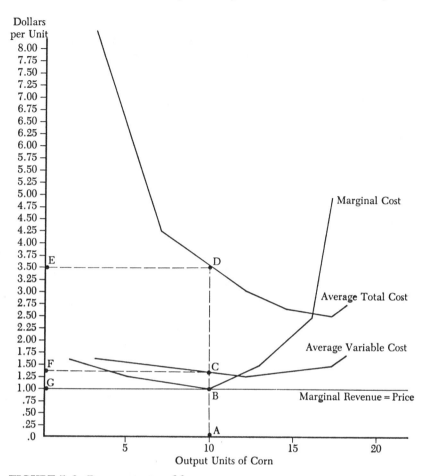

FIGURE 5–6: Revenue cost and losses

output, he or she must ascertain whether production is justified at all. To do so, the loss associated with the production of ten units of output is compared with the loss incurred by shutting down. At ten units of output, the average total cost of production is AD. Average total cost (AD), multiplied by output (OA), yields a total loss of GBDE. Total fixed costs can be found by multiplying average fixed cost (CD) by output. This results in rectangle FCDE. Since rectangle FCDE, total fixed cost, is smaller than the rectangle GBDE, loss by operating, the choice is obvious. The producer will minimize losses by shutting down production in the short run.

The same conclusion emerges when Figure 5–6 is examined from a different perspective. At the loss-minimizing output, price does not cover average variable cost. Price is indicated by line segment AB, while average variable cost is line segment AC. The farmer not only

TABLE 5–5: Profit maximization for hay production—total-cost, total-revenue approach (price of hay = $10 per unit)

(1) Units of Hay	(2) Total Fixed Cost	(3) Total Variable Cost	(4) Total Cost	(5) Total Revenue	(6) Profit + or Loss –
0	$100	$ 0	$100	$ 0	–$100
10	100	40	140	100	– 40
20	100	70	170	200	+ 30
30	100	90	190	300	+110
40	100	120	220	400	+180
50	100	190	290	500	+210
60	100	300	400	600	+200

loses all average fixed costs by producing, but also loses an additional amount (BC) on each unit. Thus, the extra loss incurred by producing equals rectangle BGCF. The general rule, again, is that when price does not cover the average variable costs of production, it is more economical for the farmer to discontinue production.

Thus, through the use of the marginal-cost, marginal-revenue approach, it is possible to determine the profit-maximizing or loss-minimizing output. In addition, by examining average costs of production and price data, it is possible to determine whether the producer should shut down or continue production in the short run while waiting to leave the industry in the long run.

A SECOND EXAMPLE: THE TOTAL-COST TOTAL-REVENUE APPROACH

A second example of profit maximizaiton or loss minimization will help to reinforce the methodology developed previously. Table 5–5 shows the production function for hay with its attendant costs.

When the price of hay is $10 per unit, the greatest difference between total revenue (column 5) and total cost (column 4) is at fifty units of hay. At this point, profits are at a maximum of $210. How will the producer react to lower prices? Earlier discussion of the simple supply-and-demand model would suggest that the producer is willing and able to supply fewer units of production on the market. The profit-maximizing or loss-minimizing level of output will decrease. Table 5–6 shows what happens when hay prices decrease to $4 per unit.

The hay producer facing a price of $4 per unit must make two decisions. He or she must first determine the optimal, or loss-minimizing, output. Once this is determined, he or she must ascertain whether the

TABLE 5-6: Loss minimization for hay production—total-cost, total-revenue approach (price of hay = $4 per unit)

(1) Units of Hay	(2) Total Fixed Cost	(3) Total Variable Cost	(4) Total Cost	(5) Total Revenue	(6) Profit + or Loss −
0	$100	$ 0	$100	$ 0	−$100
10	100	40	140	40	− 100
20	100	70	170	80	− 90
30	100	90	190	120	− 70
40	100	120	220	160	− 60
50	100	190	290	200	− 90
60	100	300	400	240	− 160

revenue derived from this output is sufficient to cover total variable costs of production. If it is, he or she is then economically better off producing that output. If it is not, he or she is economically better off shutting down. From Table 5–6, it is clear that, as the price of hay declines, the optimal output also declines. While the producer makes losses at each and every output, those losses are least at an output of forty units of hay. At this output, a comparison of total revenue ($160) and total variable cost ($120) indicates that the producer will lose less by producing than by shutting down. By producing, the loss is $60. By shutting down, the loss is $100—an amount equal to total fixed cost.

Should the price of hay fall even further, however, this might not be the case. Table 5–7 illustrates such a case. With a price of $2 per unit for hay, the decision on whether short-run production is economical is different. The output for which losses are now minimized is the smallest possible output—zero units. Comparing total revenue with total variable cost of production for all output levels shows that there is no production where TR covers TVC. Thus, the producer cannot even recover the variable costs of production at this output price. The level of output that minimizes the losses is then zero. If any output is produced at all, losses will exceed the $100 fixed cost. By shutting down, only $100 will be lost. The rational choice under these circumstances is to shut down.

A SECOND EXAMPLE: THE MARGINAL-COST, MARGINAL-REVENUE APPROACH

The marginal approach will yield the same result as the total approach for the three cases just discussed. Thus, it will be sufficient to deal with the profit-maximization situation to review the logic of the analysis.

TABLE 5-7: Loss minimization for hay production—total-cost, total-revenue approach (price of hay = $2 per unit)

(1) Units of Hay	(2) Total Fixed Cost	(3) Total Variable Cost	(4) Total Cost	(5) Total Revenue	(6) Profit + or Loss -
0	$100	$ 0	$100	$ 0	-$100
10	100	40	140	20	- 120
20	100	70	170	40	- 130
30	100	90	190	60	- 130
40	100	120	220	80	- 140
50	100	190	290	100	- 190
60	100	300	400	120	- 280

Table 5-8 translates the total information on hay production used in the last three tables into marginal and average information. It assumes a price per unit of hay of $10. The profit-maximizing output can easily be calculated by comparing marginal cost and marginal revenue.

Profits will be maximized by producing the output where MR ≥ MC.[1] For each of the first fifty units of hay produced, MR > MC. Each increment of output in this group adds more to total revenue than it does to total cost, thus increasing profits. Clearly, these units should be produced. Conversely, producing any units greater than fifty finds marginal cost greater than marginal revenue. These units add more to total cost than they do to total revenue and, consequently, reduce profits. Units of production for which this is true will not be produced by the rational producer. The profit-maximizing output is then fifty units of hay.

For more exposure to the methodology of the marginal-cost, marginal-revenue approach, the student should calculate the profit-maximizing or loss-minimizing output for the hay producer, assuming the same level of costs and a price of hay of $4 per unit and $2 per unit. Remember that two conditions exist for profit maximization or loss minimization. First, the producer will maximize profits or minimize losses by producing that output at which MR = MC. Second, the producer will continue production in the short run if, and only if, marginal revenue or price is greater than or equal to average variable cost. If this second condition is not fulfilled, the producer will find it economically advantageous to shut down.

---

1. A secondary condition to be met when losses are to be minimized is that MR, or price, must be equal to or greater than AVC or it will be to the firm's advantage to shut down.

TABLE 5–8: Profit maximization for hay production—marginal-cost, marginal-revenue approach

(1) Units of Hay	(2) Average Variable Cost	(3) Average Total Cost	(4) Marginal Cost	(5) Marginal Revenue
0	—	—		
10	$4.00	$14.00	$ 4.00	$10.00
20	3.50	8.50	3.00	10.00
30	3.00	6.33	2.00	10.00
40	3.10	5.60	3.40	10.00
50	3.80	5.80	6.60	10.00
60	5.00	6.33	11.00	10.00

THE SUPPLY SCHEDULE OF THE INDIVIDUAL PRODUCER

In an earlier discussion, the supply schedule for an industry was characterized as the horizontal summation of the supply schedule of each individual firm in the industry. Through the use of the marginal approach, it is possible to describe the supply schedule for an individual producer. Doing so requires the review of three basic points:

1. Supply is a schedule of output that a producer is willing and able to supply at various prices over a given period of time.
2. The output that will be supplied at each price is the quantity that will maximize profit or minimize loss.
3. These profit-maximizing or loss-minimizing quantities are determined where marginal revenue is equal to marginal cost and, as a secondary condition, where price is greater than or equal to average variable cost.

Given these conditions and the data in Table 5–8, it is possible to create the supply schedule for the hay-producing firm.

Since marginal revenue is equal to price for the competitive producer, each market-determined price will have a corresponding output where marginal revenue equals marginal cost. Thus, the linkage between price and quantity of product produced is established. It was previously determined that when the market-determined price of hay was $10 per unit, the individual producer was willing and able to offer fifty units of hay onto the market. This information provides one point on the supply schedule in Table 5–9 for the individual producer.

TABLE 5–9: Supply of hay—individual producer

Price of Hay Per Unit	Quantity of Hay Supplied
$10	50 Units

Other points on the individual firm's supply schedule can be determined by finding the producer's response to other prices. As the price of hay (MR) falls to $4 per unit, the producer will produce only forty units of hay. This response provides an additional point on the supply schedule shown in Table 5–10. As price falls further, the quantity of hay supplied is reduced to zero. At a price of $2 per unit, for example, it is economically advantageous for the producer to shut down. Why? Becuse the $2 price is not adequate to cover the average variable costs of production. Any price that does not cover the average variable costs will result in an output of zero, as the rational producer will shut down rather than produce under those conditions. Thus, at a price of $2 per unit, the output will be zero. The complete supply of hay is now shown in Table 5–11. To reiterate, the process by which the producer responds to different market prices is by setting output at different levels:

1. He or she chooses that output at which price equals marginal cost.
2. If the price is not greater than average variable cost at that output, he or she produces zero output, i.e., shuts down in the short run.

The individual firm's short-run supply curve then becomes the locus of points at which marginal revenue or price is equal to marginal cost, with the secondary condition of price being above-average variable cost. Thus, the supply curve is the firm's marginal-cost curve above average variable cost. As price varies, it indicates the amounts that will be offered onto the market in the short run. Figure 5–7 shows graphically the cost data previously developed for corn production. The dark, heavy portion of the marginal-cost curve identifies the firm's short-run supply curve.

LONG-RUN ADJUSTMENTS IN A COMPETITIVE MARKET

From the standpoint of the individual producer, the decision to operate in the long run is a simple one. If the producer operates at a profit, he or she will continue production in the long run. If the

TABLE 5–10: Supply of hay—individual producer

Price of Hay Per Unit	Quantity of Hay Supplied
$10	50 Units
4	40 Units

producer operates at a loss, he or she will discontinue production and leave the industry in the long run. Each producer will make this decision based on the profits or losses received in the short run.

The Case of Short-Run Losses

When the producer is receiving a loss in the short run, he or she can either continue to operate or shut down the business. In either case, the goal is to minimize short-run losses. In the long run, the situation is different. The producer's goal is to operate at a profit. It is irrational for the producer to continue operating at a loss in the long run. Thus, whatever decision the producer makes in the short run, the long-run decision must be to leave the industry.

As firms leave the industry in response to losses, the industry supply will decrease. This happens because there are now fewer firms in the industry. A decrease in industry supply, *ceteris paribus*, will increase market price. This increase in price will enable the remaining firms to cover production costs and continue operating. It should be noted that production costs are the payments the producer makes for the use of all factors of production—land, labor, capital, and management. The payment to each is as follows: land, rent; labor, wages; capital, interest; and management, normal profit. All four types of payments must be made if the firm is to operate in the industry in the long run.

TABLE 5–11: Supply of hay—individual producer

Price of Hay Per Unit	Quantity of Hay Supplied
$10	50 Units
4	40 Units
2	0 Units

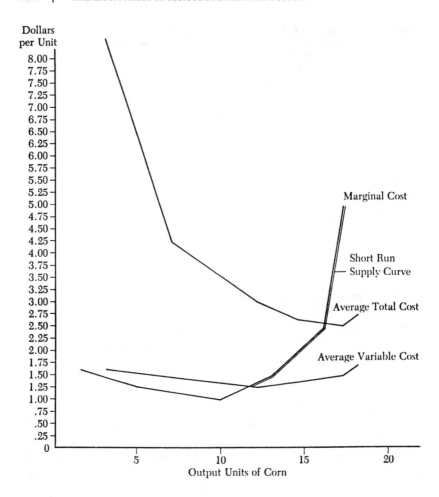

Dollars
per Unit

8.00
7.75
7.50
7.25
7.00
6.75
6.50
6.25
6.00
5.75
5.50
5.25
5.00
4.75
4.50
4.25
4.00
3.75
3.50
3.25
3.00
2.75
2.50
2.25
2.00
1.75
1.50
1.25
1.00
.75
.50
.25
0

Marginal Cost

Short Run
— Supply Curve

Average Total Cost

Average Variable Cost

5   10   15   20

Output Units of Corn

FIGURE 5-7: Short run supply curve: corn production

Any return earned in excess of that needed to make these payments is called an *economic profit*. Any return earned short of that needed to make these same payments is called an *economic loss*.

The case described previously discussed firms operating with economic losses. The effect of these losses on firms in the industry is shown in Figure 5-8. With demand D and supply S_1, a price of P_1 exists in the market. At this price, the representative firm in the industry operates at losses equal in amount to the hatched rectangle. In response to this short-run loss, firms will leave the industry in the long run. This results in the industry supply decreasing from S_1 to S_2. The new market price is P_2. At this price, the firms remaining in the industry will earn a return

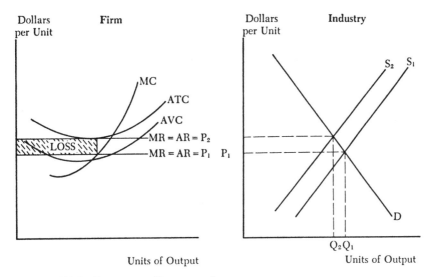

FIGURE 5–8: Long-run adjustment: loss case

that just covers all costs of production—a normal return to all factors of production received. If a price greater than P_2 had occurred, firms would have earned an economic profit. This case is examined next.

The Case of Short-Run Profits

If the firm is making an economic profit in the short run, it will have every incentive to continue operating and remain in the industry in the long run. The economic profits that exist will also be an incentive for other firms to enter the industry. With an increase in the number of firms in the industry, industry supply will increase. This increase in supply, *ceteris paribus*, will cause the market price to fall. Lower product prices will decrease the amount of revenue the firm receives. Revenues will drop to a level where firms in the industry are no longer earning economic profits.

Figure 5–9 shows how this adjustment takes place. With demand D and supply S_1, a price of P_1 exists in the market. At this price, a typical firm is earning an economic profit equal to the amount shown in the hatched rectangle. These economic profits will attract new firms to the industry. The increase in new firms will cause industry supply to increase from S_1 to S_2. The result is a decrease in price from P_1 to P_2. When this happens, there is no longer an incentive for firms to enter the industry, as they would no longer earn an economic profit.

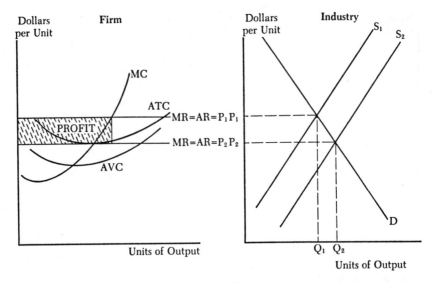

FIGURE 5–9: Long-run adjustment: profit case

Thus, while economic profits or economic losses may be present in the short run, they are definitely disequilibrium conditions in the long run. When either situation exists, forces will be set into motion in the long run to restore equilibrium. In the case of short-run economic losses, firms will leave the industry in the long run. Prices will increase so that firms remaining in the industry will cover all costs of production. In the case of short-run economic profits, firms will enter the industry in the long run. Prices will decrease so that each firm is again covering all costs of production but earning no economic profit. When this position is reached, the industry and its firms will be in long-run equilibrium. There will be no tendency to change. Firms will neither enter nor leave the industry.

SUMMARY

The purpose of this chapter was to examine how a producer makes the output decision. A framework of analysis was developed to determine the output that maximized profits or minimized losses. Distinction was made between those periods of time defined as the short run and the long run. Emphasis was on the development of models to deal with the short run since it is the time period in which most output decisions are made. In making output decisions, the producer had two approaches to use: total-revenue, total-cost approach, or marginal-revenue, marginal-cost approach. For convenience and simplicity, the marginal approach received the most attention and will throughout the remaining chapters.

Chapter 5 has served as an introduction to the decision-making process which the agricultural producer must undertake. However, analysis was applied to the simplest possible situation—that where the farmer produces only one product using only one variable input. The remaining chapters will apply the type of analytical model developed in Chapter 5 to increasingly complex and more realistic agricultural situations. Chapter 6 will develop an analogous model applied to inputs rather than outputs. Both outputs will be allowed to increase in number in this chapter.

QUESTIONS

1. Assume the following costs for a firm:

Units of Output	TFC	TVC
0	$100	$ 0
10	100	100
20	100	180
30	100	240
40	100	360
50	100	500
60	100	720

Using both the total and marginal approach, determine the following:

A. level of output to produce when price equals $15 per unit

B. level of output to produce when price equals $9 per unit

C. level of output to produce when price equals $7 per unit

2. Determine profit or loss for each of the prices given in question 1.

3. Determine the short-run supply schedule for the firm in question 1.

CHAPTER SIX

Decision-Making: The Factor-Product Decision

In the last chapter, a model was developed that allowed the producer to maximize profits by choosing a specific output. In terms of the production function in its most general form:

$$Y = f(X_1 \mid X_2, X_3, \ldots X_n)$$

emphasis was placed on choosing the level of Y that maximized profits. An alternate perspective on the same problem can be developed by looking at the input side of the production function. Since a given amount of input will produce a corresponding output, it is possible to arrive at the profit-maximizing amount of input use. Such a model allows the producer to evaluate the desirability of purchasing a greater or lesser amount of an input. Thus, it stresses the importance of input use in the production process.

Initially, examination of the input market and its effect on profit maximization will be made assuming the farmer uses only one input in the production process. This assumption simplifies the analysis so that the logic of the model may be more easily understood. In a later chapter, the number of inputs used will be allowed to vary so that the model more closely approximates reality.

Two approaches to the profit-maximizing level of input to use will be developed in this chapter. The first, analogous to the marginal approach of Chapter 5, compares the marginal return and marginal cost of an additional unit of input rather than of output. The second employs price ratios and marginal productivity to the same conclusion. Which approach to use depends on the availability of data. Before dealing with these two approaches, it is necessary to explore in some depth the meaning of an additional assumption: that the producer is a competitive buyer of inputs as well as a competitive seller of outputs.

COMPETITION IN THE INPUT MARKET

In earlier chapters, it was established that agricultural producers sold their products in a competitive market, a fact that constrained their decision-making process. As a price taker, the farmer had to accept the product price determined by the market and react to it. In this chapter, it is assumed that the farmers also purchase their inputs competitively. The very characteristics that made the farmers part of a competitive output market—a large number of firms, the small size of individual producers, and the independent decision making—also make them part of a competitive input market. Competition in the input market means that the farmers are, again, price takers. They accept the market-determined price of the various inputs they use as given. This information is then used as a basis for their decisions. They react to input prices in determining how many units of input to use to maximize profits or to minimize losses. A brief review of market determination of prices will illustrate the farmers' special circumstance.

One of the inputs used in the production process for any crop is labor. If the farmer is purchasing labor inputs competitively, he or she will accept the market-determined price as given. Tables 6–1 and 6–2 illustrate hypothetical industry supply-and-demand schedules for labor. When the market supply-and-demand schedules for labor are compared, the equilibrium price is $5 per unit. The quantity of labor exchanged at this price is 16,000 units. Each small individual firm can purchase all the labor it desires at this price without having any effect on the price paid for labor. Thus, the firm is faced with a horizontal supply curve for labor, which economists describe as being *perfectly elastic*. Figure 6–1 illustrates the interaction of market demand and supply of labor. It also shows the labor supply curve for the individual firm. It points up that, while the wage rate is determined by the market as a whole, the individual firm is a price taker facing an un-limited supply of labor at the market price. The firm could offer a higher wage. However, since it can obtain all the labor it needs at the market price, it would obviously not be in its best interest to do so. Were it to try to purchase labor at a lower price, it would find that it could not purchase any, since the labor could be sold to any number of other producers at the market price. Given these conditions, the next

TABLE 6-1: Market supply of labor

Price (Wage Rate) Per Unit	Quantity of Labor Supplied
$7	20,000 Units
6	18,000
5	16,000
4	14,000
3	12,000

question is how much labor should be hired to maximize profits or minimize losses? This question is first answered by using the marginal approach.

THE MARGINAL-VALUE-PRODUCT APPROACH

While the extra cost of another unit of labor or any input is determined by the market, the extra benefit or revenue from that unit is determined by two factors: (1) the price of the product and (2) the productivity of the input. The measure of the extra benefit or revenue was defined in Chapter 4 as the marginal value product of the input. Table 6-3 shows the link between product price, marginal physical product, and marginal value product for the production function for corn: Marginal value product declines not because of any change in the price of the output, but because of the law of diminishing marginal returns to the variable input. In this case, diminishing returns set in with the fourth unit of labor used. If the labor input had no cost, it would be advantageous for the producer to use all units for which the MPP was positive. Since labor does have a cost, the firm must decide how many units are profitable to use. It cannot do so by solely looking

TABLE 6-2: Market demand for labor

Price (Wage Rate) Per Unit	Quantity of Labor Demanded
$7	8,000 Units
6	12,000
5	16,000
4	20,000
3	24,000

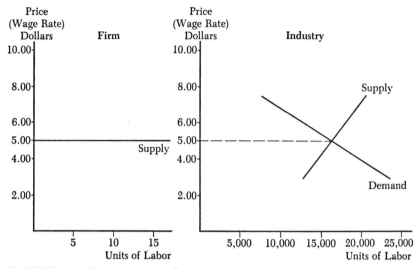

FIGURE 6-1: Determination of market and firm wage rate

at the marginal value product of each unit—it must also examine this benefit in relation to its cost. In other words, it must compare the marginal benefit with the marginal cost in making decisions about the utilization of labor.

The amount that an extra unit of input or resource adds to the firm's total cost is termed *marginal resource cost*. Since the firm purchases its inputs competitively, the marginal resource cost will be equal to the market price of the input. Purchasing additional units of labor will not bid up its price. Thus, the market price of $5 per unit equals the marginal resource cost. Referring again to Table 6–3, the producer must decide whether or not to purchase the first unit of labor, the marginal value product of which equals $9. The marginal resource cost is equal to $5. Is it advantageous for the producer to use this unit of labor? Clearly, the answer is yes. Marginal value product is greater than marginal resource cost by $4. This means the first unit of labor used adds $4 more to total revenue than it does to total cost. Using this unit either increases profits or decreases losses by this amount. Thus, the profit-maximizing producer will find it advantageous to utilize the first unit of labor.

In making the revenue cost calculations for the sixth unit of labor, the producer comes to a different conclusion. For the sixth unit of labor used, marginal physical product has declined to the point where the marginal value product is $3. When this value is compared to the marginal resource cost of $5, it becomes apparent that the use of the

TABLE 6-3: Relationship of product price, marginal physical product, and marginal value product for corn production

Units of Labor	Output Units of Corn	Marginal Physical Product of Labor	Price of Corn Per Unit	Marginal Value Product of Labor
0	0		$3.00	
		3		$ 9.00
1	3		3.00	
		4		12.00
2	7		3.00	
		5		15.00
3	12		3.00	
		3		9.00
4	15		3.00	
		2		6.00
5	17		3.00	
		1		3.00
6	18		3.00	

sixth unit of labor will have a negative effect on profits. The contribution of the sixth unit of labor to total revenue is $3; its contribution to total cost is $5. The net effect if a $2 decrease in profits. Thus, it would not be advantageous for the producer to hire the sixth unit of labor.

Table 6-4 shows the net impact on profits from the use of another unit of labor by comparing marginal value product to marginal resource cost for each unit of labor. For example, the second unit of labor has a marginal value product of $12 and a marginal resource cost of $5. Thus, the net impact on profits is $7. When the net-impact calculations are made, it becomes very clear that the producer should employ all those units of the input for which the next impact on profits is positive; in this case, five units of labor. Put another way, the producer should employ all of those units of the input for which the marginal value product is greater than the marginal resource cost. By doing so, he or she will be employing those units that contribute more to revenue than to cost. Consequently, net impact on profits will be positive.

When input is assumed to be divisible into extremely small units, the procedure for determining the profit-maximizing amount of input to use can be greatly simplified. In the logic developed thus far, the producer should employ all units of the input for which marginal value product is greater than marginal resource cost. Conversely, the producer should not employ units of the input for which marginal value product is less than marginal resource cost. In the example described in Table 6-4, marginal value product moves from being greater than to being less than marginal resource cost between five and six units of labor. Since labor units are not infinitely divisible, the producer has no choice but to sacrifice some profitable input. If it were

TABLE 6–4: Effect of input use on profits

(1) Units of Labor	(2) Marginal Value Product of Labor	(3) Marginal Resource Cost (Price) of Labor	(4) Net Impact on Profits
0			
1	$ 9.00	$5.00	+ $ 4.00
2	12.00	5.00	+ 7.00
3	15.00	5.00	+ 10.00
4	9.00	5.00	+ 4.00
5	6.00	5.00	+ 1.00
6	3.00	5.00	− 2.00

possible to infinitely subdivide the input, he or she would choose that level of input use where marginal value product equals marginal resource cost. At the point of equality between MVP and MRC, the producer would be indifferent. Adding that unit of input would have no effect on profits. Adding more labor than that amount would mean using labor that added more to cost than to revenue. Using less than that amount would mean sacrificing some profit. Thus, the profit-maximizing or loss-minimizing level of input to use is at that point where:

Marginal Value Product = Marginal Resource Cost

Since all inputs are not infinitely divisible, this condition is modified as follows:

If: MVP ⩾ MRC
Then: The producer should employ that unit of input.
If: MVP < MRC
Then: The producer should not employ that unit of the input.

The analysis of marginal value product and marginal resource cost just presented can also be done graphically. Figure 6–2 shows the information graphically and assumes that the labor input used is infinitely divisible. The decision on whether or not to employ the first unit of labor is easy: since marginal value product greatly exceeds marginal resource cost, it is in the producer's interest to employ the unit of labor L_1. In fact, according to the procedure previously discussed, labor utilization should expand to the point where MVP = MRC. This point occurs at L_2 units of labor. Increasing the amount of labor used from L_1 to L_2 increases total cost by the amount of additional labor used (L_1L_2)

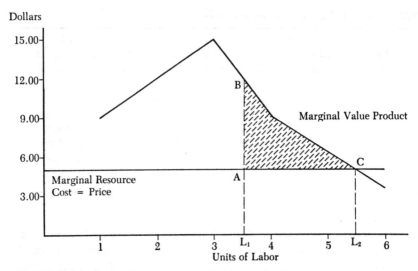

FIGURE 6-2: Marginal value product and marginal resource cost

multiplied by the price of labor (L_1A). The increased costs are represented by the area L_1L_2CA. This same expansion in labor used will increase revenues by the area represented by L_1L_2CB. This area was determined by summing up the MVP of labor used from L_1 to L_2. The difference between the two areas (the shaded area ABC) is the increased profit earned by expanding the amount of labor used from L_1 to L_2. Figure 6-2 also points up the consequences of expanding input use beyond the point at which MVP = MRC. Any unit of labor used in addition to L_2 will contribute less to revenues than it does to costs. Therefore, it should not be used, because profits will decrease.

THE PRICE-RATIO APPROACH

Thus far, the profit-maximizing or loss-minimizing level of input use has been determined through the marginal-value-product, marginal-resource-cost approach. In the main, this approach represents the application of marginal analysis to the input side of the production process. Modified, it can be used to determine the profit-maximizing level of input use in another way—the price-ratio approach. By manipulating the MVP = MRC condition, the price ratio appears.

Step 1. The condition that must be satisfied in order to determine the level of input use that maximizes profits or minimizes losses is:

$$(1.1) \text{ MVP } = \text{ MRC}$$

Step 2. Equation (1.1) can be broken down into its component parts. The additional revenue associated with an additional unit of input is the change in output multiplied by the price of the output.

$$(1.2) \quad MVP = \Delta \text{ Output} \times \text{Output Price}$$

The additional cost associated with an additional unit of input is the additional input multiplied by the price of the input.

$$(1.3) \quad MRC = \Delta \text{ Input} \times \text{Input Price}$$

Step 3. The condition in (1.1) can now be expressed as:

$$(1.4) \quad \Delta \text{ Output} \times \text{Output Price} = \Delta \text{ Input} \times \text{Input Price}$$

Step 4. If both sides of (1.4) are divided by the price of the output

$$\frac{\Delta \text{ Output} \times \text{Output Price}}{\text{Output Price}} = \frac{\Delta \text{ Input} \times \text{Input Price}}{\text{Output Price}}$$

the expression becomes

$$(1.5) \quad \Delta \text{ Output} = \frac{\Delta \text{ Input} \times \text{Input Price}}{\text{Output Price}}$$

Step 5. If both sides of equation (1.5) are divided by the change in input

$$\frac{\Delta \text{ Output}}{\Delta \text{ Input}} = \frac{\Delta \text{ Input} \times \text{Input Price}}{\text{Output Price}} \div \Delta \text{ Input}$$

the expression becomes:

$$(1.6) \quad \frac{\Delta \text{ Output}}{\Delta \text{ Input}} = \frac{\text{Input Price}}{\text{Output Price}}$$

and:

$$\frac{\Delta \text{ Output}}{\Delta \text{ Input}} = \text{Marginal Physical Product}$$

Step 6. The profit-maximizing or loss-minimizing level of input use can now be found by equating the marginal physical product of the input to the ratio of input to output prices:

$$(1.7) \quad MPP = \frac{\text{Input Price}}{\text{Output Price}}$$

Put another way:

$$(1.8) \quad MPP = \text{Price ratio is the condition necessary for profit maximization in input use.}$$

To illustrate how the price-ratio approach is used, consider the following example. If the price of the input is $10 per unit and the price of the output is $5 per unit, the price ratio is calculated in the following way:

$$\frac{\text{Input Price}}{\text{Output Price}} = \frac{\$10 \text{ Per Unit}}{\$5 \text{ Per Unit}} = 2$$

In economic terms, the quotient of 2 indicates that two units of extra output are needed to break even when one more unit of input is added. The measure of extra output for another unit of input is marginal physical product. Thus, a price ratio of 2 indicates that the producer should expand use of inputs as long as MPP is two or more. If MPP were less than two, it would be unprofitable to do so. If the MPP were one, $10 invested in additional inputs would generate $5 worth of additional output. Profits would decrease by $5. At the other hand, if MPP were three, $10 of increased input would produce $15 worth of additional output. Profits would increase by $5. In general:

If MPP > Price Ratio, it will be to the producer's advantage to expand input use.
If MPP < Price Ratio, it will be to the producer's advantage to contract input use.
If MPP = Price Ratio, the producer is using the profit-maximizing or loss-minimizing amount of input and will not gain by either expanding or contracting input use.

The use of the price-ratio technique to determine the profit-maximizing level of input use can be illustrated by the reference to the corn production example. If the price of labor is $5 per unit and the price of corn is $3 per unit, the price ratio is:

$$\frac{\text{Input Price}}{\text{Output Price}} = \frac{\$5 \text{ Per Unit}}{\$3 \text{ Per Unit}} = 1.67$$

TABLE 6-5: Marginal physical product and price ratio

Units of Labor	Output Units of Corn	Marginal Physical Product of Labor	Price Ratio	$\dfrac{P \; input}{P \; output} = \dfrac{\$5}{\$3}$
0	0			
		3		1.67
1	3			
		4		1.67
2	7			
		5		1.67
3	12			
		3		1.67
4	15			
		2		1.67
5	17			
		1		1.67
6	18			

In order to maximize profits, the producer can use only those units of input that return at least 1.67 units of output per extra unit of input. This means the marginal physical product must be at least 1.67. From the corn production data in Table 6–5, it becomes very easy to determine the appropriate amount of labor input to use.

The use of the first five units of labor is consistent with profit-maximizing behavior, since the MPP of each unit is greater than the price ratio of 1.67. The use of the sixth unit of labor is not in accord with such behavior. With a price ratio of 1.67, the sixth unit of labor does not produce the extra output required to break even. It only produces one unit and 1.67 units are needed to break even. This means that $5 worth of input generate only $3 worth of output. Employing the sixth unit of labor will diminish profits or increase losses by $2.

This analysis is presented graphically in Figure 6–3. Like Figure 6–2, it shows how the producer determines the optimum amount of labor to use, the difference being that the marginal physical product is now compared with the price ratio rather than input price with marginal value product. It is clear that at L_2 input level MPP is greater than the price ratio. This is a signal to the producer to employ more labor. Labor used should be increased from L_1 to L_2 where MPP = price ratio. The shaded area represents, in physical terms, the increase in profits from such a move. Moving beyond L_2 will reduce profits to the farmer.

CHANGES IN PARAMETERS

Once the framework of analysis is established, it is possible to show how the farmer will respond to various changes in external variables. Some of the factors subject to change are:

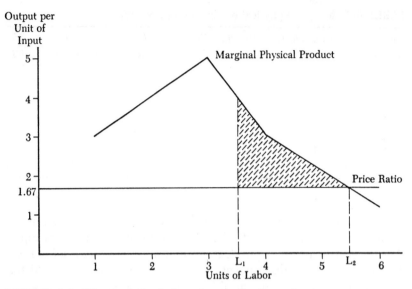

FIGURE 6–3: Marginal physical product and price ratio

1. the price of inputs
2. the price of the outputs
3. the state of technology

Changes in Input Prices

Changes in input prices have an immediate effect on the price ratio. Since input price is the dividend in the price ratio, changes in that ratio will be directly related to changes in input price. When input price increases, the price ratio will increase. When input prices decrease, the price ratio will decrease. An increase in the price ratio means that the producer can only hire inputs with greater marginal physical productivities. All other things being equal, the amount of input used must decrease. A decrease in the price ratio means the producer can hire inputs with lower marginal physical productivities. Input utilization will increase. Table 6–6 shows price ratios calculated for three different input prices. The price of labor was first increased and then decreased relative to the price of corn.

At the initial price of $5 per unit of labor (column 5), the producer uses five units of labor to maximize profits. The marginal physical product of the fifth unit of labor is two, and is well above the price ratio of 1.67. An increase in labor price to $7 per unit (column 6) will

TABLE 6-6: Effect of changes in input prices on input use in corn production

(1) Units of Labor	(2) Output Units of Corn	(3) Marginal Physical Product of Labor	(4) $\dfrac{P\ Labor}{P\ Corn} = \dfrac{\$2}{\$3}$	(5) Price Ratios $\dfrac{P\ Labor}{P\ Corn} = \dfrac{\$5}{\$3}$	(6) $\dfrac{P\ Labor}{P\ Corn} = \dfrac{\$7}{\$3}$
0	0				
1	3	3	.67	1.67	2.33
2	7	4	.67	1.67	2.33
3	12	5	.67	1.67	2.33
4	15	3	.67	1.67	2.33
5	17	2	.67	1.67	2.33
6	18	1	.67	1.67	2.33

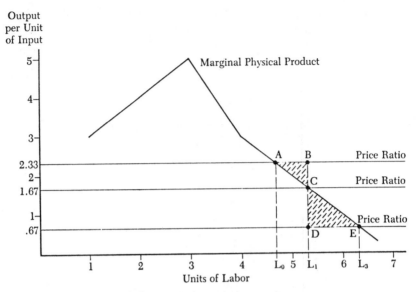

**FIGURE 6–4: Effect of changes in input prices on input use
[Price per unit of output = $5]**

change the price ratio to 2.33. At the new price ratio, the fifth unit of labor is no longer profitable. The MPP associated with the fifth unit of labor is two, less than the needed break-even amount of 2.33. In order to fulfill the condition that MPP = price ratio, the producer must reduce the amount of labor to four units. The marginal physical product of the fourth unit of labor is three. This amount now exceeds the 2.33 amount required by the price ratio. Finally, were the price of labor to fall to $2 per unit (column 4), even the sixth unit of labor would be profitable. The MPP of the sixth unit of labor is one, which exceeds the new price ratio of .67.

Figure 6–4 is based on Table 6–6 and shows graphically the effects of changes in input prices on the price ratio and the quantity of labor employed. Beginning with a price of labor of $5 per unit and a price ratio of 1.67, the producer will choose to employ L_1 units of labor in order to maximize profits. Should the price of labor increase to $7 per unit, the price ratio becomes 2.33. With this price ratio, the producer seeks a new level of employment of labor at L_0. Were the firm to persist in employing L_1 units of labor at the price ratio of 2.33, its profits would be decreased by the area of the triangle ABC. This area measures the loss of profits in physical units of production. It is the number of units of corn the firm would be short in attempting to cover the cost of L_0 to L_1 units of labor. The cost in units of corn needed to cover L_0 to L_1 labor is shown by rectangle L_0L_1BA. The return in units of corn from L_0 to L_1 labor is shown by the area L_0L_1CA. The difference is area ABC and represents the decrease in profit in units of corn.

Again, using $5 per unit of labor as a reference point, if the price of labor falls to $2 per unit, the farmer must again adjust employment of the labor input. In this case, the price ratio would decrease from 1.67 to 0.67. This means the firm will employ labor with a lower MPP—it will increase the number of units of labor used to L_3. By doing so, the amount of profit in units of corn increases by area DCE. If the firm were to ignore the price decrease and continue to employ the old amount of labor L_1, it would sacrifice this same area of profit. Thus, change in input prices has an inverse effect on the number of units of input employed. As input prices increase, causing an increase in the price ratio, the amount of input used decreases. Likewise, as input prices decrease, causing a decrease in price ratio, the amount of input used increases.

Changes in Output Prices

Changes in output prices have an immediate effect on the price ratio. Since the divisor of the price ratio is output price, changes in that ratio will be inversely related to changes in output prices. When output prices increase, the price ratio will decrease; when output prices decrease, the price ratio will increase. Table 6–7 shows the effect on the price ratio and an employment of labor as the price of corn first changes.

When the price of corn increases from $3 per unit (column 5) to $6 per unit (column 4), the price ratio declines from 1.67 to .83. This means that the firm can now profitably employ the sixth unit of labor, which has an MPP of one. Since the MPP is greater than the price ratio of .83, profits increase. The firm is now willing and able to supply more corn on the market because of the higher price of this output.

Should the price of corn decrease, the firm is willing and able to supply less corn on the market. As the price of corn declines from $3 per unit (column 5) to $2 per unit (column 6), the price ratio increases from 1.67 to 2.50. When this happens, it becomes unprofitable for the firm to employ the fifth unit of labor. The fifth unit has an MPP of two. This is not a sufficient amount of extra product for the firm to break even on its use. The price ratio indicates that the firm needs 2.5 units of output for each unit of extra input used. The fifth unit of labor returns only two units of output for an extra unit of labor used. This falls short of

TABLE 6–7: Effect of changes in output prices on input use in corn production

(1) Units of Labor	(2) Output Units of Corn	(3) Marginal Physical Product of Labor	(4) $\dfrac{P\,Labor}{P\,Corn} = \dfrac{\$5}{\$6}$	(5) $\dfrac{P\,Labor}{P\,Corn} = \dfrac{\$5}{\$3}$	(6) $\dfrac{P\,Labor}{P\,Corn} = \dfrac{\$5}{\$2}$
0	0		.83	1.67	2.50
1	3	3	.83	1.67	2.50
2	7	4	.83	1.67	2.50
3	12	5	.83	1.67	2.50
4	15	3	.83	1.67	2.50
5	17	2	.83	1.67	2.50
6	18	1	.83	1.67	2.50

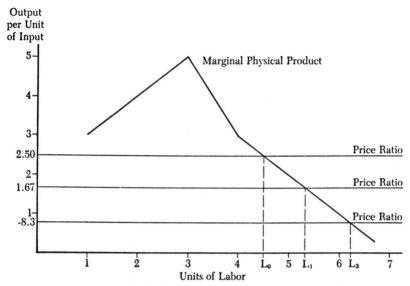

FIGURE 6–5: Effect of changes in output prices on input use
[Price per unit of labor = $5]

the required amount by .5 units of output. At a price of corn of $2 per unit, the fifth unit of input would decrease profits by $1. Thus, the firm will be forced to reduce the level of input use to four units of labor, decreasing output from seventeen to fifteen units of corn.

The analysis above is graphically summarized in Figure 6–5. Beginning with an output price of $3 per unit of corn, a price ratio of 1.67, and employment of labor at L_1 units, the producer must then adjust to changes in output price. As the price of corn increases to $6 per unit, the price ratio decreases to .83. This decrease increases the level of inputs used from L_1 to L_3. Had the price decreased to $2 per unit, or a price ratio of 2.50, the producer would be forced to decrease the number of units of labor used to L_0. Thus, the output price and amounts of input used vary directly with each other. When output price increases, so does the use of inputs. When output price decreases, so does the use of inputs.

Changes in Technology

Conceptually, technology—the manner in which inputs are transformed to outputs—can become more or less efficient. The latter case exists most often in theory since less efficient techniques are seldom adopted over existing ones. However, there have been instances where less efficient production techniques have been imposed over more efficient ones. The collectivization of Soviet agriculture following the revolution and the imposition of American farming methods on farmers in Latin America are but two examples of this illogical but real phenomenon. In either case, whether a more or less efficient technology is adopted, the primary effect is on the productivity of the inputs used. A more efficient technology makes inputs more productive; a less efficient technology makes then less productive. It follows that a more efficient technology will allow the producer to hire more inputs with a given price ratio, and that a less efficient technology will have the opposite effect. Table 6–8 shows the effects of changes in technology on the productivity of the labor factor. The less efficient technology (column 4) lowers the marginal physical product of labor for all inputs from the original level. At this new lower level of MPP (column 5) and given a price ratio of 1.67, the producer can make profitable use of only four units of labor. The MPP of the fifth unit of labor has decreased from two to one. Given the price ratio of 1.67, this means the farmer would decrease profits or increase losses through the employment of the fifth labor input. Thus, the consequence of a less efficient technology is to decrease the inputs used.

A more efficient technology (column 6) increases the productivity of inputs. This fact allows the farmer to use increased amounts of inputs more profitably. The more efficient level of technology results in more output at each level of input. Consequently, a higher level of marginal physical product for each unit of the labor input exists (column 7). Given the price ratio of 1.67, this now means that the sixth unit of input is profitable to employ. The MPP of this sixth unit has risen from one to three as a result of the new technology. This unit of labor may now be employed profitably by the producer.

Figure 6–6 shows graphically how the productivity of the labor used is affected by a change in technology. As the marginal physical product of the variable input increases or decreases with a more or less efficient technology respectively, the greater or smaller amounts of input use are used respectively. As technology becomes more efficient, the producer hires L_3 units of labor as opposed to L_1 units with existing technology. As technology becomes less efficient, the producer hires L_0 units of labor as opposed to L_1 units with existing technology.

A Complex of Changes

In the discussion of the various factors that affect the use of labor, attention was focused on one factor at a time. It was assumed that all

TABLE 6–8: Effect of technology of input use in corn production

(1) Units of Labor	(2) Present Technology Output Units of Corn	(3) MPP	(4) Less Efficient Technology Output Units of Corn	(5) MPP	(6) More Efficient Technology Output Units of Corn	(7) MPP	(8) Price Ratio
0	0		0		0		
1	3	3	2	2	4	4	1.67
2	7	4	5	3	9	5	1.67
3	12	5	9	4	15	6	1.67
4	15	3	11	2	20	5	1.67
5	17	2	12	1	24	4	1.67
6	18	1	1	0	27	3	1.67

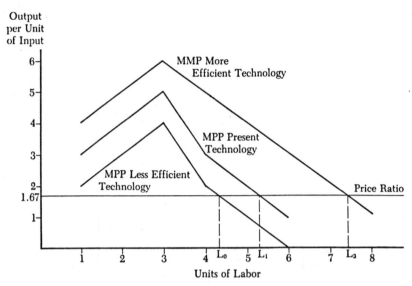

FIGURE 6–6: Effect of changes in technology input use

other things were equal—the *ceteris paribus* assumption. However, in reality, all things are seldom equal. A change in technology may foster changes in input and output prices that make prediction of its effect on input use considerably less precise than the price-ratio model would imply. For example, an improvement in technology adopted by all farmers may lead to a decline in the market price of the output produced because the market supply of the product expands. When this happens, contradictory forces are influencing the farmer's use of the variable input. By raising the productivity of the input, the improvement in technology would induce the farmer to employ more inputs. However, if output prices decrease, the price ratio will increase, inducing the farmer to employ less inputs. The net impact on employment will depend on the relative magnitude of the two changes. If the improvement in technology is more dramatic than the downward effect on output prices, employment will increase. If output prices fall more precipitously than output increases from the more efficient technology, the opposite will be true.

A more efficient technology may also affect input prices. If all farmers seek to hire more units of input because of an improvement in technology, the price of the input will increase for the market as a whole, leading to an increase in the price ratio and less input use. Again, the net effect will depend on the relative strength of the change in those factors. The introduction of complexity into the farmer's deci-

TABLE 6–9: Production function for potatoes

Units of Fertilizer	Output Units of Potatoes
0	0
1	100
2	170
3	219
4	250
5	276
6	285

sion-making process makes his or her choice of the appropriate level of input use more difficult. However, the farmer may still use the price-ratio model to good effect by examining the changes in exogenous factors through its framework.

A SECOND EXAMPLE

To review the models that have been developed to deal with the question of the profit-maximizing or loss-minimizing level of input use, it is useful to work through a second example using the tools of analysis developed. The production function under consideration shows the amount of fertilizer used as a variable input, with potatoes as the output. As in earlier discussions, it is assumed that the farmer is using only one variable input in the production of potatoes. All other inputs are held constant. Table 6–9 outlines the relationship which exists between inputs and outputs for potatoes, with a price of $2 per unit of potatoes.

From this production and price data, the first step is to calculate the marginal physical product of each unit of fertilizer used. The next step is to calculate the marginal value product associated with each level of input. The results of both of these calculations is shown in Table 6–10. This information and knowledge about the price of fertilizer allows the producer to determine the profit-maximizing or loss-minimizing level of input use by comparing the marginal value product of each unit of fertilizer with its marginal resource cost. If the price of fertilizer is $50 per unit, the producer can quickly decide on the appropriate level of input use by using inputs to the point at which marginal value product is equal to marginal resource cost. In Table 6–10, this will occur when five units of fertilizer are used. For the fifth unit of fertilizer, the MVP is $52, while the marginal resource cost of this and all units is $50.

TABLE 6–10: Marginal physical product, price ratio, marginal value product, and marginal resource cost of fertilizer for potato production

(1) Fertilizer	(2) Output Units of Potatoes	(3) MPP Fertilizer	(4) Price Ratio	(5) MVP Fertilizer	(6) MRC Fertilizer
0	0				
1	100	100	25	$200	$50
2	170	70	25	140	50
3	219	49	25	98	50
4	250	31	25	62	50
5	276	26	25	52	50
6	285	9	25	18	50

Price of Potatoes = $2 per unit.
Price of Fertilizer = $50 per unit.

Obviously, the sixth unit of fertilizer cannot be used since its cost is $50 and its revenue only $18. Since fertilizer is employed in units that are not infinitely divisible, the farmer must use that unit at which marginal value product be equal to or greater than marginal resource cost. This is clearly five units of fertilizer. Figure 6–7 shows graphically the analysis just discussed. Assuming continuous divisibility of fertilizer, slightly more than five units are used.

The second way in which the potato producer can determine the best number of units of fertilizer to use is by the price-ratio approach. The price ratio is this case is twenty-five (the price of fertilizer of $20 per unit divided by the price of potatoes of $2 per unit). By comparing the price ratio with the marginal physical product, the producer can determine whether any given unit of input should be used. The producer will find the level of input use that maximizes profits or minimizes losses—that point at which the price ratio of twenty-five is equal to or greater than the MPP of fertilizer. Referring to Table 6–10, it is apparent that this occurs at five units of fertilizer. The MPP of the fifth unit of fertilizer is twenty-six, which is greater than the price ratio of twenty-five. A price ratio of twenty-five indicates that twenty-five units of potatoes must be produced for each unit of fertilizer used in order for the farmer to break even. Thus, were the farmer to employ the sixth unit of fertilizer in the production process, he or she would decrease profits or increase losses. The sixth unit of fertilizer has a marginal physical product of only nine units. The farmer would fall short by sixteen units of potatoes of covering the cost of the sixth unit of fertilizer. At $2 per unit for potatoes, this shortage is worth $32.

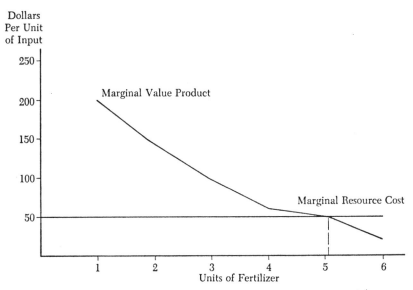

FIGURE 6–7: **Marginal value product and marginal resource cost for potato production**

For further practice in the determination of the best level of input use, the student should assess the impact of changes in input prices, changes in output prices, and changes in technology on fertilizer usage.

THE FIRM'S DEMAND FOR INPUTS

Just as it was possible to establish the firm's supply curve for the individual producing unit, it is also possible to establish the firm's demand curve for the resources that it uses. It may be helpful to recall that demand is the relationship that shows how much input will be demanded at various input prices. Each input price in a competitive input market is the marginal resource cost. To establish the demand for inputs, it is then necessary to determine how many units of input will be used at various levels of marginal resource cost. Since it is the producer's desire to maximize profits or to minimize losses, inputs will be employed until the marginal value product is equal to the marginal resource cost. Figure 6–8 shows the data developed earlier on the marginal value product of fertilizer used in potato production. Also included in this figure are three different levels of marginal resource cost. At each level of MRC, a specific level of input use can be predicted. The level of input use will be determined where MRC = MVP.

TABLE 6-11: Firm's demand for fertilizer for potato production

Price (MRC)	Quantity Demanded
$50	F_1

Thus, when MRC is at the level of $50, the producer will choose to use F_1 units of fertilizer. This provides one point, F_1, in the demand schedule for inputs. Allowing the marginal resource cost to vary generates other points on the firm's demand schedule. If MRC is $100, the amount of fertilizer demanded is F_2. If MRC is $150, the amount of fertilizer used if F_3. The resulting demand schedule is shown in Table 6-11. These points, represented by the coordinates (F_1, $50), ($F_2$, $100), and ($F_3$, $150) in Figure 6-8, are all points on the firm's marginal-value-product curve. If the MRC were allowed to vary to generate an infinite number of points on the demand schedule, they would all lie on the firm's marginal-value-product curve. In short, the marginal-value-product schedule or curve for the individual firm is the firm's demand curve or schedule for the input in question.

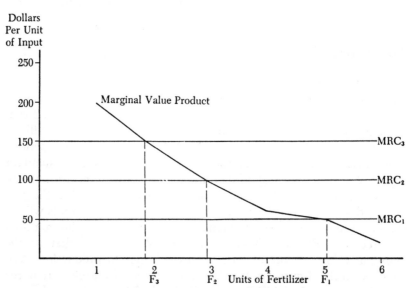

FIGURE 6-8: Marginal value product and marginal resource cost for potato production

TABLE 6–12: Firm's demand for fertilizer for potato production

Price (MRC)	Quantity Demanded
$150	F_3
100	F_2
50	F_1

SUMMARY

Before this chapter, discussion focused on the amount of output to produce to maximize profits or minimize losses. In this chapter, discussion concentrated on the amount of input to use to maximize profits or minimize losses. Again, the marginal analysis has been developed as a decision-making tool. By comparing the costs and benefits of additional units of input, the producer can determine how many units of inputs for profitable use. A comparison of the price ratio with the marginal physical product answers the same question. This chapter concludes the development of the simplest set of tools which the farmer uses in the decision-making process. The assumption that the farmer uses only one input in the production process is relaxed in the next chapter, calling for the development of more sophisticated tools of analysis.

QUESTIONS

1. Determine the marginal value product for fertilizer in the table below.

Input Units of Fertilizer	Output Units of Wheat	Price of Wheat Per Unit	Marginal Value Product
0	30	$2.00	
1	40	2.00	————
2	48	2.00	————
3	54	2.00	————
4	58	2.00	————
5	60	2.00	————
6	61	2.00	————

A. How many units of fertilizer should be applied when fertilizer is $25 per unit?

B. $15 per unit?

C. $3 per unit?

2. Determine the number of units of fertilizer to apply in Problem 1, using the marginal-physical-product, price-ratio approach given the following prices.

A. Price of wheat is $3 per unit. Price of fertilizer is $15 per unit.

B. Price of wheat is $1.63 per unit. Price of fertilizer is $5.09 per unit.

C. Price of wheat is $1 per unit. Price of fertilizer is $12 per unit.

3. Discuss the effect a change in market demand for wheat has on the demand for fertilizer. What is the demand for fertilizer when wheat is $3 per unit? $4 per unit?

CHAPTER SEVEN

Decision-Making: The Factor-Factor Model

The earlier assumption that the farmer makes use of only one variable input in the production of output is helpful in the development of simple tools of analysis. However, it is hardly descriptive of the reality of agricultural production. For each product the farmer produces, there are a number of different combinations of inputs. For example, corn can be produced using a hoe or a tractor, organic or chemical fertilizers, herbicides or cultivations. It is the purpose of this chapter to develop tools of analysis the farmer can use to determine the best combinations of inputs to use to maximize profits or minimize losses. The methodology available to the farmer is based on equal-product curves or isoquants, which help the farmer to decide on the most economical combinations of factors of production to use to produce a given product.

PRODUCTION OF CORN WITH TWO FACTORS OF PRODUCTION

The production function examined in previous chapters had one variable factor with all factors of production held constant. The general form of this production function was:

$$Y = f(X_1 \mid X_2, X_3 \ldots X_n)$$

In the corn production example of the last chapter, the output of corn was represented by Y and the input of labor by X_1. To determine how the producer can best combine more than one output, it is necessary to relax the assumptions underlying the production function above—an additional factor of production must be allowed to vary in the production process. For example, if the farmer varies both phosphate and nitrogen in the production of corn with all other factors of production held constant, the production function takes the form:

$$Y = f(X_1, X_2 \mid X_3 \ldots X_n)$$

Y again represents the output of corn produced, X_1 represents the amount of phosphate used, and X_2 the amount of nitrogen used. The other factors of the production process are held constant by assumption. Thus, X_3 to X_n constitutes the fixed bundle of inputs that hold constant as increasing amounts of phosphate and nitrogen are added to increase corn production. When increasing amounts of these two factors of production are applied to the fixed set of inputs, output will first increase at an increasing rate but, at some later point, increase at a decreasing rate and, ultimately, begin to decline.

Table 7–1 illustrates how the output of corn might vary with the application of both phosphate and nitrogen in varying combinations. From this table, it can be seen that when either variable input is allowed to increase while the other is held constant, the law of diminishing marginal returns applies. Thus, when phosphate use is held to zero and nitrogen use is increased, the marginal physical product of nitrogen declines. The first unit of nitrogen has a marginal physical product of ten, while the sixth unit has an MPP of only eight. Likewise, when the use of nitrogen is fixed at some level and the amount of phosphate used increases, the same response occurs. For example, when nitrogen used is held at three, the marginal physical product of the first two units of phosphate is thirty-two. Increasing phosphate use from ten to twelve units results in an MPP of only one unit.

Evidence of decreasing returns to scale also exists when phosphate and nitrogen are used in combination. Increasing phosphate use from zero to two units, while at the same time applying the first unit of nitrogen, increases output from zero to twenty units of corn. However, as more and more units of both inputs are applied, the rate of increase eventually declines. The increase in output produced by adding the seventh and eighth units of phosphate and the fourth unit of nitrogen is only eight units, even though the increase in inputs is the same as in the first instance. When phosphate use increases from ten to twelve units and nitrogen use increases from five to six units, corn production actually declines from ninety to eighty-five units.

Given (1) that there are a number of different combinations of phosphate and nitrogen that can be used to produce corn and (2) that

TABLE 7-1: Corn production with two inputs: phosphate and nitrogen

Units of Phosphate							
12	82	82	88	90	91	90	85
10	67	80	85	89	91	90	89
8	49	74	82	86	90	91	91
6	30	67	76	82	86	88	90 Corn = 90
4	20	49	67	78	81	84	87
2	10	20	49	67	75	80	84
0	0	10	20	35	49	59	67 Corn = 67
	0	1	2	3	Corn = 49 4	5	6

Units of Nitrogen

decreasing returns to scale exist, how does the producer determine the best combination of inputs to use? The answer can be found by using a model based on three new concepts: (1) the equal-product curve or iso-quant, (2) the marginal rate of technical substitution, and (3) the equal-expenditure line. Once these concepts are examined and understood, it will be possible to formulate a model that the farmer can use to determine the most economically advantageous combination of inputs to use in the production process.

THE EQUAL-PRODUCT CURVE

Reference to Table 7-1 reveals that there are several combinations of phosphate and nitrogen that produce the same output of corn. For example, forty-nine units of corn can be produced by using eight units of phosphate and none of nitrogen, or by using four units of nitrogen and none of phosphate. Other combinations of nitrogen and phosphate

TABLE 7-2: Corn production with variable inputs of phosphate and nitrogen

Units of Phosphate	Units of Nitrogen	Output Units of Corn
8	0	49
4	1	49
2	2	49
0	4	49

will also yield forty-nine units of output, as shown in Table 7-2. This table deals with three variables: nitrogen, phosphate, and output. It is impossible to plot this data in a two-dimensional graph. Figure 7-1, then, is a conceptual representation of the four different combinations of nitrogen and phosphate that will yield the same output. In this figure, output is plotted as if it were extending vertically outward from the page, while the two inputs are plotted within the two dimensions constituting the plane of the page. Thus, the curve shows the combinations of phosphate and nitrogen that will yield forty-nine units of corn. The term for such a curve is an *equal-product curve* or an *isoquant*, since all combinations of inputs on the curve produce the same level of output. All points on the curve are an equal distance from the plane of the page. Table 7-1 also shows other combinations of phosphate and nitrogen which produce the same level of output. Tables 7-3 and 7-4 show input combinations that produce sixty-seven and ninety units of corn, respectively. These combinations lead to two more equal-product curves, both of which are higher on the output axis and, therefore, indicative of greater output.

When these new equal-product curves are graphed on the same axis as the forty-nine-unit curve, they form the basis of an isoquant map or equal-product map. Such a map is shown in Figure 7-2. A complete isoquant map would show all combinations of the two inputs that could be used to produce all output levels ranging from zero to infinity. Several points can be made by concentrating on the three equal-product curves shown in Figure 7-2. Larger levels of output are shown by equal-product curves that lie farther from the origin to the right. It is also important to note that the isoquant curves cannot intersect. Mathematically, they cannot intersect because they lie in different planes on the output axis. Economically and technically, such an intersection would make no sense. Since all points on the equal-product curves represent the same level of production or output, intersection of the curves would imply that points of output could be equal to and greater than each other at the same time. It would also imply the use of a technically inefficient production process.

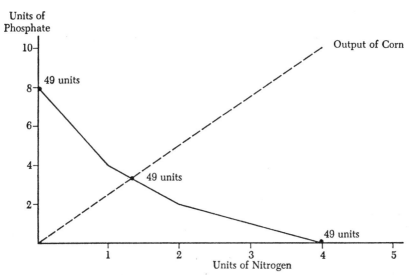

FIGURE 7–1: Equal–product curve for corn with phosphate and nitrogen as variable inputs

The equal-product map or isoquant can be compared to a topographic map of a gently sloping hill. The height of the hill represents the amount of output produced, while each equal-product curve is analogous to contour lines showing different elevations on the hill. The equal-product curves represent the locus of points on the total-product "hill" that are of equal values. Any point on a given equal-product curve is equal to any other point on that curve in that they all represent the same value of output. An equal-product curve can be shown for any level of output and can be conceptually determined as the contour line that would result were a plane passed through the "hill" representing output. It follows that there are an infinite number of equal-product curves that can be established for any production function. In practice, the producer deals with only a few.

Now that the concept of equal-product curves or isoquants has been discussed, the concepts of marginal rate of technical substitution and equal expenditure lines will be examined. Once this is done, the model for determining the best combination of inputs can fully be developed.

THE MARGINAL RATE OF TECHNICAL SUBSTITUTION

For the three equal-product curves thus far established, it is clear that one input can be substituted for the other in order to maintain a given

TABLE 7–3: Corn production variable inputs of phosphate and nitrogen

Units of Phosphate	Units of Nitrogen	Output Units of Corn
10	0	67
6	1	67
4	2	67
2	3	67
0	6	67

level of output. As indicated in Table 7–4, if a firm wants to produce ninety units of corn, it can use twelve units of phosphate and three units of nitogren. If, for some reason, it would rather use more nitrogen and less phosphate in the production process, it could use eight units of phosphate and four units of nitrogen. The output would remain the same at ninety units. The producer would have substituted one unit of nitrogen for four units of phosphate. The rate at which one input can be substituted for another in the production process is a purely technical phenomenon. It has nothing to do with relative prices but, rather, is a manifestation of the production function. The term for the rate at which one input substitutes for another is the *marginal rate of technical substitution* (MRTS). The meaning of this concept can be clarified by reference to an example in Table 7–5. This table describes a hypothetical situation where various combinations of inputs A and B are used to produce ten units of output.

Calculation of the MRTS of input A for input B—the units of B that can be saved by substituting one unit of A—is shown in column three. The notation $MRTS_{A \cdot B}$ indicates the rate at which input A can be substituted for input B as the amount of input A used increases and the amount of B used decreases. In this example, the $MRTS_{A \cdot B}$ declines from 1.5 to 1.0 to .75. This indicates that the amount of B that can be saved by the use of an extra unit of A declines as more and more units of A are brought into the production process. This phenomenon operates with such regularity that it can be described as a law of economics: *the law of diminishing marginal rate of technical substitution.* This law

TABLE 7–4: Corn production with variable inputs of phosphate and nitrogen

Units of Phosphate	Units of Nitrogen	Output Units of Corn
12	3	90
8	4	90
6	6	90

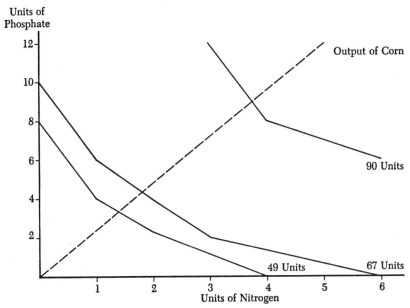

FIGURE 7–2: Equal–product curves for corn production with phosphate and nitrogen as variable inputs

formalizes the kind of behavior discussed above. It predicts that, as the producer adds additional amounts of one input, the amount of the second input saved by this increase will decline.

From another perspective, the MRTS$_{A \cdot B}$ tells the producer how much A is necessary to save an additional unit of B. When the producer decreases use of B from thirteen to ten units, two additional units of A are needed to maintain output at ten units. Thus, 2/3 of a unit of A is necessary to save one unit of B. As increasing numbers of units of A are employed in conjunction with decreasing amounts of B, the marginal productivity of A declines and the marginal productivity of B increases. This confirms an earlier demonstration that the marginal physical productivity of a factor of production declines as more and more of it is used. So, when B declines from six to three units, four units of A must be hired to substitute for the loss in product due to the decline in the amount of B used. Now, 1 1/3 units of are needed to save one unit of B.

Examples of the law of diminishing marginal rate of technical substitution are quite common in agriculture. Dairy cattle that are fed a large amount of hay and a small quantity of grain will produce a certain amount of milk each day. If the farmer wishes to save hay and still maintain the same amount of milk production, he or she can substitute grain for hay in the cows' ration. At first, increasing the amount

TABLE 7-5: Equal-product table for inputs substituting at varying rates

(1) Units of Input A	(2) Units of Input B	(3) $MRTS_{A \cdot B} = \dfrac{\Delta\ Input\ B}{\Delta\ Input\ A}$	(4) Units of Output
1	13		10
3	10	1.5 = 3/2	10
7	6	1.0 = 4/4	10
11	3	.75 = 3/4	10

of grain fed will greatly reduce the amount of hay needed for the same rate of milk production. However, as the farmer continues the substitution process of grain for hay, decreased savings in hay will occur. Another example where the law of diminishing MRTS exists is in the production of alfalfa. A yield of three tons of alfalfa can be produced by using only phosphate as a fertilizer. However, this method is likely to be quite expensive. In order to save money on phosphate, a farmer may decide to combine potassium with the phosphate in the fertilization of the crop. By adding one unit of potassium to the phosphate used, a large savings in phosphate used can be realized. Consequently, the cost of producing the three tons of alfalfa will decrease. As the farmer continues to add potassium to the fertilizer mix, the savings in phosphate will decline if the same production is to be maintained. Thus, as more and more units of potassium are used, fewer and fewer units of phosphate will be saved. The law of diminishing MRTS is again operative.

While the law of diminishing marginal rate of technical substitution is representative of most agricultural production, inputs can substitute one for another in various other ways. In some instances, the marginal rate of technical substitution may be constant. In other instances, inputs can be substituted for each other only in fixed proportions.

Constant Marginal Rate of Technical Substitution

While diminishing marginal rate of technical substitution is the rule in agricultural production, there are situations when one input substitutes for another at a constant rate no matter how much or how little of each is used. Beef animals, for example, can be fed through the winter with either hay or silage. The feed value and nutrients found in silage will bear basically the same relationship to those of hay no matter how much of either is fed. If a ton of hay has twice the feed value and nutrients of silage, then one ton of hay will save two tons of silage in

TABLE 7-6: Equal product table for inputs substituting at a constant rate

(1) Units of Input A	(2) Units of Input B	(3) $MRTS_{A \cdot B} = \dfrac{\Delta\ Input\ B}{\Delta\ Input\ A}$	(4) Units of Output
0	24		20
4	16	2 = 8/4	20
8	8	2 = 8/4	20
12	0	2 = 8/4	20

the feed. For the most part, this will be true whether hay constitutes 75 percent of the ration or only 25 percent. The marginal rate of technical substitution stays the same no matter how much is fed.

A more obvious example of a constant MRTS is tractor fuel. Two types of fuel can be used in driving a diesel engine—No. 1 and No. 2 diesel fuel. The MRTS between the two fuels will remain constant, irrespective of the amount of either fuel used. Thus, the choice of which fuel to use will depend upon their relative prices rather than on any change in the marginal rate of technical substitution between them.

Table 7-6 presents a hypothetical case of a production function using inputs for which the marginal rate of technical substitution is constant. Each time the mix of inputs changes, the amount of input A that must be substituted for input B in order to maintain twenty units of production remains constant (the $MRTS_{A \cdot B}$) at two. This means that one unit of A always substitutes for two units of B.

The equal-product information from Table 7-6 is shown graphically in Figure 7-3. The equal-product curve takes on a different shape than that normally found—it is a straight line with a constant slope. This indicates that the amount of one input saved when the other input is increased remains constant. The change in input B divided by the change in input A is the same at any point on the curve.

INPUTS SUBSTITUTING IN FIXED PROPORTIONS

Some inputs substitute in fixed proportions. They must be used together or no product will result. To plow a field, both a tractor and a tractor operator are needed. If either of the two inputs are not present, no output will be produced. Such inputs are usually described as *complementary*. When these factors of production can be combined in only

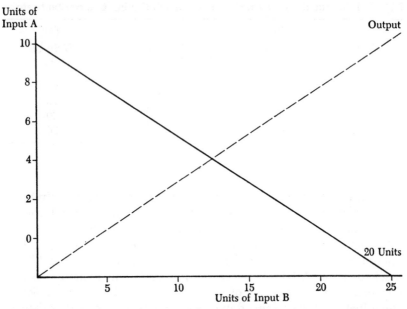

FIGURE 7-3: Equal-product curve for inputs substituting at a contant rate

one way the question of determining the optimum combination of inputs is moot. The producer has no choice; the only combination possible is determined by technical factors and is not subject to the producer's decision making. Table 7-7 shows an output grid for inputs that can only be combined in fixed proportions. The proportion shown here is 1:1. For each additional unit of input A used, the producer must also use one additional unit of input B in order to get any additional product. Other proportions are also possible. For example, there are machines that require three people to operate before any product can be produced. In this case, the required proportion would be 1:3. For inputs combined in this fashion there is no equal-product curve. All that emerges is a series of points showing the combination of inputs required for each level of output. The data from Table 7-7 is plotted graphically in Figure 7-4. Only one combination of inputs can be used at each level of output, irrespective of the price of the inputs. The producer views the required combination as one input. He or she must decide what level of input use will maximize profits or minimize losses rather than seek the best combination of these two factors of production.

In other instances, inputs must combine in a specific minimal proportion to produce an output. Once that minimum mix is met,

TABLE 7-7: Product table for inputs combining in fixed proportions

Units of A	A \\ B	0	1	2	3	4	5	6	Output
	6	0	0	0	0	0	0	30	
	5	0	0	0	0	0	29	0	
	4	0	0	0	0	25	0	0	
	3	0	0	0	20	0	0	0	
	2	0	0	14	0	0	0	0	
	1	0	7	0	0	0	0	0	
	0	0	0	0	0	0	0	0	

Units of B

other units of either input can be added without increasing or decreasing the product produced. Table 7–8 illustrates the case where A and B must be combined in a ratio of 1:1 to generate production. Once this proportion is met, other units of A or B can be added without changing the amount of output. In this case, one unit of A and one unit of B are required to produce an output of three units. One unit of A and any number of units of B equal to or greater than one unit will still produce three units of output. Likewise, one unit of B and one or more units of A will also produce only three units of output.

The relationship in Table 7–8 is shown graphically in Figure 7–5. In this figure, the equal-product curves appear as right angles. The least costly combination of inputs that can be used are those found at the corner of each right angle. Other combinations of inputs are possible, but they will use additional units of inputs without increasing output, thereby reducing profits or increasing losses.

Examples of this type of complementary are rare in agriculture. Perhaps the best example found in nature is chemical reactions. Because of

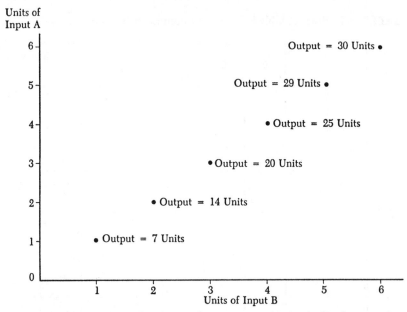

FIGURE 7-4: Equal–product points for inputs combining in fixed proportions

their chemical properties, sodium and chlorine will combine in a one-to-one ratio to produce sodium chloride—salt. If an individual were to manufacture salt by combining sodium and chlorine, one molecule of each would have to be used. One molecule of sodium and ten molecules of chlorine would produce only as much salt as one molecule of sodium and one of chlorine. The extra inputs of chlorine added to the mix would have no effect on the output of salt and would only serve to raise the cost of production.

In the case where inputs substitute for each other at a constant rate, the producer has little problem in choosing the best combination of the two inputs. The choice will depend only on the relative prices of the two inputs and the rate of technical substitution. Since that rate of substitution is constant, the choice is relatively simple. Inputs used only in fixed proportions can be viewed as a package of inputs. Thus, no decision has to be made with regard to how inputs should be combined. For inputs subject to the law of diminishing marginal rate of technical substitution, the decision on the best combination of inputs to use becomes more complex. To determine the optimum combination of factors of production in this situation, the decision maker must employ one additional tool—the equal-expenditure concept.

TABLE 7–8: Equal–product table for inputs combining in fixed proportions

Units of Input A	B→	0	1	2	3	4	5	6	
6		0	3	6	9	12	15	18	Output
5		0	3	6	9	12	15	15	
4		0	3	6	9	12	12	12	
3		0	3	6	9	9	9	9	
2		0	3	6	6	6	6	6	
1		0	3	3	3	3	3	3	
0		0	0	0	0	0	0	0	

Units of Input B

THE EQUAL-EXPENDITURE LINE

Assume the producer has a resource budget of a finite number of dollars to spend on variable inputs. The challenge is to allocate these dollars between purchases of inputs in such a way as to achieve the greatest output. To accomplish this end, information is needed about the size of the resource budget, the relative prices of the inputs used, and the production function for the inputs used. The equal-product curves previously developed provide the necessary information about the production function and the technical relationships that exist between inputs. The equal-expenditure line takes into consideration the remaining two areas—resource budget and input prices.

To explore the nature of the equal-expenditure line, consider the production function for corn with phosphate and nitrogen as variable inputs. Given a total resource budget of $100 and a price per unit of phosphate of $5 and a price per unit of nitrogen of $10, the firm can

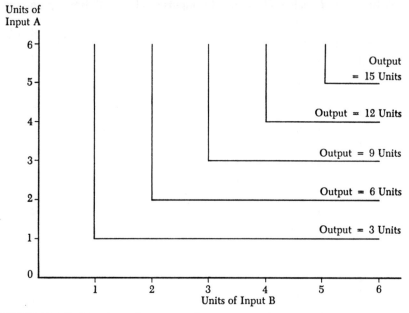

FIGURE 7–5: Equal–product curves for inputs combining in fixed proportions

purchase a number of different combinations of nitrogen and phosphate. If it wishes to buy all phosphate and no nitrogen, it can purchase 20 units of phosphate. This amount is obtained by dividing the $100 resource budget by the $5 per-unit price of phosphate. It can also purchase all nitrogen and no phosphate. In this case, it would be able to purchase 10 units of nitrogen. Again, the $100 resource budget is divided by the $10 per-unit price of nitrogen. The firm can also purchase any other combination of the two inputs as long as the total expenditures do not exceed the resource budget. Table 7–9 shows some of the combinations of the two factors of production that are possible, given the constraint imposed by the resource budget and the prices of the two inputs.

The graphical presentation of the equal-expenditure line shows all of the combinations of the two inputs that are available to the producer. Figure 7–6 shows all the possible combinations that the farmer can purchase with a resource budget of $100 and phosphate and nitrogen at $5 and $10 per unit respectively. Any combination of phosphate and nitrogen that lies on or within the equal-expenditure line is a possibility for the farmer. If the farmer purchases any combination of inputs within the shaded triangle, such as combination A, funds will be left in the resource budget. If the goal is to maximize production and, consequently, profits, the producer will seek to purchase the maximum

TABLE 7-9: Equal-expenditure outlay with nitrogen and phosphate as variable inputs

Units of Nitrogen	Expenditure on Nitrogen	Units of Phosphate	Expenditure on Phosphate	Total Expenditure
0	$ 0	20	$100	$100
2	20	16	80	100
4	40	12	60	100
6	60	8	40	100
8	80	4	20	100
10	100	0	0	100

amount of inputs possible. This means the producer will want to purchase inputs in the combinations indicated on the equal-expenditure line, such as point B. Employing one of these combinations will maximize the amount of inputs purchased and, thus, the output produced. A combination such as point C is outside the equal-expenditure line and unattainable at the prices indicated for the two inputs and the constraint of the $100 budget.

The equal-expenditure line is linear. Its slope can be derived from the two end points of the curve. To do this, it is first necessary to determine the two end points. In mathematical terms, these points are the x and y intercepts. They are found in the following way:

1. The amount of phosphate that can be purchased if the total budget is spent on phosphate (i.e., the y intercept of the equal-expenditure line) is equal to total expenditures (TE) divided by the price of phosphate:

$$y \text{ intercept } = TE/P_{phosphate}$$

2. The amount of nitrogen that can be purchased if the total budget is spent on nitrogen (i.e., the x intercept of the equal-expenditure line) is equal to the total expenditures (TE) divided by the price of nitrogen:

$$x \text{ intercept } = TE/P_{nitrogen}$$

3. The slope of the equal-expenditure line is calculated by dividing the change in phosphate by the change in nitrogen (or by dividing the y intercept by the x intercept):

$$\text{Slope} = y \text{ intercept}/x \text{ intercept}$$

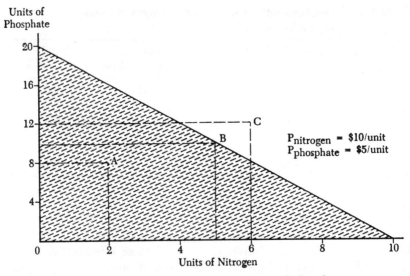

FIGURE 7-6: Equal–expenditure line for nitrogen and phosphate

4. Making the appropriate substitutions into equation 3:

$$\text{Slope} = \frac{TE}{P_{phosphate}} \bigg/ \frac{TE}{P_{nitrogen}}$$

which simplifies to:

$$\text{Slope} = \frac{TE}{P_{phosphate}} \times \frac{P_{nitrogen}}{TE}$$

Since the total expenditures cancel in this equation, the equation for slope becomes:

$$\text{Slope} = Price_{Nitrogen} \big/ Price_{Phosphate}$$

Thus, the slope is equal to the ratio of input prices.

In this instance, the slope of the equal-expenditure line is $10 (per-unit price of nitrogen) divided by $5 (per-unit price of phosphate). Since the farmer can purchase unlimited quantities of extra inputs without affecting their prices, the slope will be the same no matter how much output is produced. Thus, the equal-expenditure line has a constant slope throughout and is linear.

Two factors that will change the equal-expenditure line are: (1) a

TABLE 7-10: Input combinations for varying resource budgets

| Resource Budget | $1,000 | | $2,000 | | $4,000 | |
	Corn	SBOM	Corn	SBOM	Corn	SBOM
All Corn	10	0	20	0	40	0
All SBOM	0	5	0	10	0	20

Price of Corn = $100 Per Unit
Price of SBOM = $200 Per Unit

change in the size of the resource budget, and (2) a change in the prices of the inputs used. The way in which these two factors affect the equal-expenditure line will now be examined.

Changes in Resource Budgets and Equal-Expenditure Lines

As the size of the farmer's resource budget increases or decreases, so will the ability to purchase those inputs. Assuming the prices of the inputs used do not change as the budget changes, the slope of the equal-expenditure line will be the same for all budgets. This means that all of the equal-expenditure lines will be parallel. The difference between the lines for different budgets will be their distance from the origin. Larger resource budgets will be shown by equal-expenditure lines that are relatively further from the origin; smaller resource budgets by those that are relatively closer to the origin.

A specific example of the effect of budget changes on the position of the equal-expenditure line can be derived from the situation of the producer who uses a combination of corn and soybean oil meal (SBOM) to fatten hogs. Since all equal-expenditure lines are linear, they are uniquely determined by any two points. It is sufficient, then, to establish the x and y intercepts of each line to describe the line totally. Table 7-10 shows two intercepts for each of three possible resource budgets. It is assumed that the price of corn is $100 per unit and the price of SBOM is $200 per unit. The intercepts of the equal-expenditure lines are plotted in Figure 7-7. The outward movement of the equal-expenditure line occurs as the resource budget increases.

Changes in Input Prices and Equal-Expenditure Lines

Changes in input prices have a direct effect on the equal-expenditure lines. They change many units of inputs the farmer can purchase with

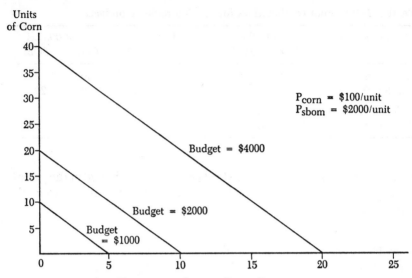

FIGURE 7-7: The effect on equal–expenditure lines
of changing resource budgets

a given resource budget. There are three ways in which input prices
can change to bring about this effect: (1) the prices of both inputs may
increase or decrease by the same relative proportion, (2) the price of
input X_1 may increase relative to the price of input X_2, or (3) the price
of input X_2 may increase relative to the price of input X_1.

Again, to use the example of the farmer who fattens hogs using a
combination of corn and SBOM, it is possible to predict the effect on
the equal-expenditure line of proportional increases in the prices of the
two inputs. When both input prices increase by the same proportion,
the ratio of one price to the other price will not be altered. In this
instance, the ratio of the price of corn to the price of SBOM does not
change. The slope of the equal-expenditure line will not change. Thus,
the effect of proportionate input price changes will be to reposition the
line. Its distance from the origin is changed but not its slope. Table
7-11 shows the effect on the intercepts of the equal-expenditure line
when the prices of both inputs increase and decrease by the same relative amount. It assumes a resource budget of $2,000.

To begin with, a price of corn of $100 per unit and a price of SBOM
of $200 per unit is assumed (column 2). Prices are then increased by 100
percent to yield column 3 and decreased by 50 percent to yield column
1. Determining the two intercepts in each case determines the linear
equal-expenditure line. The three lines derived are plotted in Figure
7-8. When input prices increase by the same proportion, the farmer

TABLE 7-11: The effect on the equal-expenditure table of changes in input price of the same relative amounts (resource budget = $2,000)

	(1) $P_{corn} = \$50$ $P_{sbom} = \$100$		(2) $P_{corn} = \$100$ $P_{sbom} = \$200$		(3) $P_{corn} = \$200$ $P_{sbom} = \$400$	
	Corn	*SBOM*	*Corn*	*SBOM*	*Corn*	*SBOM*
All Corn	40	0	20	0	10	0
All SBOM	0	20	0	10	0	5

purchases fewer units of each input with the resource budget. This situation is shown by a movement of the equal-expenditure line leftward or closer to the origin from line (2) to line (3). A decrease in input prices by the same proportion allows the farmer to buy more of both inputs with the same resource budget. This is shown in Figure 7-8 by the movement of the equal-expenditure line outward and to the right from curve (2) to curve (1).

In both cases, the new equal-expenditure lines will be parallel to the old lines when the prices of both inputs increase or decrease by the same proportion. If the price of one input changes relative to the price

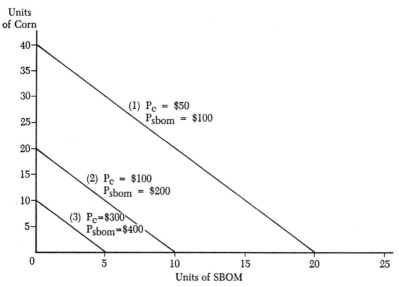

FIGURE 7-8: The effect on equal-expenditure lines of changing input prices by the same relative amounts (resource budget = $2,000)

TABLE 7–12: The effect on the equal–expenditure table of nonproportional price input changes (resource budget = $2,000)

	(1) P_{corn} = $100 P_{sbom} = $200		(2) P_{corn} = $100 P_{sbom} = $400	
	Corn	SBOM	Corn	SBOM
All Corn	20	0	20	0
All SBOM	0	10	0	5

of the other, this will not be so. The slope of the curve, being the ratio of the two input prices, will either increase or decrease. If the price of soybean oil meal increases or decreases relative to the price of corn, the relationship between the two prices will be changed and the slope of equal-expenditure line will change. Table 7-12 shows how such a change affects the number of units of input that can be purchased. Column 1 describes the starting situation where the price of corn is $100 per unit and the price of SBOM is $200 per unit. The price ratio in this case is P_{sbom}/P_{corn} = $200/$100 = 2. Column 2 shows the effect of an increase in the price of SBOM on the number of units of that input that the farmer can purchase with the total budget. When the price of SBOM increases to $400 per unit, while the price of corn stays the same, the price ratio is altered. The new price ratio is P_{sbom} / P_{corn} = $400/$100 = 4. Note that the number of units of corn that can be produced in both cases is the same.

The impact of the price change is shown graphically in Figure 7-9. The effect of the price increase is clear. As relative prices change, so does the slope of the line. As the price of soybean oil meal increased relative to the price of corn, the slope of the equal-expenditure line increased from two to four. Thus, the effect of a nonproportional change in input prices is to change the slope rather than merely the position of the equal-expenditure line. Instead of line (1) in Figure 7-9, the farmer now faces line (2). As will be shown later, such a change will limit the farmer's production.

The effect of a decline in the price of one input relative to the price of the other can be described in the same way as above. If the price of soybean oil meal declines relative to the price of corn, the producer can buy more units of SBOM with a given resource budget. Table 7-13 shows the effect of such a change on the number of units of each input that can be purchased. The resource budget upon which these calculations are based is $2,000.

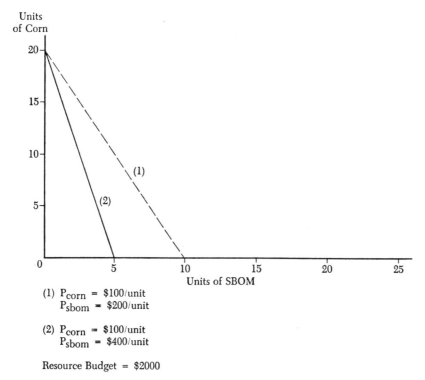

(1) P_{corn} = $100/unit
   P_{sbom} = $200/unit

(2) P_{corn} = $100/unit
   P_{sbom} = $400/unit

Resource Budget = $2000

FIGURE 7–9: The effect on equal–expenditure line of increasing the price of one input relative to the price of the other input

Plotting the information in Figure 7–10 shows graphically the effect of the changing price of one input relative to the price of the other. In the initial situation, line (1), the slope of the curve is two ($P_{sbom} \div P_{corn}$ = $200 \div $100 = 2). When the price of SBOM decreases, the slope of the line is one ($P_{sbom} \div P_{corn}$ = $100 \div $100 = 1). In the new situation, line (2), the farmer is able to purchase additional units of at least one input with the same resource budget.

PRODUCTION WITH THE LEAST-COST COMBINATION OF INPUTS

The goal of the agricultural producer is to produce at the lowest possible cost. The rationale for this is obvious. Since the difference between total cost and total revenue is profit, the rational producer will try to increase revenues and decrease costs in order to maximize

TABLE 7-13: The effect on the equal-expenditure line of nonproportional price changes (resource budget = $2,000)

	(1) $P_{corn} = \$100$ $P_{sbom} = \$200$		(2) $P_{corn} = \$100$ $P_{sbom} = \$100$	
	Corn	SBOM	Corn	Sbom
All Corn	20	0	20	0
All SBOM	0	10	0	20

profits. Increasing revenues is difficult for the individual farmer, who can only react to market-determined prices rather than influence them. Decreasing or minimizing costs of production, however, is within the farmer's abilities. Under the circumstances, where more than one input is used to produce a product, the farmer wants to use the least-cost combination of inputs to produce that product.

Producing with the least-cost combination of inputs is clearly in the farmer's interest. However, such a decision also has implications for society. The central problem of economics is scarcity, there are not sufficient resources available to allow any society or, more importantly, for "spaceship earth" to produce enough goods and services to satisfy all wants and needs. Since resource scarcities are, to a large extent, reflected by resource prices, using a more expensive production process than is absolutely necessary wastes scarce resources, which in a world of scarcity can be considered criminal. Thus, the farmer, by making the best decision on input use in terms of personal goals of profit maximization, also benefits society.

There are a great number of ways in which the farmer can determine the optimal or least-cost combination of inputs to use in the production process. Many are very cumbersome and unlikely to be of much aid to the decision maker. For example, the least-cost combination of two inputs can be found by calculating the actual cost of all possible combinations. A conclusion can then be drawn from an examination of all of the possible expenditures. This method has the advantage of simplicity. All that is required is that the farmer determine the workable combinations of inputs and multiply these amounts by input prices to determine total cost. The disadvantage is that, when extended beyond a small number of input combinations, this process becomes very time consuming. For instance, it is possible to find the costs for a series of combinations of nitrogen and phosphate that can be used to produce a given output of corn. Table 7-14 shows

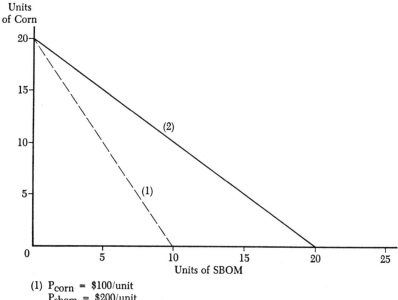

(1) P_{corn} = $100/unit
P_{sbom} = $200/unit

(2) P_{corn} = $100/unit
P_{sbom} = $100/unit

Resource Budget = $2000

FIGURE 7-10: The effect on equal–expenditure line of decreasing the price of one input relative to the price of the other input

how this is done. Given the various combinations of phosphate and nitrogen that can be used to produce an output of seventy-five units of corn, shown in columns (1) and (2), and the relative prices of $10 per unit for phosphate and $15 per unit of nitrogen, all the farmer needs to do to find the least-cost combination is to multiply the amount of each resource used by its price and add the two figures. This is done in columns (3), (4), and (5). Based on the information in this schedule, the farmer will use 5.4 units of phosphate and two units of nitrogen to obtain the least-cost combination of inputs. With this combination, the total cost of producing seventy-five units of corn is $84, the lowest possible expenditure.

Despite the attractiveness in the simplicity of this method, there are two definite drawbacks. The first, as mentioned above, is the cumbersome nature of the process. The arithmetic involved is of a low order, but the calculations are still time consuming. The second and more important drawback is that there are an almost infinite number of

TABLE 7-14: Total approach for determining least-cost combination of inputs (output of corn = 75 units)

(1) Units of Phosphate	(2) Units of Nitrogen	(3) Total Cost Phosphate	(4) Total Cost Nitrogen	(5) Total Expenditure
11	0	$110	$ 0	$110
8	1	80	15	95
5.4	2	54	30	84
4.1	3	41	45	86
3	4	30	60	90
1.6	6	16	90	106
0	9	0	135	135

Price of Phosphate = $10 Per Unit
Price of Nitrogen = $15 Per Unit

combinations of the two inputs that will produce the same output. The farmer would have to calculate total expenditures for *all* possible input combinations to eliminate the possibility of there being an even lower cost combination. Rather than making five or six simple calculations, the farmer would have to identify each of the many combinations that could be used to produce the desired output. This, in and of itself, would require a great deal of time. Through a model using a combination of the equal-product curve and the equal-expenditure line, the farmer can more quickly arrive at the least-cost combination of inputs and know that all possible combinations have been taken into account.

Before dealing with the graphic solution to the least cost combination problem, it should be recalled that such a decision benefits both the individual farmer and society. Society values its resources by pricing them through the market. Resource prices are a measure of the relative scarcity of an input. The ratio of two input prices shows how one input is valued in comparison to the other and their relative scarcity. The farmer need not known why the input is relatively scarce or abundant, but he must know how inputs relate to one another in the market. This information is obtained from input price ratio.

A second piece of information needed by the farmer is how the inputs substitute for one another in the production process. This information is provided by the marginal rate of technical substitution. With these two measures of the substitutability of inputs, the farmer can then make a decision on the combination of inputs to use that will minimize production costs and, at the same time, economize on the use of scarce societal resources. The closer the two rates of substitution, market and technical, are to being equal, the closer is the realization of the two goals. While equating the two rates may, at first, seem to be very cumbersome and difficult, it becomes much simpler when the market rate of substitution and the marginal rate of technical substitution are expressed in different forms. The market rate of substitution is the price ratio. It relates the price of input X_1 to the price of input X_2 in the following way:

$$\text{Market rate of substitution} = \frac{PX_1}{PX_2}$$

This price ratio also measures the slope of the equal-expenditure line:

$$\text{Marginal rate of technical substitution} = \frac{\Delta X_2}{\Delta X_1}$$

This ratio is the slope of the equal-product curve or isoquant. The goal, then, of equating the market rate of substitution and the marginal rate of technical substitution becomes a matter of equating the slope of the equal-expenditure line with the slope of the equal-product curve. This occurs at the point of tangency between the two curves. This principle is best illustrated by reference to an example.

The Graphic Approach

Figure 7–11 shows an equal-product curve for the production of corn, using nitrogen and phosphate as the variable inputs. This is the same equal-product information developed earlier in Table 7–14. Added to the equal-product curve are two equal-expenditure lines. One expenditure line represents a budget of $90 and the other a budget of $83. Given that there are a large number of combinations of phosphate and nitrogen that will produce seventy-five units of corn, the question is, which is the most economical combination? That is, which combination of the two inputs will produce the desired output at the least cost?

The equal-expenditure line representing a budget of $90 intersects the isoquant at points B and C. The output desired can clearly be produced with this budget. The combination of inputs indicated by point B uses P_2 units of phosphate and N_0 units of nitrogen to produce seventy-five units of corn. The total cost of this combination of nitrogen and phosphate would, of course, be $90. Likewise, combination C, which uses P_0 units of phosphate and N_2 units of nitrogen, will also produce seventy-five units of corn for the same $90 expenditure. While both combinations are possible, they do not necessarily represent the

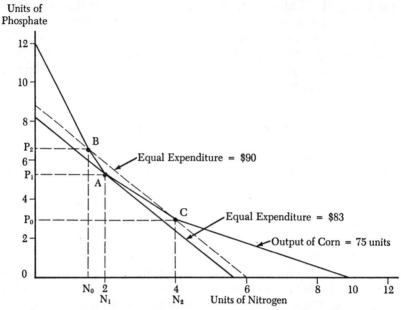

FIGURE 7–11: Determination of least-cost combination of inputs: graphic approach

most desirable or least-cost combination of the two inputs to use; there may be another of the infinite possibilities that will allow the producer to produce seventy-five units of output at a lower cost.

In order for any equal-expenditure line representative of a lower budget to be considered, it must have at least one point in common with the equal-product curve representing seventy-five units of production. The equal-expenditure line that fulfills this condition and represents the smallest budget, able at the same time to generate the required output, will have only one point in common with the equal-product curve. This point will be the point of tangency. In Figure 7–11, the equal-expenditure line meeting this condition is representative of a budget of $83 and is tangent to the equal-product curve at point A. While the required output can be produced using a larger resource budget, it cannot be produced with any smaller expenditure. If the budget were to decline below $83, the equal-product curve, representing seventy-five units of corn output, would be outside the equal-expenditure line and thus be unattainable. To summarize, the least-cost combination of inputs will be found at that point where the equal-expenditure line is just tangent to the equal-product curve, point A in Figure 7–11. The farmer minimizes the cost of producing seventy-five units of corn by using a combination of P_1 units of phosphate and N_1 units of nitrogen.

It is possible to arrive at the same conclusion in another way. As stated earlier, the farmer will derive the combination of resources defined as least cost by equating the rates of substitution in the market place and in the production process. In short, the least-cost combination of inputs will be found at that point where the price ratio of the two inputs is equal to the marginal rate of technical substitution. Since the former is the slope of the equal-expenditure line and the latter is the slope of the equal-product curve, this condition will be at the point of tangency between the two. Figure 7–11 provides greater insight into this method of determining least-cost combinations. It is clear that point B in this figure is not the least cost combination of nitrogen and phosphate. At point B, the price ratio (P_n/P_p) is not equal to the marginal rate of technical substitution $(\Delta P/\Delta N)$. Thus, point B represents a disequilibrium situation. The farmer must take action in order to correct this situation and bring the two into equality. Since a single producer cannot affect the price ratio, the farmer must concentrate on changing the marginal rate of technical substitution. At point B, the price ratio is less than the marginal rate of technical substitution. To make them equal, the MRTS must be reduced. In order to accomplish this, the farmer can decrease the amount of phosphate used and increase the amount of nitrogen used in the production process. This change will decrease the marginal productivity of nitrogen and increase the marginal productivity of phosphate and, in turn, cause the $MRTS_{n \cdot p}$ to decrease. Also, at point B, the ratio of the price of phosphate to that of nitrogen is less than the marginal rate of technical substitution of nitrogen for phosphate. This means that the farmer can add more units of nitrogen for phosphate and the saving in dollars spent on phosphate will more than offset the increased dollars spent on nitrogen. Thus, moving from point B to point A decreases the MRTS of nitrogen for phosphate and brings it into equality with the price ratio. This move also reduces the amount expended to produce seventy-five units of corn.

At point C in Figure 7–11, the price ratio is greater than the marginal rate of technical substitution of nitrogen for phosphate. In this instance, the farmer is using more nitrogen and less phosphate in the production process than would be indicated by the relative market prices of the two inputs. Thus, costs of production can be reduced by using less nitrogen and more phosphate. When this change is made, the optimum combination of inputs moves along the equal-product curve from point C to point A.

In the case of points B and C, the farmer was using the inputs in such combinations that the rates of technical substitution were inconsistent with the market prices. Only by moving to point A, where the technical trade-off between the two inputs was the same as the market trade-off, could the farmer hope to minimize individual costs and the costs to society.

The Price-Ratio Approach

It has thus far been demonstrated that the farmer can determine the least-cost combination of two inputs by comparing total cost for each possible combination of inputs—the total approach—or by using equal-product curves and equal-expenditure lines. From the latter formulation, it is possible to develop a third approach for determining least-cost combinations—the price-ratio approach.

While the farmer may be unaware of equal-product curves and unwilling to make the many calculations required for the total approach, he or she is quite familiar with the conditions under which more of one input will be used as a substitute for another. For example, when the extra dollars saved on phosphate are greater than the extra dollars spent on nitrogen, the farmer will add nitrogen to save phosphate. At long as this relationship is true, the farmer will continue to substitute nitrogen for phosphate in the production process until the extra dollars saved just equal the extra dollars spent.

The amount saved on phosphate can be measured by multiplying the amount of phosphate saved, ΔP, by the price of phosphate, P_p, or $\Delta P \cdot P_p$. The extra amount spent on nitrogen can be measured by multiplying the added nitrogen used, ΔN, by the price of nitrogen, P_n, or $\Delta N \cdot P_n$. The equilibrium condition can, thus, be expressed by equation 1:

$$(1) \quad \Delta P \cdot P_p = \Delta N \cdot P_n$$

By modifying this equation, it is possible to develop a more familiar form of where the least cost combination of inputs will occur.

If both sides of equation 1 are divided by ΔN,

$$\frac{\Delta P \cdot P_p}{\Delta N} = \frac{\Delta N \cdot P_n}{\Delta N}$$

this yields equation 2:

$$(2) \quad \frac{\Delta P \cdot P_p}{\Delta N} = P_n$$

If both sides of equation 2 are divided by P_p,

$$\frac{\Delta P \cdot P_p}{\Delta N \cdot P_p} = \frac{P_n}{P_p}$$

this yields equation 3:

$$(3) \quad \frac{\Delta P}{\Delta N} = \frac{P_n}{P_p}$$

Since

$$\frac{\Delta P}{\Delta N} = \text{marginal rate of technical substitutions of nitrogen for phosphate}$$

and

$$\frac{P_n}{P_p} = \text{input price ratio}$$

then inputs used will be in a least cost combination when:

$$(4) \quad \text{Input Price Ratio} = \text{Marginal Rate of Technical Substitution}$$

This conclusion, of course, is exactly the same one established earlier in the equal-product, equal-expenditure approach. The advantage of the price-ratio approach is that it focuses attention on how much of one input the producer must save by adding a unit of the other. The savings involved develop out of the farmer's own common-sense reasoning. This approach requires by far the simplest calculations that the farmer can make. For example, if the price ratio of inputs A and B, P_a/P_b, is two, the farmer knows that to break even two units of B must be saved when using another unit of A as a substitute. If any less than two units of B is saved, it will not be economically advantageous to make such a substitution. The marginal rate of technical substitution of the inputs for each other will provide the farmer with information on whether the amount of B saved will equal the price ratio. From past experiences, the farmer can estimate fairly well marginal rates of technical substitution, and can calculate the price ratio and make the comparison without a great amount of theoretical training. Much of the knowledge termed "experience" or "common sense" is really the codification of observations of past experience upon which theory is based. The farmer can easily make use of this awareness in the decision-making process by using the price-ratio approach.

Examples of the Price-Ratio Approach The operation of this approach is best seen through examples. The farmer using inputs A and B in the production process begins the determination of the least-cost combination of these inputs by comparing their prices and establishing the price ratio. Given a price for input A of $10 per unit and a price for input B of $5 per unit, the price ratio is:

$$\frac{\text{Price of Input A}}{\text{Price of Input B}} = \frac{\$10}{\$5} = 2$$

This result shows the farmer how many units of B must be saved to break even if one more unit of A is added. If the producer substitutes one unit of A for a saving of anything less than two units of B, the costs of production will increase, thus decreasing profits or increasing losses.

Having determined the trade-off between A and B in the marketplace, the farmer must now compare it to the trade-off in the production process. He or she must judge whether an additional unit of A will replace at least two units of B in the production process, the criteria for using it. What the farmer is, in fact, doing, albeit unknowingly, is comparing the price ratio with the marginal rate of technical substitution of A for B. At any point where one unit of A replaces more than two units of B, the farmer will be well-advised to increase the use of A.[1] At any point where one unit of A will replace less than two units of B, the use of A should not be increased.[2] In fact, the farmer should decrease its use or profits will decrease. If it is assumed that the amounts of A that can be substituted for B are infinitely divisible, then the break-even point between the time when it is profitable to use more A and the time when it is profitable to use less A comes at that point of equality between the price ratio and the marginal rate of technical substitution of A for B. That is, the $\text{MRTS}_{A \cdot B}$ equals two. To briefly summarize the three variants of the relationship and the farmer's appropriate response:

When $\text{MRTS}_{A \cdot B}$ > Price Ratio: The farmer should increase the use of A and decrease the use of B.

---

1. This will be true when the $\text{MRTS}_{A \cdot B}$ > Price Ratio.
2. In this instance, the $\text{MRTS}_{A \cdot B}$ < Price Ratio.

TABLE 7–15: The price–ratio approach for determining the least cost combination of inputs

(1) Units of Phosphate	(2) Units of Nitrogen	(3) $MRTS_{n \cdot p}$ $= \Delta P / \Delta N$	(4) Price Ratio $P_n = \$15/P_p = \$10$	(5) Total Expenditure
(1) 11	0			$110
(2) 8	1	3/1 = 3	$15/$10 = 1.5	95
(3) 5.4	2	2.6/1 = 2.6	$15/$10 = 1.5	84
(4) 4.1	3	1.3/1 = 1.3	$15/$10 = 1.5	86
(5) 3	4	1.1/1 = 1.1	$15/$10 = 1.5	90
(6) 1.6	6	1.4/2 = .7	$15/$10 = 1.5	106
(7) 0	9	1.6/3 = .53	$15/$10 = 1.5	135

When $MRTS_{A \cdot B} <$ Price Ratio: The farmer should decrease the use of A and increase the use of B.

When $MRTS_{A \cdot B} =$ Price Ratio: The farmer has arrived at the least cost combination of A B and should do nothing.

Table 7–15 shows the production relationship previously characterized in Table 7–14. It also shows the calculation of the price ratio and the marginal rate of technical substitution of nitrogen for phosphate for all combinations of inputs.

From the table, it is clear that the price-ratio approach does not always yield the precise results implied by the assumption of infinite divisibility of inputs. Nevertheless, it is still useful in determining the least cost combinations in most situations. In the production function described in Table 7–15, the farmer must choose the least cost combination of inputs from one of the seven combinations available. Should the producer contemplate a change from the combination indicated in row (1) to that indicated in row (2), he or she will base the decision on the MRTS information and price ratio found in columns (3) and (4) respectively. For the change just described, the $MTRS_{n \cdot p}$ is 3, greater than the price ratio of 1.5. By increasing nitrogen used from one to two units and decreasing phosphate used from eleven to eight units, production costs are reduced from $110 to $95. The same is true for a movement from combination (2) to combination (3). In this case, the $MRTS_{n \cdot p}$ is 2.6, while the price ratio is 1.5. Since the $MRTS_{n \cdot p}$ is greater than the price ratio, the farmer will decrease the total cost from $95 to $84 by making such a move.

A change from combination (3) to combination (4), however, will increase the farmer's costs. In this case, the $MRTS_{n \cdot p}$ of 1.3 is less than the price ratio of 1.5. The price ratio indicates that the farmer must save 1.5 units of phosphate for each additional unit of nitrogen used. In this instance, the farmer saves only 1.3 units. The difference of .2 units of phosphate represents the physical amount that the farmer will lose in making such a transaction. The dollar amount lost, or the amount by which costs increase, is the number of units of the input, .2 units of phosphate, multiplied by the per-unit price of the input, $10, or $2. As the table shows, such a move increases the farmer's costs of production by $2—from $84 to $86.

The analysis just presented is shown graphically in Figure 7–12. The data underlying this figure is from Table 7–15. The saving in resources used comes from a movement from any combination of inputs to the combination where $MRTS_{n \cdot p}$ equals the price ratio. The producer using N_1 nitrogen finds that $MRTS_{n \cdot p}$ exceeds the price ratio. The difference can be measured by the line segment AB. According to the model developed earlier, this is a signal to the farmer to increase the amount of nitrogen to N_2. At this point, the $MRTS_{n \cdot p}$ = the price ratio. How has the producer benefited through this change? In physical terms, the farmer has saved units of phosphate by using more units of nitrogen. The amount of phosphate saved per unit of nitrogen is represented by the area under the MRTS curve from N_1 to N_2. It is the odd-shaped area $N_1 BCN_2$. At the same time that the producer saves phosphate, however, the use of nitrogen is increased, resulting in an increase in nitrogen cost. In physical terms, the amount of phosphate needed to offset the increased nitrogen cost can be found by multiplying the change in nitrogen used (N_1N_2) by the input price ratio. This yields rectangle N_1ACN_2. The difference between these two areas is the area represented by ABC. In physical terms, this area represents units of phosphate saved above that needed to offset the increased cost in nitrogen used in moving from N_1 to N_2.

To determine whether nitrogen use should be increased from N_2 to N_3, the producer must compare the savings in phosphate against the increased costs of nitrogen. Graphically, the amount of phosphate saved by increasing nitrogen use from N_2 to N_3 is the area under the MRTS curve defined as N_2CEN_3. The amount of phosphate the farmer would have to save to cover the increased costs of nitrogen in moving from N_2 to N_3 is N_2CDN_3. Since the latter area is larger than the former area, the farmer will lose, in physical terms, the amount of phosphate represented by the triangle CDE. Clearly, the farmer is better off to use inputs at the point where the price ratio is equal to the marginal rate of technical substitution.

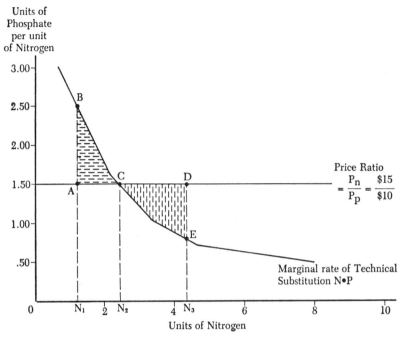

FIGURE 7–12: Determination of least–cost combination of inputs:
the price–ratio approach

The Effect of Changing Input Prices

The price ratio is based on the prices of the inputs used. Thus, any change in input prices will have a direct and immediate effect on the combination of inputs described as "best" or "least cost." With inputs A and B, prices can change in three possible ways:

1. The prices of input A and B increase by the same proportion.
2. The price of input A increases relative to the price of input B.
3. The price of input B increases relative to the price of input A.

In the first instance, when the price of both inputs increase proportionally, there will be no effect on the price ratio or the least-cost combination of inputs. However, a change in the price of input A relative to that of input B will have an effect. With the price ratio of P_a/P_b, an increase in P_a relative to P_b will increase the ratio. This will act as a signal to the producer that A is relatively more scarce than B. The producer will respond by altering the optimum combination of A and B to include less A and more B.[1] An increase in the price of B relative to A will, obviously, have the opposite effect. In the price ratio P_a/P_b, an increase in P_b relative to P_a will decrease the price ratio. This will signal the producer to make greater use of A and less use of B in the production process. By doing so, the least-cost combination is altered and total costs decrease.

Focusing on the equal-product, equal-expenditure approach, any change in relative input prices will affect the location of the point of tangency between the two. The result will be a change in the relative amounts of A and B used, the same as that described above. When input prices change by the same proportion, the slope of the equal-expenditure line will be unchanged. However, its position in reference to the origin will change. Depending on whether input prices decrease or increase, the producer may be able to increase the amount of output or may find that the output must be curtailed because the "real" budget has diminished.

THE OPTIMUM LEVEL OF OUTPUT

In previous chapters, discussion centered on how the farmer maximizes profits by choosing the best output. In this chapter, concern has been given to the input market—how does the farmer choose the least-cost combination of inputs? Again, the goal is profit maximization from the input side. If the farmer minimizes costs by choosing the optimal input combination, at least part of the task of profit maximization has been achieved. It is possible, however, to make the tie between choice of the least-cost combination of inputs and profit maximization more explicit. To do this, the farmer need only acknowledge that input combinations can be measured in dollar terms as costs and that an infinite number of production levels exist that can be converted to dollar values or revenues.

Simply put, for each equal-product curve or level of production, there is a least-cost combination of inputs. The expansion path shows the producer all of these least-cost combinations. Using this information, the producer must calculate the total costs and revenues of each combination to determine which level of output is the most profitable. Figure 7–13 describes how some of the options available look to the producer. The farmer producing output with inputs A and B has a choice of three levels of output—sixty, seventy-five, and ninety units.

1. The student can easily modify Figure 7–12 to see how an increase in the price ratio produces this effect.

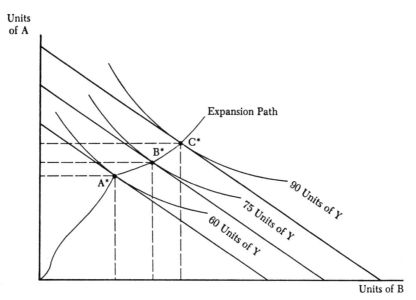

Units
of A

Expansion Path

C*

B*

A*

90 Units of Y

75 Units of Y

60 Units of Y

Units of B

FIGURE 7–13: Determination of expansion path

For each level of output, there is a least-cost combination of inputs A and B indicated by A*,B*, and C* respectively. Now that the producer knows the least combination of inputs for each output, the following must be determined: (1) the cost of each combination, (2) the revenues for each output, and (3) the profit for each level.[1] The producer will then produce that level of output which is most profitable.

To provide meaningful calculations, the totally theoretical representation in Figure 7–13 must be translated into concrete terms. Table 7–16 shows the least-cost combinations of inputs A and B for sixty, seventy-five, and ninety units of corn respectively. It also shows the calculation of costs, revenues, and profits for each level of output.

Once the farmer has made the calculations of total cost and revenues for each least-cost point along the expansion path, it is easy to determine which output should be produced. An output of seventy-five units of corn yields $7 more profit than either of the other two options.

As mentioned above, the choice is easy. First, the producer determines the least-cost combinations of inputs available to produce varying levels of output, then decides which level of output will maximize profits or minimize losses. This is accomplished by comparing

---

1. In order to maintain simplicity and clarity, this analysis will make the very restrictive assumption that there are no fixed costs or other variable costs.

TABLE 7-16: Determination of profit-maximizing least-cost combinations

COSTS			REVENUES		
Least-Cost Combinations		Cost of Inputs			
Units of Phosphate	Units of Nitrogen		Units of Output	Total Revenue	Profit
3.6	1.6	$36 + $24 = $ 60	60	$120	$60
4.7	2.4	$47 + $36 = $ 83	75	150	67
6.6	3.6	$66 + $54 = $120	90	180	60

Price of Phosphate = $10 Per Unit
Price of Nitrogen = $15 Per Unit
Price of Corn = $2 Per Unit

total costs and revenues for each possible level of output and selecting the output with the greatest total profit. As noted in earlier chapters, however, this is but one way to determine the profit-maximizing or loss-minimizing output. Another way in which the most profitable output can be determined is through the marginal approach. In Table 7-17, information on the total cost of each of the least-cost combinations of inputs is expressed in terms of average variable and marginal costs, while the price of corn becomes the marginal revenue of the firm.

Given the information on marginal costs and marginal revenues, the farmer can decide on the output that maximizes profits. This decision is based on the relationship of marginal revenue to marginal cost. If MR is greater than MC, expansion of output will increase profits. If MR is less than MC, expansion of output will decrease profits. If MR = MC[1], output should remain at its present level as profits are maximized.

In the situation described in Table 7-16, the producer must decide whether sixty units of corn maximizes profits, or if it would be worthwhile to expand production to the next level of output, seventy-five units. For such an expansion, the marginal revenue of $2 clearly is greater than the marginal cost of $1.53. This being the case, the farmer will find an increase in output increases profits. The next increase is not as propitious. In expanding from seventy-five to ninety units of output, the farmer encounters a marginal cost of $2.47. In this case, marginal cost is greater than marginal revenue. Such an expansion of output would diminish the farmer's profit.

1. In this example, output is characterized as "lumpy," i.e., not continuously divisible. The student should understand that many more equal-product curves are possible and that it would be possible to find the level of output where MR = MC.

TABLE 7–17: Optimum output for two variable inputs—the marginal approach

Output of Corn	Total Cost of Both Inputs	Average Variable Cost	Marginal Cost	Marginal Revenue	Profit
60 Units	$ 60	$1.00			$60
75 Units	83	1.11	1.53	2.00	67
90 Units	120	1.33	2.47	2.00	60

See Table 7–16 for optimum combinations of inputs and all other prices.

Once the farmer recognizes the potential impact of the two increases in output described above, it becomes apparent that the profit-maximizing output is seventy-five units. At this output, profit is $67, while at the other two alternatives, it is only $60.

Sufficient tools have now been developed to allow the student to determine the effect of different exogenous factors on the producer's profit-maximizing output. For practice and review, the student should be able to explain the impact of the following: (1) changes in input prices, (2) changes in output prices, and (3) changes in technology.

LEAST-COST COMBINATIONS FOR MORE THAN TWO VARIABLE INPUTS

In discussing the optimum combination of inputs a producer can employ, the assumption limiting the number of variable inputs to one was relaxed. A second input was allowed to vary. The production function under consideration was:

$$Y = f(X_1, X_2 \mid X_3 \ldots X_n)$$

While the relaxation of this assumption introduced a substantial amount of complexity into the decision-making model, it helped to point up the methodologies and tools of analysis that are required in the farmer's day-to-day decision making. Allowing two inputs to vary comes closer to reality. While the production function used in this chapter has one output, corn, using two variable inputs, phosphate and nitrogen, the real-world farmer faces a much more complex set of decisions. Some producers in fact produce multiple outputs using multiple variable inputs. To give a very simple example, the farmer may produce corn, but with labor, herbicide, and capital varying along with phosphate and nitrogen. The production function then becomes:

$$Y = f(X_1, X_2, X_3, X_4, X_5 \mid X_6 \ldots X_n)$$

where:

$$X_1 = \text{phosphate}$$
$$X_2 = \text{nitrogen}$$
$$X_3 = \text{labor}$$
$$X_4 = \text{herbicide}$$
$$X_5 = \text{capital}$$

and

$$X_6 \ldots X_n = \text{all fixed inputs}$$

Needless to say, this added complexity makes the farmer's decisions more difficult. It also precludes the use of the graphic models developed in this chapter. Mathematically, however, the tools of analysis developed thus far can be employed in a situation with multiple variable inputs, enabling the producer to determine the appropriate amounts of each input to use.

Earlier in this chapter, it was shown that the producer was using the least-cost combination of two inputs, X_1 and X_2, when the marginal rate of technical substitution equaled the price ratio. Since:

$$\text{MRTS} = \frac{\Delta X_2}{\Delta X_1}$$

and

$$\text{Price Ratio} = \frac{PX_1}{PX_2}$$

the condition for the least-cost combination is:

$$\frac{PX_1}{PX_2} = \frac{\Delta X_2}{\Delta X_1}$$

To focus on the dollar amount of X_2 that must be saved to make up for the increased expenditure on X_1, this equation can be restated as:

$$PX_1 \cdot \Delta X_1 = PX_2 \cdot \Delta X_2$$

where $PX_1 \cdot \Delta X_1$ equals extra expenditure on X_1, and $PX_2 \cdot \Delta X_2$ equals savings on X_2. As increased numbers of variable inputs are introduced, it is obvious that the farmer must meet the same conditions of cost and benefit among all variables as were necessary with just two variables. Thus, when X_3 is allowed to vary, the farmer will use three inputs in a least-cost combination when:

$$PX_1 \cdot \Delta X_1 = PX_2 \cdot \Delta X_2 = PX_3 \cdot \Delta X_3$$

Thus, the least-cost combinations of inputs for any number of variable inputs will exist when:

$$PX_1 \cdot \Delta X_1 = PX_2 \cdot \Delta X_2 = PX_3 \cdot \Delta X_3 = \ldots = PX_n \cdot \Delta X_n$$

After determining the least-cost combinations of the several inputs, the producer must find the levels of production that will maximize profits or minimize losses. In an earlier chapter, it was demonstrated that the producer would find the profit-maximizing level of input use at the point where marginal return from that input was equal to the marginal cost of that input.

SUMMARY

This chapter represents a movement from the simplistic world of theory into the more complex world of reality, with emphasis on the input market. In this instance, however, the questions raised concern the development of models to deal with the situation of multi-variable inputs in the production process. The question is, how does the agricultural producer decide on what combination of inputs to use in order to minimize production costs? Two basic models have been developed to answer this question. The first uses equal-product curves and equal-expenditure curves to determine the least-cost combination of inputs graphically. From the logic of this model comes the price-ratio model. This model allows the producer not only to avoid the use of graphs, but also fits well with the common sense and knowledge of the experienced farmer.

The introduction of multi-variable inputs to the farmer's decision making should not obscure the fundamental point that the farmer rationally evaluates a proposed action by examining its possible costs and benefits. In the next chapter, the farmer's output decision will be complicated by the production of multiple outputs. However, the models developed in this chapter will, with slight modification, be useful in determining the combination of products to produce.

QUESTIONS

1. From the following information, calculate the marginal rate of technical substitution of labor for machinery.

Units of Labor	Units of Machinery	$MRTS_{L \cdot C}$
2	14	
5	12	_____
9	10	_____
16	8	_____
30	6	_____

How many units of labor and machinery should be used in each of the following price combinations?

A. Price of labor = $10 per unit; price of machinery = $20 per unit

B. Price of labor = $5 per unit; price of machinery = $20 per unit

C. Price of labor = $10 per unit; price of machinery = $5 per unit

Determine answers by using the total approach and by comparing input price ratio with marginal rate of technical substitution.

2. Using equal-product curves and equal-expenditure lines, show that the least combination of inputs need contain only one of the inputs when the two inputs involved are perfect substitutes for each other.

3. Show graphically the effect of a change in input prices on the expansion path for a farm. Do so when prices change in the following ways:

A. Price of input A doubles; price of input B stays the same.

B. Price of input B doubles; price of input A stays the same.

C. Price of both inputs A and B doubles.

CHAPTER EIGHT

Decision-Making: The Product-Product Model

In the last chapter, a greater element of reality was introduced into the decision-making model by relaxing the assumption that the farmer used only one input in the production process. Analogously, it is now time to bring the output decision closer to reality by acknowledging that the farmer may produce more than one kind of product. In fact, in modern agriculture, the farmer producing only a single product is something of a rarity. The focus of this chapter will be on the allocation of the farmer's scarce resources between two outputs. In order to maintain concentration on the output market, it will be assumed that the bundle of resources available to the farmer is fixed. The form of the production function is then:

$$Y_1, Y_2 = f(\mid X_1, X_2, X_3 \ldots X_n)$$

where Y_1 and Y_2 are two outputs, for example, corn and soybeans, and the Xs represent the various inputs available to the farmer. The vertical bar, which precedes the listing of available inputs, indicates that these inputs are fixed. Thus, the problem now facing the farmer is choosing that combination of outputs which will maximize profits, given the fixed bundle of resources available as inputs. To make this choice, the farmer must gather information on two sets of product relationships— the technical production relationships between the two products and their market relationship.

TABLE 8-1: Production function for corn and soybeans

Units of Input X_1	Output Units of Corn	Units of Input X_1	Output Units of Soybeans
0	0	0	0
1	15	1	9
2	29	2	17
3	42	3	24
4	54	4	30
5	65	5	33
6	75	6	35

THE PRODUCTION-POSSIBILITIES CURVE

As indicated above, the first step the producer must take to determine the profit-maximizing combination of outputs is to discover the technical production relationships that exist between the fixed bundle of inputs and the two outputs. Initially, the farmer must determine the production function for each output. If Y_1 and Y_2 represent corn and soybeans respectively, and X_1 represents the fixed bundle of inputs, then the task is to determine the nature of the two production functions:[1]

$$Y_1 = f(X_1)$$

and

$$Y_2 = f(X_1)$$

Table 8-1 shows the relationship between various levels of X_1 and the output of corn and soybeans. Both production functions exhibit the law of diminishing marginal returns.

The farmer will be interested in the various combinations of corn and soybeans that can be produced with a given bundle of resources. For example, if the farmer has four units of input X_1 available, there are several ways in which this bundle can be used to produce corn and soybeans. All four units of X_1 could be employed in the production of

---

1. It would be more accurate to describe X_1 as a bundle of inputs that is fixed in composition and size. However, the amount of X_1 used in each production function is allowed to vary from zero up to the total fixed amount available. This variation is allowed for the purpose of establishing the production functions.

TABLE 8–2: Possible combinations of corn and soybeans using four units of input X_1

Total Units of X_1 Used	Units of X_1 Used for Corn	Output Units of Corn	Units of X_1 Used for Soybeans	Output Units of Soybeans
4	0	0	4	30
4	1	15	3	24
4	2	29	2	17
4	3	42	1	9
4	4	54	0	0

corn and none in the production of soybeans. This would result in an output of fifty-four units of corn and zero units of soybeans. By shifting one unit of input X_1 from corn to soybeans, three units of input X_1 would go to corn production and one unit to soybean production, with a resultant output of forty-two units of corn and nine units of soybeans. Table 8–2 summarizes the possible combinations of corn and soybeans that can be produced when the farmer has four units of input X_1 available. When the information in Table 8–2 is graphed in Figure 8–1, the result is the production-possibilities curve. This curve indicates all the possible combinations of two outputs that can be produced from a given bundle of inputs.

Three points are of interest in Figure 8–1. It is possible for the farmer to produce the combination of corn and soybeans shown by point A, which lies within the shaded area bounded by the production-possibilities curve. While the production of any combination of corn and soybeans within this shaded area is possible, it is unlikely the farmer will seek to produce such combinations but rather will attempt to keep inputs fully employed and productive. Thus, the producer will want to produce more of either or both outputs by moving production toward a point on the production-possibilities curve itself.

A second point of interest in Figure 8–1 is point C, which is not within the space confined by the production-possibilities curve. Thus, by definition, it is impossible for the farmer to produce the combination of corn and soybeans indicated by point C because it would require more resources than the available four units of input X_1.

To maximize production from the allocation of resources, the farmer will attempt to produce a combination of corn and soybeans as close to the fringe of the product-possibilities curve as possible, preferably on the curve itself, such as the combination shown by point B, the third point of interest.

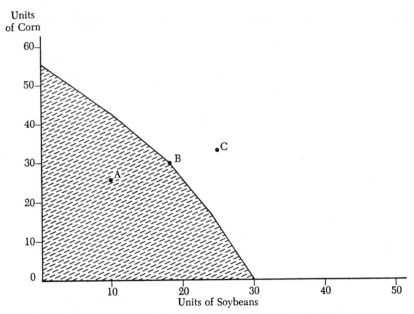

FIGURE 8-1: Production–possibilities curve for corn and soybeans
using four units of input X_1

Another way to view the production-possibilities curve is as an equal-resource or iso-resource curve, since it represents all the combinations of output that can be produced from a given bundle of resources. Since every point on the iso-resource or production-possibilities curve represents the same level of resource use, the cost of inputs for any combination of outputs indicated on or within the curve will be exactly the same. Thus, it is in the farmer's interest to maximize the amount of output produced with these inputs since input costs are the same for all levels of output.

The production-possibilities curve described in Figure 8-1 represents only one level of resource availability—four units of input X_1. Obviously, there are many other possible production-possibilities curves, as many as there are resource bases. When the producer's resource base is larger or smaller than that indicated in Figure 8-1, the production-possibilities curve changes in its position relative to the origin. It moves either outward as resource availability expands or inward as it contracts. Using production-function information from Table 8-1, a production-possibilities table can be developed showing the combinations of corn and soybeans that can be produced when six units of input X_1 are available (see Table 8-3).

The production-possibilities curve representing six units of input X_1, along with that representing four units of input X_1, is graphed in

TABLE 8–3: Possible combinations of corn and soybeans using six units of input X_1

Total Units of X_1 Used	Units of X_1 Used for Corn	Output Units of Corn	Units of X_1 Used for Soybeans	Output Units of Soybeans
6	0	0	6	35
6	1	15	5	33
6	2	29	4	30
6	3	42	3	24
6	4	54	2	17
6	5	65	1	9
6	6	75	0	0

Figure 8–2. This graph clearly shows how changes in resource availability affect the producer's capabilities. As the resource base available expands from four to six units of X_1, the production-possibilities curve moves outward and to the right. Any shrinkage in the resource base reverses the process and decreases the producer's possibilities, moving the curve inward toward the origin.

Changes in Technology and the Production-Possibilities Curve

The position of the production-possibilities curve with respect to the origin will change when technology used in the production of either corn or soybeans is altered. If a more efficient method of producing either product is discovered, the farmer will be able to obtain more product with the same resources. Hence, the production-possibilities curve will change shape. In essence, the intercept of the product whose technology has been improved will increase. Table 8–4 illustrates the effect a change in the technology of corn production has on the production function for corn previously developed.

When technology changes, the output of corn is greater at every level of input use. Under the old technology, the use of two units of X_1 produced twenty-nine units of corn; under the new technology, those same two units of X_1 will produce thirty-nine units of corn. This phenomenon is operative at each and every level of input use. This change in the production function for corn will be felt in the combinations of corn and soybeans that the farmer can produce from six units of X_1. Table 8–5 shows the new technology and resulting combinations of corn and soybeans obtainable with six units of X_1. Obviously, the producer can produce the same output of soybeans and a greater output of

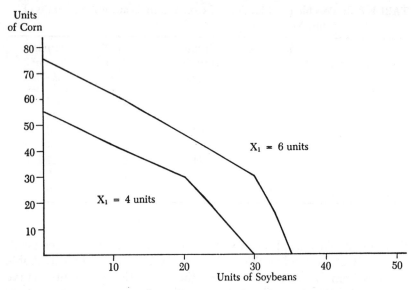

FIGURE 8–2: Production–possibilities curve for corn and soybeans
using four and six units of input X_1

corn for every combination of the two products produced. When the
production-possibilities curve based on Table 8–5 is graphed in Figure
8–3, the effect is clearly illustrated. The curve moves outward from the
origin with a greater gap on the corn axis. The only point in common
between the two production-possibilities curves is where all six units of
X_1 are devoted to soybean production. Since the technology of soybean
production did not change, thirty-five units of soybeans is still the

TABLE 8–4: The effect of a change in technology on the production function
of corn

OLD TECHNOLOGY		NEW TECHNOLOGY	
Units of Input X_1	Output Units of Corn	Units of Input X_1	Output Units of Corn
0	0	0	0
1	15	1	20
2	29	2	39
3	42	3	57
4	54	4	74
5	65	5	90
6	75	6	105

TABLE 8–5: Possible combinations of corn and soybeans using six units of
input X_1 given new technology for corn production

Total Units of X_1 Used	Units of X_1 Used for Corn	Output Units of Corn	Units of X_1 Used for Soybeans	Output Units of Soybeans
6	0	0	6	35
6	1	20	5	33
6	2	39	4	30
6	3	57	3	24
6	4	74	2	17
6	5	90	1	9
6	6	105	0	0

maximum possible soybean production. It is left for the student to
determine how other changes in technology, particularly negative
changes, affect the farmer's production-possibilities curve.

THE MARGINAL RATE OF PRODUCT SUBSTITUTION

As was indicated earlier, the first step the farmer must take to determine the profit-maximizing combination of outputs to produce is to
determine the technical details of production for the two crops. This
has been done. The production-possibilities curve establishes the technical production data for both products. It shows the relationship
between the two outputs. In the last chapter, inputs were examined
from two aspects:(1) how they substituted for each other in the production process and (2) how they substituted for each other in the marketplace. Though this chapter is concerned with optimum combinations
of outputs rather than of inputs, the comparisons made will be analogous. Rather than seeking to find how much more of input B must be
used when the amount of input A used declines, the question will be
how much of product B must be sacrificed in order to produce more of
product A. In a sense, this is a measure of the opportunity cost of A.
Analogous to the marginal rate of technical substitution (MRTS), the
marginal rate of product substitution (MRPS) measures the change in
one output that must be made to produce more of the other output. For
example, the marginal rate of product substitution of corn for soybeans
measures the units of soybeans that must be given up to produce an
additional unit of corn. In making this calculation, the change in the
output of soybeans is divided by the change in the output of corn.

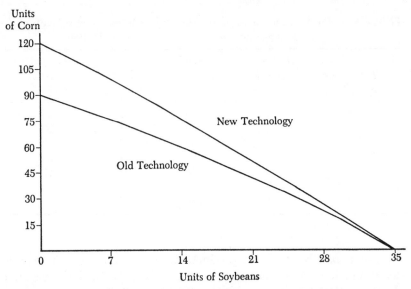

FIGURE 8-3: Production–possibilities curve for corn and soybeans using six units of X_1 with old and new technology for corn production

Thus, the marginal rate of product substitution of corn for soybeans ($\text{MRPS}_{\text{corn-soybeans}}$) is:

$$\text{MRPS}_{\text{corn-soybeans}} = \frac{\Delta \text{ Output of soybeans}^1}{\Delta \text{ Output of corn}}$$

Table 8-6 reproduces the production possibilities of corn and soybeans using six units of X_1. It shows the calculation of $\text{MRPS}_{\text{corn-soybeans}}$ for changes between the different combinations of corn and soybeans.

The marginal rate of product substitution of corn for soybeans shown in this table indicates how many units of soybeans must be sacrificed in order to obtain one more unit of corn. Thus, a MRPS of 0.13 indicates that the producer must give up 0.13 units of soybeans to produce an additional unit of corn. Because of the law of diminishing returns, which applies to both production functions, the amount of soybeans that must be sacrificed to obtain an additional unit of corn

---

1. In the notation used here, the product listed first is the one whose production is increased; the product listed second is the one whose production is decreased. Thus, the MRPS_{1-2} means that product one increases at the expense of product two. The product being increased forms the denominator of the equation while the product being decreased forms the numerator.

TABLE 8–6: Marginal rate of product substitution of corn for soybeans

Output Units of Corn	Output Units of Soybeans	$\dfrac{\Delta Output\ Soybeans}{\Delta Output\ Corn}$	$MRPS_{C\text{-}S}$
0	35		
15	33	−2 / 15	−0.13
29	30	−3 / 14	−0.21
42	24	−6 / 13	−0.46
54	17	−7 / 12	−0.58
65	9	−8 / 11	−0.73
75	0	−9 / 10	−0.90

will increase as greater amounts of corn are produced. This fact illustrates the law of increasing marginal rate of product substitution. If the phenomenon under consideration were the $MRPS_{\text{soybeans-corn}}$, the units of corn sacrificed for an additional unit of soybeans would also increase as larger amounts of soybeans were produced. Before leaving the discussion of how the products substitute for each other in the production process for the discussion of how they substitute for each other in the marketplace, it should be noted that there are several types of relationships that exist between products. These relationships will be discussed next.

PRODUCT RELATIONSHIPS

There are four basic types of relationships which two products can have to one another: (1) competitive, (2) complementary, (3) supplementary, and (4) joint. The nature of the relationship existing between the products will influence the kinds of decisions that the producer makes in determining the optimum product mix. Thus, it is important to examine in greater detail these relationships.

Competitive Products

Two products are competitive when an increase in the production of one can be accomplished only by a decrease in the production of the other. The relationship between corn and soybeans developed earlier is an example of competitive products. More corn could be produced if fewer soybeans were produced. This fact is true because a fixed bundle of resources was used to produce both products. Production of additional units of one product required the diversion of resources from the production of the other. The land available to the producer could be used for corn production or for soybean production but not for both at the same time. As previously noted, the marginal rate of product substitution is a measure of how the two products substitute for each other. Competitive products substitute for each other in three ways. They can substitute for each other at an increasing rate, a constant rate, or a decreasing rate. The MRPS will reflect which of the three ways competitive products substitute for each other in the production process.

The first way in which competitive products may substitute for each other is at an increasing rate. This happens when the amount of product B given up to get an extra unit of product A increases as more and more A is produced. Put another way, the $MRPS_{A-B}$ will increase as more A is produced. The production-possibilities curve developed earlier for corn and soybeans shows two competitive products substituting for each other at an increasing rate. As noted, the production-possibilities curve is concave to the origin because each of the products is produced with a production function exhibiting decreasing marginal returns. As increasing amounts of input X_1 are used in the production of corn, the marginal physical product of X_1 in corn production declines. Likewise, as decreasing amounts of input X_1 are used in the production of soybeans, the marginal physical product of X_1 in soybean production increases. Thus, as units of X_1 are diverted from the production of soybeans to the production of corn, increasing amounts of soybeans must be sacrificed to obtain an additional unit of corn. The result is an increasing $MRPS_{soybeans-corn}$. Many products in agriculture are competitive and substitute for each other at an increasing rate. If a limited amount of fertilizer is available for the production of wheat and barley, these two products will be competitive. Since the production functions for both products exhibit diminishing marginal returns to fertilizer, the products will substitute for one another at an increasing rate. Likewise, if the farmer has available a fixed amount of labor that can be devoted to the production of crops or livestock, more of one product can be produced only at the expense of the other. The amount of crops sacrificed for livestock will increase as more and more livestock is produced.

A second way in which competitive products may substitute for each other is at a constant rate. In this instance, the amount of product B that must be sacrificed to obtain an additional unit of A will remain the same no matter how much A or B is produced. Since the two products substitute for each other at the same rate throughout all ranges of production, the $MRPS_{A-B}$ will remain constant. Products will substitute for each other at a constant rate when the production functions for both products are linear. The production-possibilities curve for two

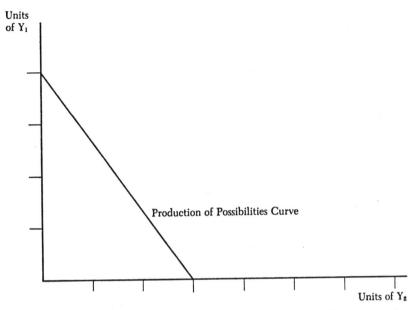

FIGURE 8–4: **Production–possibilities curve for products substituting at a constant rate**

products substituting at a constant rate is shown graphically in Figure 8–4. The result is a straight-line production-possibilities curve.

As an example, a farmer may have sixty acres of land equally suited to the production of wheat or oats. From this land, it is possible to obtain a yield of forty bushels of wheat per acre or eighty bushels of oats per acre. If the farmer devotes an additional acre of land to wheat production eighty bushels of oats must be sacrificed. This will be true for each and every acre of land in the sixty-acre plot. For each extra bushel of wheat produced, a constant two bushels of oats must be given up. The MRPS$_{wheat-oats}$ will be constant at a value of two. Under these circumstances, the producer will maximize profits by producing only one of the crops. The choice will be determined by the relative prices the two products carry in the marketplace and their relative yields per acre. A farmer who chooses to produce both products when they substitute at a constant rate does so for some reason other than profit maximization, for example, diversification to reduce the risks inherent in relying on only one crop.

A third way in which competitive products may substitute for each other is at a decreasing rate. When products substitute in this manner, increasing units of A can be produced at a smaller and smaller cost in terms of the production of B sacrificed. This would result in a

Units of Y₁

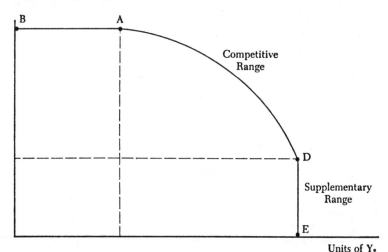

FIGURE 8-5: Production-possibilities curve for two supplemental products

continually decreasing MRPS and a production-possibilities curve convex to the origin. This phenomenon occurs very rarely in agriculture. It occurs most often over short periods of time when the stock of capital utilized in the production process is so small that production is still in the stage of increasing returns. Another possibility is that the two products may be produced in such a way as to be destructive to each other. An example of this is antipathetic symbiosis, which occurs when cedar trees and apple trees are produced close together. The cedar tree is capable of harboring disease organisms that are very detrimental to the production of apples. When this is the case, only one of the products should be produced.

Supplementary Products

Products are supplementary to one another when the production of one does not increase or decrease the production of the second. This generally occurs only over a small range of the production possibilities, after which the products become competitive again. Figure 8-5 describes a hypothetical situation in which products Y₁ and Y₂ are supplementary over range BA and range DE, and competitive over range AD. It is to the farmer's advantage to make use of the supplemental ranges and produce at least to the point where the two products become competitive.

An example of supplemental production may occur when the farmer raises both cattle and hogs. The hogs are put in the same feedlot as the cattle and fed nothing more than the nutrients they can forage from the beef cattle droppings. To hog producers, this is known as the "Iowa Free Lunch." If the hogs were not allowed to forage in the droppings, the corn and nutrients contained therein would simply be wasted. Putting a few hogs in the lot to fatten does nothing to diminish the amount of beef produced. Thus, to begin with, the relationship of hogs to cattle is supplementary. However, as the number of hogs increases, they will begin to compete with cattle for limited time, feed, and space resources and thus become competitive products.

A second example of supplementary production may occur when the farmer purchases a combine to harvest corn and soybeans in the fall and wheat in the summer. In this case, there is no competition for combining between the two harvest periods. In fact, to the extent that corn and soybeans are harvested at different times during the fall, their harvest with the combine would be supplementary. However, as the number of acres of one or both of the crops increases, the relationship will become competitive. The use of the combine to harvest corn will interfere with its use in harvesting soybeans.

Complementary Products

Products are complementary to one another when an increase in the production of one also increases the production of the other. In this case, the MRPS will be positive. In general, complementary production occurs only over a number of production periods rather than during one production season. An example of complementarity would be the inclusion of hay and grain in a crop-rotation system. In this instance, the two products are complementary because of a kind of mutual symbiosis. Including a legume such as alfalfa in the crop rotation will help to add nitrogen to the soil. This, in turn, will increase the yield of the grain crop that follows the alfalfa in the crop-rotation cycle. In addition to adding nitrogen to the soil, crop rotation might also reduce disease organisms in the soil, increase soil drainage, reduce insect problems, or in other ways improve the field for the combing grain crop. In essence, the hay crop is complementary to the grain crop because it provides external benefits the grain crop can use. Similarly, people who receive educations provide benefits to society beyond their direct contributions as more productive workers. For example, they are less criminally motivated and tend to participate in volunteer activities to a greater extent than those with less formal education. Thus, educated people and societal well being are complementary products. Increases in the production of one also increases the production of the other.

While maximizing the benefits of complementary relationships is not subject to decision making during one production period, it is clear that knowledge of these relationships does influence the farmer's choice over a number of production periods. It is to the producer's advantage to choose carefully those products which, in a sense, provide "free" externalities. Even a casual examination of crop planning in modern agriculture indicates that this is so.

Joint Products

The last relationship between two products is that of joint production. When two products are produced jointly, the production of one guarantees the production of the other. From one perspective, this is the case of the production of what are commonly called by-products. When the farmer produces oats, a by product is oat straw that can be used for animal bedding. Producing mutton also produces wool. Since the products are produced jointly, the farmer does not have to determine how much of each to produce. The decision cannot be made to produce some lambs with wool and some without wool, but rather only which level of production, if any, is profitable. Thus, the relative prices of the two joint products, mutton and wool, will have no impact on the farmer's decision making in the short run. The decision will concern only whether to raise sheep and, if so, how many sheep will be the most profitable to produce.

Over a longer period of time, however, the relative market prices of the two joint products will affect the farmer's choice of which breed variety of the product to produce. If the price of wool increases relative to the price of mutton, the farmer may choose a breed of sheep that produces more wool and less mutton. Likewise, if the price of straw increases relative to the price of oats, the farmer may plant a variety of oats that produces more straw relative to grain. Once the choice of breed or variety is made, the farmer will again be in the position of deciding only the total amount of joint products to produce to maximize profits.

THE EQUAL-REVENUE LINE

Thus far, the technical details of production have been established through individual production functions and production-possibilities curves. The rate at which products substitute for each other technologically is indicated by the marginal rate of product substitution. The final piece of information that the producer requires to determine the optimum combination of products to produce concerns how they substitute for each other in the marketplace. The product relationship for which this knowledge is most critical is that of competitive products substituting at an increasing rate for each other. For competitive products substituting at a constant or decreasing rate for each other, the producer's best decision is to produce one or the other of the products. Supplementary or complementary products should be produced through the relevant ranges until they become competitive to each other. Likewise, joint products are produced independent of product prices in the short run.

For those products most common in agriculture, which substitute at increasing rates, the producer must have information on product prices before the most profitable combinations of the two products can be determined. The vehicle through which this information can be expressed is the equal-revenue line or iso-revenue line.

It is easiest to develop the concept of an equal-revenue line by assuming the producer has as a goal a certain amount of revenue. Once the producer has decided on the desired level of revenue, the combination of products which will produce that revenue must be determined. The market provides information about the prices of these products. Once this information is known, the combination of products that will yield the desired amount of revenue can easily be found. For example, if the price of corn is $1 per unit, the price of soybeans $2 per unit, and the desired level of revenue is $100, there are many combinations of the two products that will produce the desired result. Table 8–7 shows some of these combinations.

It is plain that these combinations do not represent all of the possible combinations of corn and soybeans that will generate $100 in revenue. A more comprehensive representation could be established by graphing these and all other possible combinations as an equal-revenue or iso-revenue line.

An equal-revenue line is easily determined from the available data by determining either the two end points of the curve or one end point and the slope. If the farmer produces two products, Y_1 and Y_2, with prices P_{Y_1} and P_{Y_2}, respectively, and if the total revenue desired is TR, then the intercepts showing how many units of each product must be produced to generate the desired revenue can be found in the following manner:

Intercept on the Y_1 axis (the amount of Y_1 that must be produced to generate TR if no Y_2 is produced) = TR / P_{Y_1}

TABLE 8-7: Equal-revenue combinations for corn and soybeans

Total Revenue	Units of Corn	Revenue from Corn	Units of Soybeans	Revenue from Soybeans
$100	0	$ 0	50	$100
100	20	20	40	80
100	40	40	30	60
100	60	60	20	40
100	80	80	10	20
100	100	100	0	0

Price of Corn = $1 Per Unit
Price of Soybeans = $2 Per Unit

Intercept on the Y_2 axis (the amount of Y_2 that must be produced to generate TR if no Y_1 is produced) = TR / P_{Y_2}

Since the slope of the curve is found by dividing the Y_1 intercept by the Y_2 intercept:

$$\text{Slope} = \frac{TR}{P_{Y_1}} \div \frac{TR}{P_{Y_2}}$$

$$= \frac{TR}{P_{Y_1}} \cdot \frac{P_{Y_2}}{TR}$$

$$= \frac{P_{Y_2}}{P_{Y_1}}$$

Thus, when the data in Table 8-7 is expressed graphically in Figure 8-6, the intercepts are determined as above and the slope is equal to the ratio of the two product prices. Since the farmer's output has no effect on the products' market prices, the price ratio is assumed to be constant no matter how many units of product are offered on the market or how much revenue the producer desires.

Influences on the Equal-Revenue Line

The slope and position of the equal-revenue line is determined by two factors: (1) the amount of revenue the farmer desires and (2) the relative prices of the two products produced. Clearly, there are an infinite number of equal-revenue lines reflecting a particular level of revenue

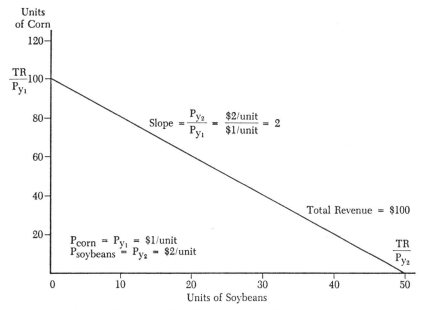

FIGURE 8-6: Equal-revenue line for corn and soybeans

and product prices. Just as clearly, the influences that will move the line from one position to another are the same two factors—level of revenue and product prices.

Changes in the amount of revenue desired will move the equal-revenue line inward or outward with respect to the origin. As the producer decides on higher levels of revenue, the curve will move outward from the origin. As the producer decides on lower levels of revenue, the curve will move inward toward the origin. Table 8–8 shows the situation of the farmer who is producing beef cattle and hogs. With the price of beef cattle at $400 per unit and the price of hogs at $200 per unit, Table 8–8 illustrates the combinations of the two products necessary to generate revenues of $2,000, $4,000, and $8,000. For example, $4,000 of revenue can be generated by producing ten units of beef and zero units of hogs or by producing zero units of beef and twenty units of hogs.

When this information is plotted and graphed in Figure 8–7, the effect of changes in desired revenue is easy to understand. While the line changes position with respect to the origin, the slope of all three equal-revenue lines is the same. The ratio of the price of hogs to the price of beef has not changed. Since this product price ratio is the slope of the equal-revenue line, all three lines will be parallel. The line representing $8,000 in revenue will be twice as far from the origin as

TABLE 8–8: Product combinations required for various levels of revenue

Total Revenue Desired	$2,000		$4,000		$8,000	
	Units of Beef	Units of Hogs	Units of Beef	Units of Hogs	Units of Beef	Units of Hogs
All Beef Produced	5	0	10	0	20	0
All Hogs Produced	0	10	0	20	0	40

Price of Beef = $400 Per Unit
Price of Hogs = $200 Per Unit

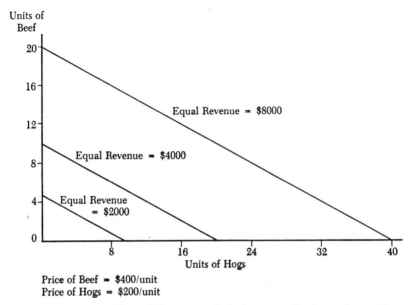

Price of Beef = $400/unit
Price of Hogs = $200/unit

FIGURE 8–7: The effect of changes in desired revenue levels on the position of the equal–revenue lines

the line representing $4,000 in revenue, and it will be four times as far from the origin as the line representing $2,000 of revenue.

Changes in the prices of the two products produced will also influence the position and the slope of the equal-revenue line. The prices of two products, A and B, may change in three ways: (1) both prices may change by the same proportion, (2) the price of A may increase relative to the price of B, and (3) the price of B may increase relative to the price of A. In the first instance, when the prices of both products increase or decrease by the same proportion, the effect on the equal-revenue line will be to shift it in a parallel direction. The equal-revenue line will shift inward when both product prices increase by the same proportion and outward when both decrease by the same proportion. In both instances, the slope of the line, i.e., the ratio of the two prices, will remain unchanged. Such a price change will only serve to decrease, in the case of a price increase, or increase, in the case of a price decrease, the amount of each product the farmer must produce in order to achieve the desired level of revenue. Thus, the effect of proportionate product price changes will be to alter the position of the equal-revenue line with respect to the origin, but not to change its slope.

When the price of A increases relative to the price of B or vice versa, the effect on the equal-revenue line will be on the slope of the line. As

TABLE 8-9: Effect of nonproportional price changes on equal-revenue combinations

	Old Price		New Price	
	Units of Beef	Units of Hogs	Units of Beef	Units of Hogs
All Beef	5	0	4	0
All Hogs	0	10	0	10

Desired Revenue = $2,000
Price of Beef = $400 Per Unit; of Hogs = $200 Per Unit
Price of Beef = $500 Per Unit; of Hogs = $200 Per Unit

the ratio of the two product prices is the measure of the slope of the line, any change in one price relative to the other will increase or decrease this ratio and, consequently, change the slope. A simple example will illustrate this process. If the price of A is $5 per unit and the price of B is $2 per unit, the slope of the equal-revenue line will be found in the following manner:

$$\text{Slope} = P_A / P_B = \$5 / \$2 = 2.5$$

Now, if the price of A increases to $6 per unit and the price of B remains unchanged, the slope of the equal-revenue line will change to the following:

$$\text{Slope} = P_A / P_B = \$6 / \$2 = 3.0$$

It can be seen that product A now makes a larger relative contribution to the desired amount of revenue than it did formerly. Table 8-9 illustrates the effect of product price changes on equal-revenue combinations. This table, based on the information in Table 8-8, shows the effect of increasing beef prices relative to hog prices. As can be seen, less beef production is now needed to generate the desired revenues. Two thousand dollars can now be produced from four units of beef rather than five units.

When this information is plotted in Figure 8-8, it is clear that the effect of an increase in the price of beef relative to the price of hogs is to decrease the slope of the equal-revenue line. It is left to the student to trace out the effects of other product price changes on the equal-revenue line. Suffice it to say that any nonproportional price changes will have their impact on the slope of the equal-revenue line.

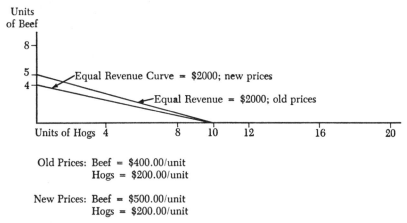

Old Prices: Beef = \$400.00/unit
        Hogs = \$200.00/unit

New Prices: Beef = \$500.00/unit
        Hogs = \$200.00/unit

FIGURE 8–8: Effect of nonproportional price change on equal–revenue lines

PROFIT-MAXIMIZING COMBINATIONS OF OUTPUT

Earlier in this chapter, it was noted that the farmer required a certain set of information in order to determine the combination of outputs that would maximize profits. Thus far, this chapter has centered around the development of the required information. The production-possibilities curve established the technical relationships between products. This relationship was expressed through the marginal rate of product substitution. Substitutions between products in the market-place were expressed through product price ratios and equal-revenue lines. The task that remains is to put this information together in such a way that the producer can utilize it in determining the combination of products to maximize profits or to minimize losses.

The process for doing this is similar to that developed in the last chapter for determining least-cost combination of inputs. There are three basic approaches. The first, the total approach, mathematically determines the amount of revenue associated with each and every combination of output. The combination with the greatest amount of revenue is then selected. The second is the graphic approach. It makes use of the two graphical tools developed—the production-possibilities curve and the equal-revenue line. Finally, the third approach is the marginal approach. Here, the producer uses the marginal rate of product substitution and the product price ratio. These two measures are compared to determine the profit-maximizing combination of products to produce. While all of these approaches will yield the same result, one may be more appropriate than the others depending on the information available.

TABLE 8–10: Determination of revenue-maximizing combination of outputs—the total approach

Output Units of Corn	Output Units of Soybeans	Revenue from Corn	Revenue from Soybeans	Total Revenue
0	35	$ 0	$70	$70
15	33	15	66	81
29	30	29	60	89
42	24	42	48	90
54	17	54	34	88
65	9	65	18	83
75	0	75	0	75

Price of Corn = $1 Per Unit
Price of Soybeans = $2 Per Unit

The Total Approach

The most obvious way the producer can determine the combination of outputs that maximize profits is through visual examination of all possible revenue outcomes. The method is simple. The farmer determines all combinations of the two outputs that are feasible within the input constraint, then multiplies the various amounts of output by their respective market prices and adds to find the total revenue for each possible combination. Since each combination is produced from the same resource base, the cost of production will be the same for all alternatives. Therefore, the combination that yields the greatest amount of revenue will also yield the greatest level of profit. To illustrate this method, Table 8–10 shows the combinations of corn and soybeans available to the producer using six units of input X_1. The revenue for each product in the combination is calculated along with the total revenue. The product prices assumed are $1 per unit of corn and $2 per unit of soybeans.

Once the farmer has determined the revenue from each possible combination of corn and soybeans, all that remains is to choose the combination with the greatest revenue. This will clearly be forty-two units of corn and twenty-four units of soybeans. This combination produces a revenue from corn of $42 (forty-two units of corn multiplied by a per-unit price of $1), and a revenue from soybeans of $48 (twenty-four units of soybeans multiplied by a per-unit price of $2). This yields a total revenue of $90. Since the costs of production are the same for all combinations, and since no other combination produces a total revenue greater than $90, profits will be maximized or losses minimized by the production of this combination of corn and soybeans.

While the appeal of this approach is its simplicity, that same simplicity makes it very cumbersome. First, it can be used for only a relatively small number of output combinations. As the number of combinations expands, the amount of time spent performing the calculations also expands, making the farmer's task tiresome. Second, although the number of combinations of the two products for a given resource base is infinite, the total approach selects only isolated points along the production-possibilities curve. While $90 is clearly the greatest revenue produced by the seven combinations listed in Table 8–10, there may be unspecified combinations that will produce a greater revenue. Thus, while the total approach is useful when the number of combinations possible are few, it is much less useful when it is assumed that outputs are continuous and infinitely divisible. For larger numbers of alternatives, the marginal approach is more useful than the total approach.

The Graphic Approach

In Chapter 7, the decision concerning the least-cost combination of inputs was based on finding the point where inputs substituted for each other in the production process at the same rate they substituted for each other in the marketplace. This same logic applies to the decision concerning the profit-maximizing combination of outputs. Only this time, the producer compares the rate at which products substitute for each other in the production process with the rate at which they substitute for each other in the marketplace. The producer will maximize profits by equating the marginal rate of product substitution with the produce price ratio. Thus, the condition for profit maximization or loss minimization is:

Marginal Rate of Product Substitution = Product Price Ratio

The marginal rate of product substitution is a measure of the slope of the production-possibilities curve, while the product price ratio is a measure of the slope of the equal-revenue line. Given that, the condition will be met at the point of tangency between the two measures, where the slope of the production-possibilities curve is equal to the slope of the equal-revenue line.

Figure 8–9 shows both the production-possibilities curve for corn and soybeans and several equal-revenue lines. The production-possibilities curve is based on a resource constraint of six units of X_1. Thus, the cost of production are the same for all combinations of output shown by the curve. The producer's goal, then, is to maximize revenue from the six units of input, which in this case is the same as profit maximization or loss minimization.

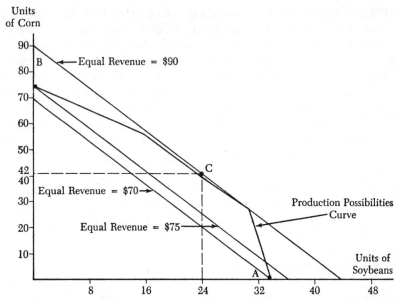

FIGURE 8–9: Determination of revenue–maximizing combination of outputs: the graphic approach

The producer can obtain any level of revenue represented by an equal-revenue line that has a point or points in common with the production-possibilities area. For example, point A shows a combination of thirty-five units of soybeans and zero units of corn. The total revenue associated with this combination is $70, thirty-five units of soybeans at $2 per unit. Any combination of corn and soybeans along the equal-revenue line will, by definition, also produce $70 of revenue. The question that the producer must now ask is whether the constraints imposed by the production-possibilities curve and the ratio of product prices will yield yet a higher level of revenue.

It is obvious from Figure 8–9 that the producer can achieve a greater revenue than $70. Producing at point B with seventy-five units of corn and zero units of soybeans yields $75 in revenue, seventy-five units of corn at $1 per unit. Can the equal-revenue line be moved even further outward, representing even more revenue, and still remain within the production-possibilities area? The answer to this question is yes. The equal-revenue line can be moved outward to the point of tangency. This will occur at point C. At this point, forty-two units of corn and twenty-four units of soybeans are produced. This combination results in a revenue of $90, the highest revenue possible when using only six units of input. At the point of tangency, the rate of substitution of the products in the production process equals the rate of substitution of the products in the market. Thus, profits will be maximized or losses minimized.

This conclusion can be substantiated from a different perspective. At point B, the ratio of the price of soybeans to the price of corn is greater than the marginal rate of product substitution of soybeans for corn. By producing less corn and more soybeans, the producer increases revenue. The loss in revenue from decreased corn output is more than offset by the gain in revenue from increased soybean output. As more and more soybeans are produced, however, the gap narrows. The MRPS will increase as more and more soybeans are produced until it is equal to the price ratio at point C. At this time, it will no longer pay the producer to increase soybean production.

At point A, the producer is producing too many soybeans and not enough corn. At this point, the MRPS is greater than the price ratio. By decreasing soybean output and increasing corn output, the producer will again generate greater additional revenues from the increased corn output than will be sacrificed in lost revenues from soybean output. The MRPS will also decrease until it is again equal to the price ratio at point C.

The Marginal Approach

The marginal approach rests on the same basis as the graphic approach; namely, that the farmer must compare the rates at which products substitute for each other in the production process with the rates at which they substitute for each other in the marketplace. This enables the farmer to arrive at the optimal decision regarding the combinations of output to produce. In using the marginal approach, it is necessary to compare dollar values of increases or decreases of one product against those of the other product.

When deciding to increase the production of one of the outputs, the farmer knows the cost of such an increase will be measured by the amount of the other product that must be sacrificed. The producer will increase the production of product A at the expense of product B when the additional revenues from the increased production of A are greater than the sacrificed revenues from the decreased production of B. The physical measure of how many units of B must be sacrificed to produce another unit of A is the marginal rate of product substitution of A for B. This measure must be compared to the product price ratio. In this case, the price ratio of A to B tells the producer how many units of B can be sacrificed for one unit of A in the marketplace and still break even. If the MRPS is less than the price ratio, the increased revenues from the production of A more than compensate for the lost revenues

from the production of B. Should the MRPS be greater than the price ratio, the increased revenues from the production of A will not compensate for the lost revenues from the production of B. To summarize:
 If:

$$MRPS_{A\text{-}B} < \text{Price Ratio} = \frac{P_A}{P_B}$$

then the producer will increase revenues by producing more A and less B, and if:

$$MRPS_{A\text{-}B} > \text{Price Ratio} = \frac{P_A}{P_B}$$

then the producer will increase revenues by producing less A and more B.

Since the production-possibilities curve developed earlier is continuous, changes in the product mix of A and B can be infinitely small. The point at which the $MRPS_{A\text{-}B}$ becomes greater rather than less than the price ratio is the point of equilibrium for the product mix. Since all proposed increases in A up to this point should be made and all proposed increases in A following this point should not be made, the point of equality between $MRPS_{A\text{-}B}$ and the price ratio signals the farmer to produce neither greater nor lesser amounts of A.

Put another way, the farmer will increase production of A until the gain in revenue from the production of A is just equal to the loss in revenue from the decrease in the production of B. The gain in revenue from more A can be measured by multiplying the change in A produced by its price. The loss in revenue from less B can be measured in A produced by its price. The loss in revenue from less B can be measured by multiplying the change in B produced by its price. Thus, the farmer should produce to the point where:

$$(1) \quad \Delta A \cdot P_A = \Delta B \cdot P_B$$

If both sides of equation 1 are divided by ΔA

$$\frac{\Delta A \cdot P_A}{\Delta A} = \frac{\Delta B \cdot P_B}{\Delta A}$$

it reduces to:

$$(2) \ P_A = \frac{\Delta B \cdot P_B}{\Delta A}$$

If both sides of equation 2 are divided by P_B

$$\frac{P_A}{P_B} = \frac{\Delta B \cdot P_B}{\Delta A \cdot P_B}$$

it reduces to:

$$\frac{P_A}{P_B} = \frac{\Delta B}{\Delta A}$$

Since

$$\frac{P_A}{P_B} = \text{Price Ratio}$$

and

$$\frac{\Delta B}{\Delta A} = \text{MRPS}_{A\text{-}B}$$

the equilibrium condition becomes $\text{MRPS}_{A\text{-}B}$ = Price Ratio.

This is, of course, the same condition for determining the profit-maximizing or loss-minimizing combination of outputs established using the graphic approach. The application of the marginal approach to the same data as previously examined will help to point up the differences in the two approaches. Table 8–11 shows the output of corn and soybeans when six units of X_1 are available. In addition to this basic information, the $\text{MRPS}_{\text{corn-soybeans}}$, the price ratio, and the total revenue are shown for each combination of corn and soybeans. The price ratio of corn to soybeans of .5 is calculated by dividing the \$1 per-unit price of corn by the \$2 per-unit price of soybeans. The farmer facing this set of conditions cannot give up more than .5 units of soybeans for another unit of corn and break even on the exchange. The $\text{MRPS}_{\text{corn-soybeans}}$ tells how many units of soybeans must be given up to produce an additional unit of corn. By comparing the actual amount that must be given up with the maximum amount that can be given up in order to break even, the farmer can make a judgment about each

TABLE 8-11: Determination of revenue–maximizing combination of outputs—the marginal approach

Output Units of Corn	Output Units of Soybeans	$MRPS_{corn\text{-}soybeans}$ $\Delta SB / \Delta C$	Price Ratio P_c = $1 Per Unit P_s = $2 Per Unit	Total Revenue
0	35			$70
		−0.13	0.5	
15	33			81
		−0.21	0.5	
29	30			89
		−0.46	0.5	
42	24			90
		−0.58	0.5	
54	17			88
		−0.73	0.5	
65	9			83
		−0.90	0.5	
75	0			75

and every potential change in product mix. Thus, to decide whether to increase the amount of corn in the combination from zero to fifteen units, the farmer compares the price ratio of 0.5 to the MRPS of 0.13. In this case, MRPS is greater than the price ratio, so the farmer increases corn production. This trade-off will result in more revenue from the additional corn than is lost from fewer soybeans. All systems are go, and the farmer changes the product mix accordingly.

In considering a move from forty-two to fifty-four units of corn, the farmer again compares the MRPS$_{corn\text{-}soybeans}$ with the price ratio, which indicates that revenues will be reduced if more than 0.5 units of soybeans are sacrificed to produce one more unit of corn. The MRPS$_{corn\text{-}soybeans}$ indicates that the farmer wants to increase corn output from forty-two to fifty-four units, 0.58 units of soybeans will have to be sacrificed for each additional unit of corn. Such a move would result in lost revenues from the decreased soybean production, which is in excess of the revenues gained from increased corn production. Thus, the change from forty-two to fifty-four units of corn will not be made by the rational producers.

In Table 8-11, the producer will continue to substitute corn for soybeans in the product mix as long as the MRPS$_{corn\text{-}soybeans}$ is less than the price ratio. The producer will stop substituting when the price ratio exceeds the MRPS. Thus, a combination of twenty-four units of soybeans and forty-two units of corn should be produced to maximize profits. In moving to this combination, the MRPS of 0.46 is still less than the price ratio of 0.5.

The marginal approach can also be illustrated graphically to show the amount of revenues lost and gained by a given transaction. Figure 8-10 is a plot of the information on the marginal rate of product substitution and the price ratio found in Table 8-11.

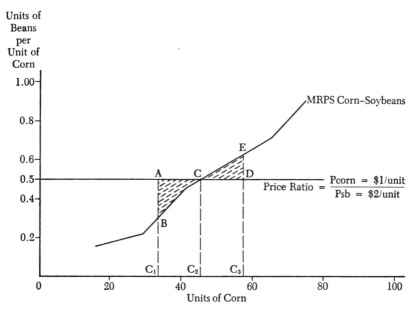

FIGURE 8-10: Marginal rate of product substitution and price ratio

If the producer is producing C_1 units of corn, the price ratio at that output is greater than the $\text{MRPS}_{\text{corn-soybeans}}$ by an amount represented by the line segment AB. This is a signal to produce more corn. Corn production should be increased until the MRPS equals the price ratio. This happens at C_2 units of corn. It is possible to measure graphically the amount of gain to the farmer from such a change. The amount of soybean production sacrificed as corn production is increased from C_1 to C_2 is shown by the area under the $\text{MRPS}_{\text{corn-soybeans}}$ curve, represented as C_1BCC_2. The value of the additional corn production is measured in terms of physical units of soybeans—the change in corn, C_1C_2, multiplied by the product-price ratio. The result is rectangle C_1ACC_2. The shaded area ABC represents the gain to the farmer from increasing corn production from C_1 to C_2. Again, this gain is measured in physical units of soybeans.

In other words, the area C_1BCC_2 represents the amount of soybeans that must be sacrificed if corn production is increased from C_1 to C_2. The extra amount of corn produced, C_1C_2, can be traded in the marketplace for soybeans at a rate determined by the price ratio. In this case, the result is C_1C_2 multiplied by $P_c P_{sb}$, which translates graphically into area C_1ACC_2. The amount of soybeans the producer can obtain by trading the extra corn produced exceeds the amount of soybeans sacrificed by the triangular area ABC. By the same logic, expansion of corn production from C_2 to C_3 will decrease revenues. In this instance, the amount of extra corn produced would yield fewer units of soybeans when traded in the marketplace than the amount of soybeans that must be sacrificed in order to produce the additional corn. Graphically, the amount of soybeans sacrificed when corn production is increased from C_2 to C_3 is the area C_2CEC_3. The amount of soybeans that the additional corn could be traded for is represented by the area C_2CDC_3. Thus, area CDE represents the amount of soybeans that the producer would lose by expanding corn production from C_2 to C_3.

The marginal approach is, perhaps, the easiest and most accurate way in which the producer can determine the profit-maximizing or loss-minimizing combination of products. Its logic is irrefutable. The producer must get back more in revenue than is given up in revenue to make a change in the product mix. Since most decisions are made concerning the addition of a little more or less of a product, the marginal approach is called into action most often. While it lacks the simplicity of the total approach, the number of calculations required is lessened considerably while the accuracy of prediction is increased.

Changes in Output Prices

When output prices change, the marginal approach will predict the same modifications in producer behavior as the graphic or total approach, albeit through a different mechanism. This section will deal with two types of output price changes: (1) proportional changes in the prices of products A and B, and (2) an increase in the price of product A relative to the price of product B. It is left up to the student to examine the effects of an increase in the price of product B relative to the price of product A.

When the prices of both ouptuts increase or decrease by the same proportion, the effect on the combination of two products that maximizes profits or minimizes losses will be zero. The reason for this is plain. When the optimal product mix is found using the marginal approach, the procedure used is to establish equality between the marginal rate of product substitution and the ratio of product prices. Proportionate increases or decreases in the prices of the two outputs will have no effect on the marginal rate of product substitution, which is determined solely by the production functions of the two products. Nor will it have an effect on the price ratio. For example, in this chapter, if both product prices double, the ratio of the two prices will remain the same.

Under old prices:

$$P_c = \$1 \text{ per unit and } P_{sb} = \$2 \text{ per unit}$$

$$\text{Price Ratio} = \frac{P_c}{P_{sb}} = \frac{\$1}{\$2} = 0.5$$

If prices double:

$$P_c = \$2 \text{ per unit and } P_{sb} = \$4 \text{ per unit}$$

$$\text{Price Ratio} = \frac{P_c}{P_{sb}} = \frac{\$2}{\$4} = 0.5$$

With the same marginal rate of product substitution and the same price ratio, the model predicts the same combination of corn and soybeans will maximize profits or minimize losses. Proportionate changes in output prices will leave the optimal product mix unchanged.

For nonproportional price changes, or when the price of one product changes relative to the price of the other, the price ratio will change. Consequently, this will also affect the optimal combination of the two products. For example, if the price of corn increases and the price of soybeans stays the same, corn becomes a relatively more attractive product and the new product mix will contain more corn and less soybeans. The change in mix will occur because of the effect the increase in the price of corn has on the price ratio. Table 8–12 shows the effect of nonproportional price changes on product mix.

An increase in the price of corn from $1 to $1.50 per unit with the price of soybeans unchanged at $2 per unit will increase the price ratio from 0.5 to 0.75. This is a signal to the producer once again to examine the product mix. Corn should now be substituted for soybeans as long as no more than 0.75 units of soybeans have to be sacrificed for each additional unit of corn produced. When the price ratio was 0.5, the farmer could not substitute corn for soybeans beyond the fourth combination listed—forty-two units of corn and twenty-four units of soybeans. With the new price ratio, further substitution becomes profitable. In fact, the producer will find it profitable to substitute corn for soybeans in the product mix until sixty-five units of corn and

TABLE 8–12: Effect of a nonproportional price change on product mix

Output Units of Corn	Output Units of Soybeans	$MRPS_{C\text{-}S}$ $= \dfrac{\Delta S}{\Delta C}$	Price Ratios	
			$P_c = \$1$ $P_s = \$2$	$P_c = \$1.50$ $P_s = \$2.00$
0	35			
15	33	0.13	0.5	0.75
29	30	0.21	0.5	0.75
42	24	0.46	0.5	0.75
54	17	0.58	0.5	0.75
65	9	0.73	0.5	0.75
75	0	0.90	0.5	0.75

nine units of soybeans are being produced.[1] As the producer increases the amount of corn from fifty-four to sixty-five units, the marginal rate of product substitution$_{corn\text{-}soybeans}$ is 0.73. The price ratio tells the producer to continue to substitute corn for soybeans as long as less than 0.75 bushels of soybeans are sacrificed for each additional unit of corn. Thus, it will be profitable to increase corn production to sixty-five units. However, for the next increase in corn output, the MRPS$_{corn\text{-}soybeans}$ is 0.90. To obtain an additional unit of corn, 0.90 units of soybeans would have to be sacrificed. With a price ratio of 0.75, this will not be advantageous. Thus, the impact of an increase in the price of corn relative to that of soybeans will be to change the product mix that maximizes profits or minimizes losses. The new mix will include more corn and less soybeans.

In summary, nonproportional price increases or decreases will act as a signal to the producer to examine the relationship between the MRPS and the price ratio to determine whether the product mix presently being produced is consistent with the new changes in output prices.

EXPANSION PATHS

The producer who knows the optimal combination of products to produce with a given production-possibilities curve, can determine the best possible combinations for a number of different curves. As previously noted, an increase in the resource base causes the production-possibilities curve to move outward to the right. The farmer

---

1. To show that this is true, the student should calculate the total revenue for each combination of outputs under both the old and new prices.

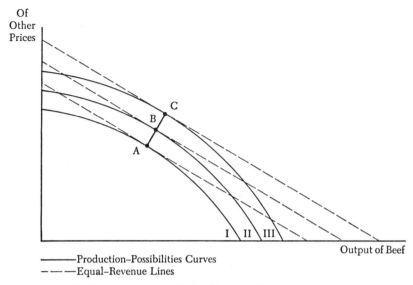

─────── Production–Possibilities Curves
─ ─ ─ ─Equal–Revenue Lines

FIGURE 8-11: Expansion path for beef production

looking to the future will be concerned about the direction production should take as the resource base increases. In a sense, the producer's concern is with the combinations of products that will be most profitable on each of several production-possibilities curves. The locus of the points representing these combinations is known as the *expansion path.* A specific example will be helpful in showing how the expansion path is determined. A beef producer might be interested in the effect an increase in the amount of permanent pasture has on the production of beef and other farm enterprises.

Figure 8–11 shows a family of three different production-possibilities curves. Curves I, II, and III represent, respectively, low, medium, and high levels of permanent pasture. As the resource base of permanent pasture increases, production possibilities also increase. Given the equal-revenue lines indicated by the dashed lines, the optimum combinations of beef and other products are identified by the points of tangency A, B, and C. Thus, an increase in the amount of permanent pasture causes production to expand along the heavy line from point A to point B to point C. Since increased permanent pasture favors beef production more than the other farm enterprises, the expansion path will favor beef production. Interested students can construct expansion paths for production combinations that result from: (1) changes in product prices, (2) change in technology, and (3) changes in the amount of fixed inputs available. This can be done for the corn and soybean example used throughout this chapter.

REVENUE-MAXIMIZING PRODUCT MIX FOR MORE THAN TWO PRODUCTS

Discussion thus far has dealt solely with possible combinations of only two products. In reality, the farm-firm is a multi-product firm. It produces not only more than two products, but also many by-products of the direct products. While the graphical analysis developed cannot be extended beyond two products, the mathematical conditions inherent in the marginal approach can be generalized to the production of n products. As was indicated in the discussion of marginal approach, the producer will maximize profits or minimize losses by producing that combination of products where:

$$MRPS_{A-B} = \text{Price Ratio}$$

If this condition is not satisfied, production is in a disequilibrium situation where revenues can be increased by changing the product mix. If the price ratio exceeds the $MRPS_{A-B}$, the firm will increase revenues by producing more A and less B. If the price ratio is less than the MRPS, it will increase revenues by producing more B and less A. Thus, when the firm is dealing with more than two products, it must satisfy this equilibrium condition for each and every product. The equilibrium condition for n products is more easily expressed if restated in somewhat different terms. Equilibrium is also met when the dollar trade-off between the two products is equal. That is, when

$$\Delta A \cdot P_A = \Delta B \cdot P_B$$

When the farmer is producing n products, the dollars acquired from increased production of one must be equal to the dollars sacrificed through the decreased production of any of the others. In other words, equilibrium exists with n products when the farmer is producing them in a combination so that:

$$\Delta Q_1 \cdot P_1 = \Delta Q_2 \cdot P_2 = \ldots = \Delta Q_n \cdot P_n$$

Where the ΔQs represent the changes in the quantity of a specific output, the Ps represent the price of that output. When the resources available are allocated between outputs in this manner, equilibrium will be established. The producer will not be able to increase revenues by reallocating resources from one output to another.

SUMMARY

The purpose of this chapter has been to bring the output decision closer to reality by acknowledging the fact that the farmer produces more than one type of output. The methodologies developed to determine the profit-maximizing or loss-minimizing combinations of output to produce are analogous to those formulated in the last chapter to determine the least-cost combination of inputs. All proposed actions must be weighed in terms of added costs and added revenues before a decision is made. While the introduction of two products and the concept of product mix complicates the farmer's decision-making process somewhat, the models used in this chapter stem from the very basic cost-benefit tool of analysis.

QUESTIONS

1. From the production functions below, determine the production-possibilities schedule given a resource base of four and six units.

Units of Resource	Product One	Units of Resource	Product Two
0	0	0	0
1	20	1	40
2	35	2	75
3	48	3	105
4	58	4	130
5	66	5	150
6	71	6	160
7	73	7	165

2. Determine the marginal rate of product substitution of Product One for Product Two, $\Delta Q_2 / \Delta Q_1$, when the firm has a resource base of six units. Now, determine the combination of products that maximizes profits for the firm with the following product prices:

   A. Price of Product One is $5 per unit
      Price of Product Two is $10 per unit

   B. Price of Product One is $10 per unit
      Price of Product Two is $5 per unit

C. Price of Product One is $7 per unit
   Price of Product Two is $7 per unit

What method for solving this problem is the most convenient to use?

3. Determine graphically the expansion path for the farm when it has a resource base of four units and six units, given the price of each product is $7. Explain what happens to the expansion path when a more efficient technology for Product One is used.

CHAPTER NINE

Linear Programming Applied to Agriculture

The last two chapters have dealt with the application of economic models to situations of increased complexity. Chapter seven focused on decision making when multiple inputs were used, while chapter eight explored the case where multiple outputs were produced. In the real world of the agricultural producer, such complexity is the rule of the day rather than the exception. Farmers are always trying to determine the best combinations of a large number of inputs to use and, likewise, the best combination of a large number of products to produce. Two events have made these kinds of decisions easier to handle. The first was the advent of electronic data processing, which allows the farmer access to the performance of a vast number of mathematical calculations in a relatively short period of time. The second is the creation of a technique known as linear programming, which provides the farmer an analytical framework with which to evaluate the opportunities afforded by multiple inputs and outputs.

A well-developed, sophisticated analytical tool, linear programming has found increasing favor among agricultural producers. It is now common for farmers to go to local colleges and universities to plug their possible choices into the already prepared linear programming models. The computer printout is fast becoming part of the equipment of the modern farmer. It is, in many ways, more important to the profitability of the farm than the tractor or combine.

As previously noted, linear programming is a complex and sophisticated tool. The interested student would do well to seek the large body of literature on the subject or to study it in formal course work. It is beyond the scope of this text to examine the subject in any detail so as to formally implant these techniques. Thus, this chapter will present two simple examples of the linear programming technique applied to the familiar problems of choice between multiple inputs and between multiple outputs. In both cases, only the bare essentials of linear programming have been presented to demonstrate how this tool can lead the farmer to more rational decisions in an increasingly complex world.

COST MINIMIZATION

One example of the type of problem for which linear programming is well suited is the minimization of the cost of a given activity. Linear programming is a set of techniques based on matrix algebra used to define minimum or maximum solutions for problems involving many constraints. Linear programming assumes the number of techniques of production available to the producer is finite. Each of the products produced may be produced through a finite number of production processes—each with a unique set of input requirements or coefficients. Each technique can be used to produce any level of output. It is additionally assumed that if inputs in a given production technique are varied, then output will vary proportionately. Thus, if five units of capital and ten units of labor produce twenty units of outputs, ten units of capital and twenty units of labor will produce forty units of output. Finally, the linear programming model assumes production techniques are separate and do not interact with one another. To illustrate the use of linear programming and to make these assumptions more meaningful, an example simple enough for mathematical and graphical solution is necessary.

A farmer producing pork will have a choice of a number of different techniques, each using a different set of inputs. If the pork producer has available three different techniques, each using different amounts of labor and capital, it is possible to construct a table showing the input requirements or coefficients of each technique. This is done in Table 9–1.

To produce 100 units of pork, Technique One uses labor and capital in a ratio of 1:3, Technique Two in a ratio of 1:1, and Technique Three in a ratio of 4:1. Using the concept of equal-product curves, it is possible to show how these three techniques will produce various levels of output. This is done in Figure 9–1.

Since each technique produces proportionate increases in output as inputs are increased, each technique can be represented by a ray from the origin. The amounts of labor and capital listed in Table 9–1 that must be used to produce 100 units of pork are shown in Figure 9–1:

TABLE 9-1: Linear programming table for pork production (input requirements for 100 units of pork)

	Technique One	Technique Two	Technique Three
Hours of Labor	4	8	16
Hours of Capital	12	8	4

Point A_1 for Technique One, Point A_2 for Technique Two, and Point A_3 for Technique Three. When these points are linked together, they form an equal-product curve.[1] Two other equal-product curves are also shown: curve $B_1B_2B_3$ represents fifty units of pork production; curve $C_1C_2C_3$ represents 150 units of pork production. Once the equal-product map is completed, the next step is to define the goal function and to apply it to the equal-product map showing the constraints imposed by the three available techniques.

Once the equal-product curves have been established, an equal-expenditure line is used to find the technique or combination of techniques that will produce the required 100 units of pork at the lowest possible cost to the producer. Figure 9–2 shows the equal-product curve for 100 units of pork developed previously. Several equal-expenditure lines have been added to indicate how the producer selects the least cost technique. Equal-expenditure line TE_1 represents a total expenditure of $48. While this is the smallest total expenditure represented, it obviously cannot be the solution because it does not share a point or points in common with the equal-product curve representing 100 units of pork production. The remaining expenditure lines—TE_2, TE_3, and TE_4—all have at least one point in common with the equal-product curve. However, TE_2, representing a total expenditure of $56, is the lowest input cost that the farmer can incur and still produce 100 units of pork. This equal-expenditure line is tangent to the equal-product curve at the ray representative of Technique Two. Here, the desired output of 100 units of pork is produced using eight units of labor and eight units of capital. While TE_3 and TE_4 are capable of generating the desired output, the input cost represented by these

1. In this example, it is assumed that Technique One represents the most extreme use of capital and Technique Three the most extreme use of labor in pork production. Thus, beyond the limit set by T_1, any additional capital used will add nothing to production. Thus, the vertical portion of the equal product curves beyond T_1. The use of more labor than that indicated by T_3 will also produce no increase in production. Hence, the horizontal portion of the equal product curves beyond T_3.

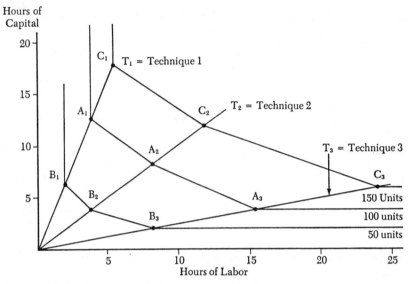

FIGURE 9–1: Alternate techniques pork production

curves is $60 and $64, respectively. Thus Technique Two, with an outlay of $56, will be the least costly way to generate the desired output.

While graphical solutions are possible only for situations with limited variables, another way to solve the problem is to set the desired outcome up in algebraic form. The farmer's goal is to minimize the total cost of producing 100 units of pork by choosing the best technique or best combination of techniques available. The objective function is:

Minimize TC

The alternative production techniques are included by describing the cost of one unit of pork produced by each technique. To accomplish this, it is necessary to know the prices of the two inputs. If the price of labor is $3 per unit and the price of capital is $4 per unit, the cost of producing one unit or pork by each technique may be found. Using Technique One, four hours of labor and twelve hours of capital were required to produce 100 units of pork. Thus, $60 worth of inputs were required to produce 100 units of pork. One unit of pork can be produced with $0.60 worth of inputs. The requirements of Technique One can then be described as:

$$\$.60 \ Q_1$$

where Q_1 is the quantity of pork produced by Technique One.

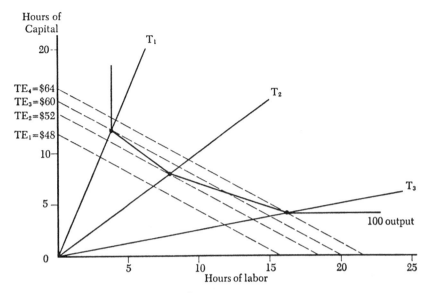

Price of capital = $4 per unit
Price of labor = $3 per unit

FIGURE 9-2: Cost minimization for pork production

Through the same process, it is possible to calculate the cost of inputs for one unit of pork production using Techniques Two or Three. Since Technique Two uses eight units of each input, the cost of producing 100 units of pork will be $56 [(8 · $3) + (8 · $4)]. Therefore, the cost of producing one unit of pork using Technique Two is $0.56. The cost of input requirements for Technique Two is then:

$$\$.56\ Q_2$$

Technique Three uses sixteen hours of labor and four hours of capital. The cost of producing 100 units of pork is $64 [(16 · $3) + (4 · $4)]. This means that the cost of inputs required to produce one unit of pork by this method is:

$$\$.64\ Q_3$$

The full objective function describing the goal and the available means of achieving that goal can be stated:

$$\text{Minimize TC} = \$.60\ Q_1 + \$.56\ Q_2 + \$.64\ Q_3$$

This objective function is subject to two further constraints. Since the producer desires to produce 100 units of pork, the pork produced by the three techniques must equal 100 units, i.e.:

$$Q_1 + Q_2 + Q_3 = 100$$

Also, the computer must be told to reject any negative solutions since they are not relevant in the economic world. Nonnegativity is stated in the second constraint as:

$$Q_1 \geqslant 0$$
$$Q_2 \geqslant 0$$
$$Q_3 \geqslant 0$$

When this information is plugged into the computer, the machine can run through a number of calculations to determine the best technique to produce 100 units of pork at minimum cost. In this very simple problem, the answer is obvious. Technique Two, which produces the output at a cost of $0.56 per unit, is the lowest cost technique to use. There are many situations, however, where the constraints are more complex and call for the power of the computer.

REVENUE MAXIMIZATION

The problems solved in chapter eight were rather simple and easy to solve because only two products were produced from a given bundle of inputs. In many instances in agriculture, the producer will be concerned with more complex problems. For example, a variety of products such as hogs, beef, corn, and soybeans may be under production. The producer will also be concerned with the effect on the optimum product combination as changes occur in the amount of fixed inputs available or in product price. When it is necessary for the agricultural producer to consider the production of many different products at one time, the revenue-maximizing approaches developed in Chapter 8 will not be feasible. The problem is, however, well suited to the application of linear programming techniques.

In linear programming, some inputs are viewed as fixed and some as variable. The fixed inputs would be those inputs such as land, capital, and management that are available only in fixed amounts. Variable inputs would be inputs such as fertilizer and feed that could be purchased until capital is exhausted. Using the linear programming method, the costs of the variable inputs needed to produce a certain product are deducted from the price of the product. Thus, linear programming will maximize net returns to the producer's bundle of fixed

TABLE 9–2: Production techniques and inputs available

Input	Measure	Supply of Inputs	Inputs Required to Product One Unit of	
			Beef	Grain
Land	Acres	90	1.5	1
Labor				
Dec-Mar	Hours	400	8	0
Apr-July	Hours	400	0	8
Aug-Nov	Hours	420	6	6
Machines	Hours	300	3	5

inputs. For illustrative purposes, the example considered will be simple.

A useful example is the agricultural producer producing beef and grain. The amount of beef and grain produced depends on the techniques of production and the amount of fixed inputs available. Table 9–2 shows the producer faced with five constraints: limited acreage of land, limited supply of labor in three different time periods, and limited amount of hours of machine time. Given the total supply of each of these inputs available and the inputs required in the production process, the producer can determine the maximum amounts of beef and grain that can be produced with these fixed inputs. This has been done in Table 9–3.

The production-possibilities combinations of beef and grain in Table 9–3 were obtained by dividing the fixed supply of inputs available by the input requirements for one production process with the other process being operated at zero production. For example, if the producer uses the entire ninety acres of land for beef, the maximum amount of beef that can be produced will be sixty. This figure was obtained by dividing ninety acres by 1.5 acres for each unit of beef. Likewise, if all ninety acres of land is used to produce grain, ninety units of grain is the maximum grain production attainable (90 acres ÷ 1 acre per unit of grain). When sixty units of beef are produced, no land is available for grain production. Thus, grain output is zero. When all land is used for grain production, sixty units of grain and zero units of beef result. The other maximums in Table 9–3 were obtained in the same manner. The table also shows that beef production requires no April-July labor. Beef and grain production exhibit a supplementary relationship for this input. The amount of grain produced during this period does not depend on beef production. Likewise, December-March labor does not restrict grain production because grain requires no labor during this

TABLE 9–3: Production possibilities for beef and grain

Input	Measure	Supply of Inputs	Units of Beef	Units of Grain
Land	Acres	90	60	90
Labor				
Dec-Mar	Hours	400	50	*
Apr-July	Hours	400	*	50
Aug-Nov	Hours	420	70	70
Machines	Hours	300	100	60

*Input is not a restriction

time. Here, grain and beef exhibit a supplementary relationship. Earlier experiences have shown that the producer should take advantage of the supplementary relationships that exist between the two products. Table 9–3 also shows the most limiting input to beef production is hours of labor available in December through March, while April-to-July labor is the most crucial input in grain production.

By connecting the points of maximum beef and grain production, it is possible to show graphically the production-possibilities curve. This has been done in Figure 9–3. The lines represent production possibilities for beef and grain for each one of the five inputs. At point A, production of beef will be limited to a maximum of fifty units by the amount of December-to-March labor available. At point F, production of grain will be limited to a maximum of fifty units by the amount of April-to-July labor available. The producer can move from point A to point B on the production-possibilities curve and increase grain production from zero to fifteen units without decreasing beef output. However, to expand grain production above this level would necessitate reducing beef production. In moving along line BC, grain production becomes competitive with beef for the use of the land input. Taking more land for grain production leaves less land for beef production. If grain production is increased again, it will once more reduce beef production. If the producer moves from point C to point D, the beef and grain enterprises will now be competing for the limited labor available in August through November. In moving from point D to point E, machine time available becomes the limiting input. And, finally, in moving from E to F, April-to-July labor will limit grain to fifty units. Thus, the curve represented by points ABCDEF is the production-possibilities curve. Combinations of beef and grain that can be produced must lie within the area represented by ABCDEF. Any combination of beef and grain outside this area cannot be produced because it requires more of the limited inputs than are available. For

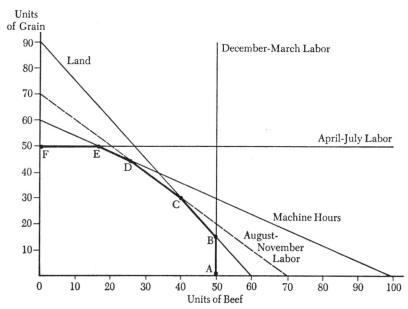

FIGURE 9–3: Production possibilities for beef and grain

example, point G uses more August-to-November labor, more machine hours, and more April to July labor than are available while point H uses more August to November labor and land than are available.

Once the production-possibilities curve has been established, the optimal solution can be found graphically by adding a series of equal-revenue lines to Figure 9–3. To do this, it is necessary to make assumptions about prices and variable costs for each unit of grain and beef produced. Once this is done, the return above variable costs, i.e., contribution to fixed costs and profits, can readily be determined. For this example, it is assumed that the price and average variable cost of each product is fixed per unit and does not change as the producer changes output of grain and beef. It is assumed that the prices of grain and beef are $550 and $350 per unit respectively, while the average variable per-unit cost of grain and beef is $150 and $50, respectively. This means that a unit of grain provides the producer with a return above average variable costs of $400 ($550 – $150 = $400), while a unit of beef provides $300 ($350 – $50 = $300).

With this information at hand, the farmer can focus on the problem of determining how many units of grain and beef to produce to generate the greatest return to the available land, labor, and machine inputs. For linear programming purposes, the problem is stated in algebraic terms. First, consider the objective function, in this case, the maximization of revenue from a given bundle of inputs: revenue (R) = $300Q_{Beef}$ + $400Q_{Grain}$. This equation was obtained by taking the per-unit return above AVC for each product and multiplying times the unknown quantity of beef and grain yet to be produced.

In addition to the objective function, the constraint set must also be considered. The constraint set is a list of algebraic statements indicating the limiting factors that must be considered. In this case, the only constraints to be concerned with are nonnegativity and the amounts of fixed inputs available. The constraints are:

(1) $1.5 Q_B + 1Q_G \leqslant 90$ (Land Acres)
(2) $\qquad 8Q_B \leqslant 400$ (December-March Labor Hours)
(3) $\qquad 8Q_G \leqslant 400$ (April-July Labor Hours)
(4) $6Q_B + 6Q_G \leqslant 420$ (August-November Labor Hours)
(5) $3Q_B + 5Q_G \leqslant 300$ (Machine Hours)
(6) $Q_B \geqslant 0 ; Q_G \geqslant 0$

The above equations separate the attainable from the unattainable beef and grain possibilities. For example, equation (1) combines beef and grain input coefficients for land with the total acres of land available. The 1.5 says that, for each unit of beef produced, 1.5 acres of land will be used; the 1 says that, for each unit of grain produced, one acre of land will be used. The 90 indicates that ninety acres of land are available in total to produce beef and grain. Thus, the maximum attainable units of beef and grain are sixty and ninety, respectively. The other constraints can be interpreted in a similar manner. Once the constraints and the objective function are known, a solution to the problem could be found by using the simplest method. Linear programming theory indicates that the optimum solution to the problem will be at one of the corners of the production-possibilities curve shown in Figure 9–3. The solution could also be determined mathematically by calculating the return above variable costs at each corner of area ABCDEF and choosing the corner with the greatest total return above variable costs. Since the problem is sufficiently simple, a graphic solution is presented in Figure 9–4. This figure reproduces the production-possibilities curve developed in Figure 9–3. The optimal solution can now be found by adding a series of equal-revenue lines to the diagram. The equal-revenue lines are based on the objective function revenue (R) = $300Q_{Beef}$ + $400Q_{Grain}$.

Each equal-revenue line shows the various combinations of beef and grain that provide the same total return above variable costs. The objective is now to find the point on the production-possibilities curve ABCDEF that lies on the highest equal-revenue line. A quick inspection shows that if the producer operates at point B on the production-

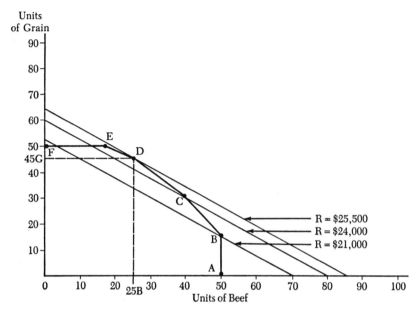

FIGURE 9-4: Most profitable combination of beef and grain

possibilities curve, the result will be a total revenue above variable costs of $21,000; at point C, $24,000; and at point D, $25,500. Since points B, C, and D are all produced from the same bundle of fixed inputs, combination D represents the optional combination of products. At this point, forty-five units of grain and twenty-five units of beef will be produced.

In the problem just presented, it was not necessary to use linear programming to find the optimal solution. However, this will not always be the case. As product-combination problems become more complex, linear programming will become indispensable to farmers and farm managers in determining the optimum combinations of products to produce.

Index